THE PARADISO
OF
DANTE ALIGHIERI

THE PARADISO
OF
DANTE ALIGHIERI

With a translation
into English triple rhyme and
a brief introduction
by

GEOFFREY L. BICKERSTETH

★

"Glorious the song, when God's the theme"

★

CAMBRIDGE
AT THE UNIVERSITY PRESS
1932

CAMBRIDGE
UNIVERSITY PRESS

University Printing House, Cambridge CB2 8BS, United Kingdom

Cambridge University Press is part of the University of Cambridge.

It furthers the University's mission by disseminating knowledge in the pursuit of education, learning and research at the highest international levels of excellence.

www.cambridge.org
Information on this title: www.cambridge.org/9781107536692

© Cambridge University Press 1932

First published 1932
First paperback edition 2015

A catalogue record for this publication is available from the British Library

ISBN 978-1-107-53669-2 Paperback

PREFACE

The text of the *Paradiso* adopted for this translation
and printed facing it is that of G. Vandelli, the editor
responsible for the Divine Comedy in the Italian Dante
Society's *testo critico* of *Le opere di Dante* published by
R. Bemporad and Son (Florence, 1921). For permission
to reproduce it here I am indebted to the courtesy of
Professor Michele Barbi, president of the editorial com-
mittee for the *edizione nazionale* of the poet's complete
works. Apart from its other merits, for a description of
which the reader may be referred to Professor Barbi's
preface to the above-mentioned volume, Vandelli's text
has from my point of view the advantage of preserving
the *trecento* orthography, so important for correct appreciation of the harmony and rhythm of the verses. The
translation endeavours everywhere to follow it faithfully, not only in all disputed readings, but in punctuation, the spelling of Italian names and in the use of
capital letters.

The claim of the translation to originality in form is
explained in the introduction. It owes something to
previous versions. I have from time to time deliberately
echoed Cary in line, phrase or word; and have also
occasionally borrowed a rendering from the prose-
translations of Norton, Tozer, Wicksteed and others.
But, apart from the commentators consulted, too
numerous for individual mention here, I have perhaps
been chiefly aided in arriving at the poet's meaning by
Fay's *Concordance of the Divine Comedy* and Blanc's
Vocabolario dantesco, both works in which Dante is
made to serve as his own interpreter.

My principal guides in the artistic appreciation of the poem have been de Sanctis and Professor Karl Vossler. The seventh chapter of the former's *Storia della letteratura italiana* still remains by far the best short introduction to the poetry of the Divine Comedy which has ever been written. As for Vossler's great work *Die göttliche Komödie*, it unquestionably deserves Giovanni Gentile's description of it as "the most powerful instrument which we possess for helping us to understand the art of Dante". Both of these books have recently been translated into English.

My friend Professor Cesare Foligno very kindly read through the introduction and the translation in manuscript. Those passages of the former which deal with the rhythms and scansion of Dante's verse, a subject of special difficulty to an Englishman, owe not a little to his lucid and sympathetic criticism. If what I have written is still wanting in clarity or open to objection by orthodox Italian prosodists, it can only be in places where I have for some reason failed to make proper use of his suggestions.

G. L. B.

THE UNIVERSITY
GLASGOW
October 1932

CONTENTS

Non è pileggio da picciola barca
   quel che fendendo va l' ardita prora,
   nè da nocchier ch' a se medesmo parca.

No sea-way for a bauble-boat is this
   cut by my daring keel, but one to prove
   the steersman's mettle in extremities.

INTRODUCTION

THE translation accompanying the present reprint of the *Paradiso* is primarily intended for the reader with whom the third and greatest cantica of the Divine Comedy counts (outside the Bible) as the supreme expression in literature of the Christian faith, and who uses it as such for study and meditation—

> contento ne' pensier contemplativi.

"Post Dantis Paradisum", said Cardinal Manning, speaking of it from this point of view, "—post Dantis Paradisum nihil restat nisi visio Dei."

And, secondly, the translation is specially addressed to those whom the *Paradiso* fascinates and delights as the supreme achievement of the poet's art, the greatest 'deed' which the human imagination has ever 'determin'd, dar'd and done' through the medium of words.

These two aspects of the Divine Comedy as a whole, and of its last cantica in a very special degree, tend to be obscured by study of the commentaries, which have buried the poem and its ultimate purpose under mountainous glosses on its theology, its philosophy and its symbolism, moral, political and otherwise. And yet as Vossler, perhaps the most learned of living Dantists, has well said: "We know that the Divine Comedy is infinitely more than a didactic poem; it is an act of the most personal piety. We know that the innermost impulse was mystical, not educational. The moralising and popularising philosopher becomes, by his mighty flight, a divinely inspired seer.... It is the peculiarity of artistic genius that it reaches, in happy moments, a height for

which its own understanding has no measure or rule....
Even so it may have been for Dante a marvel how he
arrived at the divine Italian terzets for which his theory
of art, progressive though it was, failed to account".

'The divine vision' and 'the divine Italian terzets' in
which it is expressed—to compel, and at the same time
to assist, the English reader's concentration upon these
is, then, the chief aim of the present translation. For
this reason it has the original Italian text printed beside
it, is accompanied by no notes (which would but distract
attention and can easily be obtained elsewhere) and is
composed in *terza rima*, written not in the English, but
after the Italian manner.

The original text is supplied not only for easy reference, but also that none may suppose the English
version is intended to stand instead of it. For it is a
truism that, in one sense, poetry cannot be translated.
A translation, though as beautiful as, or even more
beautiful than, its original—the Authorised Version of
the Bible, for instance—can, of its very nature, never
be precisely the same thing. Even in the same language
to alter the way of saying a thing is inevitably to alter at
the same time the thing said. But, apart from this obvious fact, a translation in verse, if, while not reading as
a translation, it faithfully, however faintly, reflects (as
prose can never do) not only the content but also the
very form of the original, still remains the most direct
and effective of all devices by which foreign poetry as
art can be rendered interesting to readers unacquainted,
or but superficially acquainted, with the language and
metre in which it is written.

Therefore, on the technical side, my aim has been two-
fold: at once to render the verbal meaning of the Italian

with fidelity (which is not the same as absolute literalness) and to write to Dante's melody—that is, of all the wealth of meaning which derives from the varied rhythm, tones and cadences of the Italian verses, to echo so much as my ear and command of English idiom and skill in versification would allow. From this, as from all other points of view, the translation must be its own excuse. If it cannot justify itself, none else can perform this office for it, least of all its author. But, to avoid possible misunderstanding, it is perhaps fair to permit him some introductory explanation of the principles by which he has been guided in his work, more especially as, despite the attention devoted to Dante's poetic style by English students, the poet's verse-form, the reason for it and the laws which govern it have been almost entirely neglected and by the average reader seem little understood.

The first point to be grasped, or Dante's main artistic purpose will be entirely missed, is that in pattern his verse is neither epic nor dramatic, and still less is it lyrical. It was chosen because it admitted all these modes, but its norm is none of them; it is satiric, but 'satiric' as the term was understood by our great classical satirists, Dryden and Pope, in whom, as the late W. P. Ker very happily put it, "the narrow sound of satire (a phrase of Swinburne's) opens out to a large sea. The beauty of his (Pope's) satiric poetry is its reflection of the whole world, not steadily or as the great masters render it in Epic or Tragedy, but with all the lights of the greater modes represented here and there—so that anywhere you may be caught away, for a moment, to different regions". In just the same way it may be said that the narrow sound of the Italian *sirventese* opens out to the large sea of Dante's Divine Comedy. For the *sirventese*, as an established poetic type, passed on its characteristic features to the Comedy both in content and form. Taken over from Provençal literature, the Italians made it predominantly narrative, sententious and didactic. In subject it dealt with passing events, that is, actual events, and not with a romantic, ideal or sentimentalised world of the poet's own invention. So too the Comedy, though a vision, is a vision of the real, described by an eyewitness, who, as such, is mainly concerned to give an accurate report, and at the same time sound reason for the truth, of everything, however unprecedented, that he has actually beheld.

Exact description and rational argument, 'per chiare parole e con preciso latin', often seemingly prosaic (if judged by 'romantic' standards), must therefore constitute the staple of the poem, as in fact they do. It is Dante's mighty imagination fired by his passionate conviction of the truth of what he is describing and arguing, which through restriction within these rigidly prescribed limits gives to his style its characteristic note of suppressed power. Only our great classical satirists, minor poets though they be in comparison with Dante, provide us with anything similar in English poetry. Of these perhaps his nearest congener is Dryden in such a poem as *The Hind and the Panther*, where (as the last two paragraphs of its preface indicate) the author aimed at a style which would equally admit of the 'majestic turns of heroic poesie'; deal 'plainly' with subjects that were 'matters of dispute'; possess, when required, the 'freedom and familiarity' of 'domestic conversation' and be no less at home with 'the common places of satire'—all of them objects which he achieved within the strict limits of the heroic couplet. Clearly, therefore, the translator of the Comedy into English, if seeking in his own language for a native form and manner corresponding, must look to the poets mentioned, despite their total want of 'l' alta fantasia',* rather than to our great 'romantics', Spenser, Shakespeare, Milton or Shelley, whose style is as far removed from Dante's as are their metres.

For, metrically also, the Comedy must be considered as related to, if not derived from, the *sirventese*. The latter was composed of linked stanzas, of two or three verses each, with 'cauda' or tail. The stanza, in its commonest form, consisted of three hendecasyllables, monorhymed, the third with a *quinario* (five-syllabled verse) as 'cauda'. This did not rhyme with the verse to which it was attached, but supplied the rhyme to, and thereby the link with, the stanza following, thus:

$$AAAb, BBBc, CCCd, etc.$$

Dante's own stanza, of three hendecasyllables in triple rhyme (*terza rima*), which repeats itself continuously from start to finish of the canto and is linked by the rhymes thus:

$$ABA, BCB, C\ldots YX, YZY, Z$$

(closing, not with a quatrain, but in a single verse) was a development rather than a variant of the other. For it is not found in any extant *sirventese* and was presumably invented by Dante himself as suiting the symbolism of numbers (with special reference to the Trinity and Unity of the Godhead) by which the whole structure of the Comedy is determined.

If technically, then, the Divine Comedy cannot be

* Cp. *Purg.* XVII, 13–25; *Par.* XXXIII, 142.

classified as epic or drama or lyric, but is, properly
speaking, "a great complex of narrative, personal, religious, moral, satirical and didactic *sirventesi*", each
consisting of some forty to fifty rhyme-linked, three-
verse stanzas, and all reduced to one organic whole by
an imagination working within the strict limits which
the chosen form prescribes, certain obvious results follow
for any translator who regards form and matter as in-
dissoluble in poetry and desires to achieve an adequate
rendering of both. Neither blank verse (supposing he
could write it) nor any of the great traditional English
narrative stanzas—e.g. the rhyme-royal, the Spenserian
or the octave—and still less any lyric or elegiac stanza
will serve his purpose. On the contrary, their associations
are such that they would inevitably defeat it. And
since rhyme he must have and a stanza in which the
rhythms do not overrun the stanza-endings, he is left
with only two possible metres—either the heroic couplet
as handled by Dryden and Pope, or Dante's own *terza
rima*. And surely—since, as Shelley said, in specific reference to translation of the Divine Comedy "it is an
essential justice to an author to render him in the same
form"—the latter must be deemed preferable, unless
there are insuperable objections.

Such objections have been held to exist: and they may
be briefly stated as follows, beginning with the weightiest.
It has been argued that English thought-forms do not
naturally fit themselves to the *terza rima* measure. If
they did, why should Shelley, the only great English
poet who ever composed a long poem in *terza rima*, have
imposed upon it the rhythms of blank verse? Again,
does not the fact that English poets do not construct
their sonnets, though originally imitated from the Italian,

on *terza rima* cadences, prove that they find it difficult to bring the triple-rhyme melody to its close? And, further, is not this difficulty obviously connected with the scarcity of rhyming words in English as contrasted with their abundance in Italian? And, finally, even suppose the rhymes to be found without resort to mistranslation or ugly inversions, is not the frequency of the triple rhyme unpleasant to the English ear?

The one convincing answer to these objections would be an actually existing example of *terza rima* to which, though written in English, none of them was by qualified judges felt to apply. And such is the answer that has been attempted in the present translation of the *Paradiso*. However far it falls short of its aim, it can at least claim to be a genuine and consistent attempt to write English triple rhyme in Dante's form and manner. These, of course, require to be understood before they can be imitated; and a full enquiry into the particular features of his craftsmanship as 'fabbro del parlar materno' would involve consideration not only of his management of rhythm and rhyme, but also of the part played in his versification by the length and shortness of syllables, vowel and consonantal music, intonation, alliteration, assonance, sentence-structure, inversion, repetition, archaisms, neologisms, word-play, proper names and so on. But though the translator ought to have made a minute study of all these and be every-where ready with a practical solution of the nice pro-blems they are perpetually raising for him, it is with the rhythm and the rhyme that he must chiefly concern himself, if he is to produce the general effect of Dante's versification in easy and idiomatic English. We will therefore briefly consider both.

In Dante's verse, as in English, what determines rhythm is the relation of the word-values accentually to one another, not the absolute time as measured by the metre. For the latter is a pure abstraction, with which the actual movement of the verse, though for ever suggesting it, hardly ever in fact coincides. Nor, indeed, when once the translator has satisfied himself, by reading both aloud, that the English ten-syllable (or five-stressed) line is the metrical equivalent of the Italian hendecasyllable, need he think of the metre again. For, whichever method of scansion* be adopted, Italian or English, the ear recognises that it is confronted in both verses with the same rhythmical movement of the line as a whole. It is true that a verse with a rhythm like

In forma dűnque | di cándida rŏsa,

if scanned after the English fashion, may at first seem unmetrical. But let it be read aloud with due respect for the caesura, in the right *tempo* throughout and, above all, with the lingering inflexions which the Italian voice gives to the words 'dűn-que' and 'cán-dida' (cáhn-děě-dăh), and even by the English ear it will be acknowledged to fit the required measure.†

---

* The usual English method is to scan the verse by the number of its feet and stresses. The Italian prosodist knows nothing of feet, but measures the verse, and classifies it as 'short' or 'long', according to the number of its syllables (allowing for elision) and of its (primary) 'rhythmic' accents. Of these, in any long verse, e.g. the hendeca-syllable, there must be two, and two only; one falling always on the tenth syllable, the other, according to the position of the caesura, on the fourth or sixth. Secondary accents occur within both the phrases into which the caesura cuts the hendecasyllable. But though these accents of course affect the rhythm, they are *metrically* invalid; for they vary in number and incidence, whereas the primary accents are in both these respects fixed.

† A hendecasyllabic verse of this form (i.e. with rhythmic accent on the fourth, and a secondary accent on the seventh, syllable) has been criticised as constituting a *stonatura* even by Italian prosodists;

The translator, therefore, who,

come a buon cantor buon citarista,

would fain make his own verse keep time with Dante's
rather than breaking up the latter into abstract metrical
units, should aim at distinguishing its real rhythmical
phrases; and to these he must chiefly guide himself by
the sense and natural grouping of the words, by the
necessary pauses (not always marked by punctuation)
and by sensitive discrimination between the primary
and secondary stresses. For it is the phrasal rhythms—
controlled, doubtless, in delivery by a conscious or sub-
conscious feeling for the metre into whose units they are
theoretically divisible—that enable him to appreciate
the melody to which the poet is writing and under the
influence of which alone, though by means that defy
exact analysis, the thought-form and the rhythmical
come into simultaneous existence.

But even if he attends as he must to the phrasing (for
it constitutes the very soul of poetry), the translator will
entirely fail to reproduce the characteristic movement
of the Dantesque *terzina* unless he makes his rhythms
exactly coincident with this. For the real rhythmical unit
is not the verse, but the stanza, as the linking of its
phrases over and over again makes clear. This fact in
itself would make a line-for-line translation, even if in

but this is mere pedantry, according to G. Mari. He points out that,
though the form is relatively rare, both Dante and Petrarch were
fond of it, especially if the seventh syllable, thus accented, is pre-
ceded or followed by a monosyllable or by an accented syllable.
(For a similarly accented verse where neither of these conditions is
observed cp.

Ma non con quésta | modérna favélla.)

The rhythm in question is very rare in English blank verse, but is
occasionally imitated by Milton, who had carefully studied, and
could himself write, Italian verse: cp. *P.L.* vi, 866, 906; vii, 527;
x, 178, 202.

verse it was possible, not only needless but actually wrong; for it ignores Dante's own practice. Within the *terzina* he readily separates by the line-ending the adjective from its noun (XIII, 19), the adverb from its verb (XVI, 100; XVIII, 97) and the same from its conjunction (XIV, 16; XVIII, 31): he will sometimes end the verse with the copulative (VIII, 44), the relative (II, 11; IX, 94), the article (XI, 13) or even (XXIV, 16) with part of a word,* whereas between the *terzine* he allows no synaphea, or at least not in the *Paradiso*. The whole rhythmical period however, by no means always coincides with one *terzina*. It may extend to two or more *terzine*—on occasion, to as many as eight (XIII, 1–24), though always on the condition, that its unit (the *terzina*) be preserved rhythmically intact. To observe this condition would be scarcely possible even for Dante, if he wrote in long complex sentences, clause within clause. But he does not. His purpose—plain description, syllogistic argument—suits with a sentence-structure, mostly paratactic or, if otherwise, having the simple relationship of short propositions connected, for the most part, by 'as' and 'so' or 'so' and 'that'. Thus, in one case the simile, in the other the premise and conclusion, or cause and consequence, fall easily into three verses apiece, although, as already remarked, many more than one *terzina* may be required before the whole rhythmical movement comes with the final cadence to a full stop.

Now, it is undoubtedly true, that the English translator, unless he has trained ear and mind by long practice

---

* Cp. Milton's one instance of the same partition of a single compound word in *P.L.* x, 581:

> Ophion, with Eurynome (the wide-
> Encroaching Eve perhaps),

which I have imitated in my translation of the verse above quoted.

to adjust his thought-forms almost unconsciously to successive units, each of three verses exactly, will find his own rhythms tending by nature to overrun the limit. From the time of Shakespeare, and more especially of Milton, their free rhythms have not only set the norm for English blank verse, but have imposed themselves on the heroic verse-couplet and the longer stanza as well. Shelley's *terza rima* is for this reason not *terza rima* at all, but rhymed blank verse, as utterly different from Dante's, as his Spenserian stanza in *Adonais* is in pace and movement different from Spenser's in the *Faerie Queene*.

Yet there is no reason in theory why, if English poetry can adjust its rhythms to the closed couplet or to a series of closed couplets, it should not equally well adjust them to the closed *terzina*. It does in fact do so, sometimes for several 'triplets' together, in the satires of Dryden and Pope, who though writing in couplets often needed an extra verse to complete the rhythm, and that not always an alexandrine. Thus, apart from the rhyme (which we are not at present considering), when, in *The Hind and the Panther*, Dryden writes:

> Can I believe eternal God could lye
> Disguis'd in mortal mold and infancy?
> That the great Maker of the world could die?

he has composed a Dantesque *terzina*. And if it be argued that, while capable of managing a single odd terzet without inconvenience, the English poet would be much embarrassed if required to build up a series of them forming one rhythmical structure, we must reply again that Dryden discovered no difficulty in the feat: for in the poem already quoted we have such a series as

And like his Mind his outward form appear'd
When, issuing Naked to the wondring Herd,
He charmed their Eyes; and, for they lov'd, they fear'd:

Not armed with horns of arbitrary might,
Or Claws to seize their furry spoils in Fight,
Or with increase of Feet t'o'ertake 'em in their flight;

Of easy shape, and pliant ev'ry way,
Confessing still the softness of his Clay,
And kind as Kings upon their Coronation-day;...

It is true that he then closes with a couplet: but we need
not suppose that any technical obstacles would have
prevented him from writing a poem as long as a canto
of the Comedy in *terzine* had he so desired. Couplets,
however, happened to be the new fashion; so he preferred them.

We are driven to conclude, therefore, that the sup-
posed difficulty of writing English *terza rima* in the
Italian manner must lie not in the stanza itself, but in
its rhyme-scheme—a difficulty greatly increased under
the conditions imposed by translation, where the writer
is bound by his original. That the difficulty exists cannot
be denied. But it is necessary here to distinguish. No
one, surely, can seriously maintain that a language is
deficient in words of a like-sounding termination, which
boasts of the *Faerie Queene* and such a poem as Byron's
Don Juan. For in these immensely long works the stanza
of the one requires four, of the other three, verses to be
written on the same rhyme. It is certainly true that
Italian contains a vastly greater number of rhyming
words than English, and further allows of identical
rhymes, which English by custom does not. But even
so the Spenserian stanza is proof positive that English
possesses rhymes enough for *terza rima* purposes. Their

relative scarcity as compared with Italian, while no
excuse for using bad English rhymes, will, however,
justify the translator of Dante in departing from the
latter's practice in one respect, and one only. He may
permit himself to do what Dante very rarely does (in the
Paradiso, at any rate), and that is repeat the same set of
rhymes in the same canto. But even this liberty must
not be abused. The same rhyme should be avoided in two
consecutive *terzine*, or, from being two stanzas, they
would become one. He may, further, allow himself eye-
rhymes* and rhymes of open-vowel with close-vowel
syllables: and that, without apology, for two reasons:
firstly, because he has the authority of all the greatest
English poets for so doing; and, secondly, these kinds of
rhyme, precisely because they are not true rhyme, please
(or have, by habit, come to please) the English ear. And
this apart from the fact that there are certain common
but important words—notably 'love', the key-word of
the *Paradiso*—which he would otherwise scarcely ever
be able to place at the end of a line at all. It may further
be remarked in passing, that a judicious use of the eye-
rhyme completely disposes of the objection, referred to
above, that the frequency or too rapid recurrence of the
rhyme in *terza rima* will prove trying to the English ear.
All that in this respect the translator need remember is
to avoid over-insistent rhymes (unless, as in Dante's own
manner, introduced for a special purpose) and also any
rhyme which attracts attention to itself by its sheer
ingenuity. For the latter, in English, is permissible in
comic verse only and therefore—however appropriate to

* Often, originally, true rhymes, and even now sometimes such in
dialect; and parallel to the Latin, archaic, or dialectical forms em-
ployed by Dante for the sake of easier rhyming.

certain passages of the *Inferno*—must be deemed entirely out of place in a translation of the *Paradiso*.

The real difficulty of writing Dantesque *terza rima* in English is not to find the rhymes but to imitate Dante in his artistic use of them. He employs rhyme in this respect for at least three clearly distinguishable purposes. The first has already been referred to. The rhyme links the stanzas formally by "an infinitely subtle simplicity. It is unique in combining, or rather achieving a compromise between, the completely continuous form of blank verse and the discontinuous 'eddying' form of all stanzaic measures". The rhymes from this point of view are no less essential to the structure of the poem than are its quadruple rhyme and alexandrine to the structure of the Spenserian stanza. The *Faerie Queene* could not be rebuilt in blank verse or in a stanza of other rhyme-scheme without complete destruction of its character. No more can the Divine Comedy. And yet this purely formal function of the rhyme is in a sense less important than the second role which Dante makes it play in the poem, namely to point the sense and guide the meaning.

Although it is true that in well-written verse the important word (or thought), wherever it be placed in the line, will inevitably get the emphasis it requires, yet in the Italian hendecasyllable the metre itself involves that the end of the line should be specially emphatic. For the tenth syllable is the only one which must invariably bear the stress. The fourth or sixth comes next in importance. Dante makes the rhyme reinforce the final stress, with the result that in nine cases out of ten the rhyme-word—and, of the three in the *terzina*, often one in particular—is the outstanding or key-word of the

argument. So true is this that in whole passages together
you may follow the drift of the thought by a mere glance
at the rhymes. It would be foolish to suggest that the
translator must always so manipulate his thought as to
emphasise by rhyme the very same idea that Dante does.
For translation is art, not mechanism; and the translator, like any other good craftsman, must conceal his
art and make his rhymes seem to occur as easily and
inevitably as in his original. This they can only do, if,
while adopting so far as he may Dante's principle of
linking the important idea with the rhyme, he remains
free to emphasise by this means whatever word the logic
of his own rendering of Dante's argument raises to
special importance. Yet there are countless passages,
where unless he can contrive to place at the end of the
line the same word as Dante does, he will not in the
strict sense be translating him. One instance will illustrate what is meant.

In St Peter's famous denunciation of Boniface VIII
(XXVII, 22) the saint refers to the pope as follows:

> Quelli ch' usurpa in terra il luogo mio,
> il luogo mio, il luogo mio, che vaca
> ne la presenza del Figliuol di Dio....

The 'luogo mio', thrice repeated for the sake of emphasis, must obviously be retained by the translator,
who (since, rendered literally, the words fall naturally
into English verse) might be inclined to translate it

> He that usurps on earth my place, my place,
> my place, etc.

But this is precisely what he must not do. For the
rhythm, the grammatical inversion, but chiefly the
rhyme, all show that the emphasis falls on the possessive,

not the noun. What St Peter says is 'the place that is
mine'. He is not concerned with the papal see as such,
but to underline the contrast between himself and
Boniface as occupants of it. Nor is 'my place' a mistranslation of the meaning only. It also fails to render
the feeling of indignation which is expressed not merely
by the repetition of the words, but by the *sound* of the
rhyme-word. The deep, open 'o' of 'luogo' passing into
the long-drawn-out, close, high-pitched 'i' of 'mio' (and
dropping back to short 'o' again) conveys the very
inflexion of the apostle's voice, rising on the rhyme-
word to a shr*i*ek (gr*i*do) of fury, which trembles indeed
on the verge of the comic. Boniface represents not God
but Satan, 'il perverso (another rhyme-word) che cadde
di qua su', whereas St Peter was truly the vicar of God,
as the triple rhyme, 'io—mio—Dio', subconsciously im-
presses through the ear on the mind by association of
ideas. If the translator cannot, throughout the poem, be
constantly using the rhyme for this sort of effect, he had
better not attempt *terza rima* at all. Where a new topic
of conversation is introduced on the rhyme (e.g. XXIV,
38), or where the key-word of the sentence is reserved
for the final cadence (e.g. XXIX, 18), or where this comes
as a climax (e.g. XVI, 66; XX, 30), he can hardly forsake
his author without betraying him.

The third way in which Dante exploits the rhyme
must be studied in connexion with the music of his verse.
If it be rhythm rather than intonation, or the reverse,
or both in equal degree, from which a poet's tune derives
its characteristic quality may be matter for dispute.
But there can be no question that in *terza rima*, as Dante
writes it, the rhyme profoundly influences, by emphasis-
ing, the cadences. In fact his rhymes are so essentially

part of his music, and so especially beautiful is the third rhyme when it brings the melody to a full close, that the translator may well despair of reproducing even the echo of the echo of such loveliness. All the same he must make the attempt, especially in passages of philosophical argument, where the rhymes are as important as the rhythms in aiding the mind to appreciate the music no less than the logic of the thought. If the reader doubts this let him turn to such a passage of sustained argument as XIII, 37–111, and try to estimate what it would lose in meaning by being deprived of the rhymes.

Nor may the translator excuse himself for failure in his duties here by either of the two pleas, often advanced but equally false, that the English language is inherently less musical than the Italian and that about philosophical theory there is something unavoidably prosaic. With regard to the first it is doubtless true that Italian is more richly vowelled than modern English, and that over and over again in the Comedy lines like

per le sorrise parolette brevi

defy literal translation: not because English is incapable of producing the same quality of sound when handled by a master, but because the thought here has to be rendered as well as the melody, and consequently the right-sounding words may not be available. But English, though not so rich in vowels, has an immense advantage over the Italian language in its mixed Teuton and Latin vocabulary, its consonantal music and above all its monosyllables. Nor could the greatest of all extant poetic literatures have been composed in English, were this not by nature better adapted for poetic composition than any other modern language. The English translator who thinks of Italian as musical and his own language as, relatively speaking, harsh, either possesses no ear or has never read English poetry.*

As for the commonly expressed opinion that the poetry of the *Paradiso* is impaired (or interrupted) by the intrusion of dry disquisitions devoted to obsolete philosophical theories, it is enough to reply that every problem—theological, metaphysical, moral, or scientific—raised by Dante is as much a living problem at the present time as it was in his own day and will be centuries hence; and on the relationship of poetry to philosophy to quote the following observations on the subject by Santayana, which the twenty years or more that have elapsed since he made them have far from rendered out of date. "There is a kind of sensualism or aestheticism that has decreed in our day that theory is not poetical; as if all the images and emotions that enter a cultivated mind were not saturated with theory. The prevalence of such a sensualism or aestheticism would alone suffice to explain the impotence of the arts. The life of theory is not less human or less emotional than the life of sense; it is more typically human and more keenly emotional. Philosophy is a more intense sort of experience than common life is, just as pure and subtle music, heard in retirement, is something keener and more intense than the howling of storms or the rumbling

---

* By 'musical' I refer of course to the sound of words in themselves as the material medium of the art of poetry, not to their incidental suitability for being converted to its own ends by the kindred but quite distinct art of music. In the sense of 'more easily *sung*' Italian may well be more musical than English. But in either language 'numerous verse', if truly poetry, is, and always has been, of its very nature

> More tuneable than needed lute or harp
> To add more sweetness.

of cities. For this reason philosophy, when a poet is not mindless, enters inevitably into poetry, since it has entered into his life; or rather, the detail of things and the detail of ideas pass equally into his verse, when both alike lie in the path that has led him to his ideal. To object to theory in poetry would be like objecting to words there; for words, too, are symbols without the sensuous character of the things they stand for; and yet it is only by the net of new connexions which words throw over things, in recalling them, that poetry arises at all.''*

Of Dante's vocabulary it is characteristic that no word, learned or popular (even vulgar), can be too expressive or too clear. All his senses are summoned to help his thought, and it has been aptly remarked that in no other poem, comparable for size with the Comedy, does the individual word seem each one to be so much an independent creation, so clearly an unique, fully developed, definite, living picture. In the *Paradiso*, where he makes such constant use of light, sound and movement, his numerous terms for these are as nicely distinguished in sense as his philosophical and scientific terminology is technically correct. His illustrations never, as Coleridge complained that his own did, 'swallow up his thesis'. Metaphors, however beautiful, are always primarily means to an end —the clearer presentation of the things described, or the more lucid exposition of the thought. If a speaker asks a question, the reply is always rigidly restricted to answering what has been asked, and that with the utmost

---

* On the relationship of the philosophical discussions in the *Paradiso* to the religious purpose of the poem Wicksteed has well said: "At the touch of Dante's staff, the flintiest rock of metaphysical dogma yields the water of life, and in his hands the subtlest discussion of casuistry becomes a lamp to our feet".

economy of phrase. The frequent simile is so constructed as to illustrate the one or two points of likeness observed between the objects compared, and no more. Nothing in the simile is superfluous and nothing, if properly understood, inappropriate. Thus, to take as a single example the famous image of the lark in xx, 73, the likening of so small a bird to the vast eagle imprinted on the orb of Jupiter might seem incongruous to absurdity unless we grasp the true point for comparison, which is a double one: the singing of the eagle *while it flies* and the *reason* for the cessation of its song. The lark is then seen to be the one and only bird which will serve the poet's purpose. The flight of the lark is not so much described as actually suggested in the rhythm of the verse, and the joy, that makes her silent, by the sound of it. Dante never seems embarrassed by his rhyme, or forced by it to use words other than precisely those which his argument requires,* though sometimes (as in vi, 48, where he needs a rhyme for a proper name) it may suggest a metaphor which might not otherwise have occurred to him.

These are all features of Dante's style which the reader, without even glancing at the original Italian, should be able to gather from a competent translation of it or, indeed, of any one of its *terzine*; for in style each *terzina* is the whole poem in miniature. Nor can there be any question but that the translator, in seeking to reproduce them in English, will be immensely aided by using Dante's own metre. In fact only thus will he be able to deal at all adequately with certain special pro-

---

* The author of the *Ottimo commento* (in his note on *Inf.* x, 85) says he himself had heard Dante claim that "never had a rhyme made him say other than he would, but that many a time and oft in his rhymes he had made words say for him what they were not wont to express for others".

blems in expression with which the poet's love of word-
play frequently confronts him. For Dante, like his
masters the Provençal troubadours, delights at times in
exhibitions of verbal dexterity, which his translator
should imitate if by any means it is possible.

Sometimes (as in I, 115–117; XII, 91–93) each verse of
the *terzina* begins with the same word: sometimes (as
in XIII, 94, 97, 100; XV, 100, 103, 106, 109) each one of a
series of *terzine* begins with the same word, of which the
most notable example is the thrice repeated 'Lì si
vedrà', 'Vedrassi' and 'E' of XIX, 115–133: sometimes
each of a series of double *terzine* begins with the same
words (as in XX, 40–70). As remarkable, and as necessary
to imitate, are those intricately yet neatly constructed
verses, in which changes are rung, by stress and rhyme
alike, on a single repeated idea, as in XX, 96–99, 'vince—
vince—vinta—vinta—vince'; XXI, 49–50, 'vedea—
veder—vede'; XXXIII, 5–6, 'fattore—farsi—fattura'.
The descending rhythms of the verses from which the last
example is taken should be specially noted—the famous
opening sentence of the prayer to the Virgin: 'Vérgine
madre—úmile e alta—términe fisso', followed up in the
fourth line by the emphatic 'tu', and closing in the sixth on
the cadence 'fattura'. Then there are sound-jingles, which
must be reproduced if possible; like the 'chiusa chiusa',
'canto canta' of V, 138–9, and the 'luce la luce' of VI, 128.
Only actual puns, depending as they do on the similarity
and difference of Italian words, are probably untrans-
latable (cp. the 'vóti e vòti' of III, 57, and the 'pietà—
spietato' of IV, 105, where 'pity' is no true rendering of
the Italian 'pietà'). It is easy, on the other hand, to make
the word 'Christ', as Dante does, rhyme only with itself
and to reproduce the emphatic 'vidi' of XXX, 95–7–9.

Proper names should be anglicised, where they have their true English equivalent, such as Pietro—Peter, etc. Where this is lacking, not only must the Italian name be retained, but retained with its right accent; being so placed in the verse, that the verse will not scan, unless the name be accented correctly. More difficult are the philosophical terms, which must of course be rendered with scrupulous accuracy, though here the translator should be able to rely upon the reader's possessing at least a working knowledge of the language of the schools. But Dante in the *Paradiso* invents a series of words to express the process by which one thing becomes, or is unified with, another, and these it is very hard to know how to anglicise. Such words are for the most part verbs compounded of the preposition 'in' with a noun, adverb or pronoun, like 'imparadisare' (xxviii, 3), from which Milton coined 'imparadise', 'invogliare', 'insemprarsi', 'immiarsi', 'intuarsi', 'inluiarsi', etc. To 'in-will' on the analogy of 'in-form' is a daring but perhaps legitimate English equivalent: but in the case of 'in-me, in-thou', etc. the translator must secure the effect by stressing the pronoun either through position or rhyme. There are a few passages* which it is best to render as nearly as possible word for word because they admit of several interpretations.

In conclusion I return to where I began. The present version of the *Paradiso* is not addressed to those who regard translation as useless, because impossible: but to those who, recognising its limitations, allow it, when

---

* Such, among others, are the difficult xxvii, 136–8 (where in rendering v. 138 I adopt the sense placed upon it by Professor J. E. Shaw in *Modern Philology*, vol. xxviii, No. 11) and xxxii, 70–1 (where, for the sake of easier apprehension, I have, while retaining, slightly modified, the boldness of the metaphor).

working strictly within these, the full dignity of an art only less exacting in its requirements than original composition. How exacting these are the conscientious translator knows better than his severest critic. Nor, in the case of the *Paradiso*, will the expenditure of infinite pains enable him (though otherwise qualified) to meet them. He needs to share Dante's faith and to pray for something of his spirit—

Entra nel petto mio, e spira tue.

For if the mighty Florentine himself confessed that his sacred poem had made him lean through many years, how should his humble translator expect to render him even feebly without tasting of the same discipline?

" Visionary power
Attends the motions of the viewless winds,
Embodied in the mystery of words:
There, darkness makes abode, and all the host
Of shadowy things work endless changes,—there,
As in a mansion like their proper home,
Even forms and substances are circumfused
By that transparent veil with light divine,
And, through the turnings intricate of verse,
Present themselves as objects recognised,
In flashes, and with glory not their own."

PARADISO

★

CANTO I

La gloria di colui che tutto move
　per l' universo penetra e risplende
　in una parte più e meno altrove.　　　　3
Nel ciel che più de la sua luce prende
　fu' io, e vidi cose che ridire
　nè sa nè può chi di là su discende;　　　6
perchè appressando sè al suo disire,
　nostro intelletto si profonda tanto,
　che dietro la memoria non può ire.　　　9
Veramente quant' io del regno santo
　ne la mia mente potei far tesoro,
　sarà ora matera del mio canto.　　　　12
O buono Apollo, a l' ultimo lavoro
　fammi del tuo valor sì fatto vaso,
　come dimandi a dar l' amato alloro.　　15
Infino a qui l' un giogo di Parnaso
　assai mi fu; ma or con amendue
　m' è uopo intrar ne l' aringo rimaso.　　18
Entra nel petto mio, e spira tue
　sì come quando Marsia traesti
　de la vagina de le membra sue.　　　　21
O divina virtù, se mi ti presti
　tanto che l' ombra del beato regno
　segnata nel mio capo io manifesti,　　　24
venir vedra'mi al tuo diletto legno,
　e coronarmi allor di quelle foglie
　che la matera e tu mi farai degno.　　　27

PARADISE

*

CANTO I

His glory, in whose being all things move,
  pervades creation and now more, now less,
  resplendent shines in every part thereof.
Within the heaven his brightest beams caress
  was I, and things beheld which none returning
  to earth hath power or knowledge to express;
because, when near the object of its yearning,
  our understanding is for truths made strong,
  which memory is too feeble for relearning.
Yet of the realm that saints and angels throng
  so much as I could treasure up in mind,
  shall now be made the matter of my song.
Apollo, to my crowning task be kind;
  make me thy chosen vessel, round whose brow
  thy darling bay might fitly be entwined.
So far with one Parnassian peak hast thou
  met all my needs: but I require the twain,
  to dare the struggle that awaits me now.
Enter my breast in such a mood as when
  thou from the scabbard of his limbs didst tear
  forth Marsyas; breathe in me that matchless strain.
O power divine, let me but so far share
  thyself, that I, dim memory though it be,
  the blessèd kingdom may in words declare,
and thou shalt see me come to thy loved tree
  and crown myself with laurel, then indeed
  made fit to wear it by my theme and thee.

Sì rade volte, padre, se ne coglie
  per triunfare o cesare o poeta,
  colpa e vergogna de l' umane voglie,   30
che parturir letizia in su la lieta
  delfica deità dovria la fronda
  peneia, quando alcun di sè asseta.   33
Poca favilla gran fiamma seconda:
  forse di retro a me con miglior voci
  si pregherà perchè Cirra risponda.   36
Surge ai mortali per diverse foci
  la lucerna del mondo; ma da quella
  che quattro cerchi giugne con tre croci,   39
con miglior corso e con migliore stella
  esce congiunta, e la mondana cera
  più a suo modo tempera e suggella.   42
Fatto avea di là mane e di qua sera
  tal foce quasi, e tutto era là bianco
  quello emisperio, e l' altra parte nera,   45
quando Beatrice in sul sinistro fianco
  vidi rivolta e riguardar nel sole:
  aquila sì non li s' affisse unquanco.   48
E sì come secondo raggio suole
  uscir del primo e risalire in suso,
  pur come pellegrin che tornar vuole,   51
così de l' atto suo, per li occhi infuso
  ne l' imagine mia, il mio si fece,
  e fissi li occhi al sole oltre nostr' uso.   54
Molto è licito là, che qui non lece
  a le nostre virtù, mercè del loco
  fatto per proprio de l' umana spece.   57
Io nol soffersi molto, nè sì poco,
  ch' io nol vedessi sfavillar dintorno,
  com ferro che bogliente esce del fuoco;   60

For Caesar's triumph or for poet's meed
  so seldom is it gathered, mighty sire,
  (woe worth the sordid ends of human greed)
that the Peneian frondage should inspire
  with gladness the glad Delphic deity,
  whene'er in any man it wakes desire.
From tiny spark a flame may leap full high:
  haply some bard, praying in worthier wise,
  may after me from Cirrha win reply.
Through divers openings dawns on mortal eyes
  the world's bright lamp; but that we see display
  four circles with three crosses joined, supplies
his beams with happier course, wherein, with ray
  of happier star conjoined, he mouldeth fair
  the mundane wax more after his own way.
This point, or near it, had caused morning there,
  here eve: and all of half the heavens were white
  on that side, and on this all darkling were,
when I saw Beatrice, with visage bright
  turned leftward, gazing full upon the sun:
  eagle thereon so never fixed his sight.
As forth the first the second ray will run
  and upwards re-ascend, like pilgrim fain
  to turn home, when his outward voyage is done,
so to her gesture, through the eyesight ta'en
  into my fancy, was my own inclined,
  and I gazed sunward, past the wont of men.
There much is granted, which our senses find
  denied them here, through virtue of the spot
  fashioned of old expressly for mankind.
So long I gazed—tho' long I bore it not—
  as to perceive him sparkling all around,
  like iron which from the furnace flows white-hot;

e di subito parve giorno a giorno
  essere aggiunto, come quei che puote
  avesse il ciel d' un altro sole adorno.   63
Beatrice tutta ne l' etterne rote
  fissa con gli occhi stava; ed io in lei
  le luci fissi, di là su rimote.   66
Nel suo aspetto tal dentro mi fei,
  qual si fè Glauco nel gustar de l' erba
  che 'l fè consorto in mar de li altri Dei.   69
Trasumanar significar per verba
  non si poria; però l' essemplo basti
  a cui esperienza grazia serba.   72
S' i' era sol di me quel che creasti
  novellamente, amor che 'l ciel governi,
  tu 'l sai, che col tuo lume mi levasti.   75
Quando la rota che tu sempiterni
  desiderato, a sè mi fece atteso
  con l' armonia che temperi e discerni,   78
parvemi tanto allor del cielo acceso
  de la fiamma del sol, che pioggia o fiume
  lago non fece mai tanto disteso.   81
La novità del suono e 'l grande lume
  di lor cagion m' accesero un disio
  mai non sentito di cotanto acume.   84
Ond' ella, che vedea me sì com' io,
  a quietarmi l' animo commosso,
  pria ch' io a dimandar, la bocca aprio,   87
e cominciò: "Tu stesso ti fai grosso
  col falso imaginar, sì che non vedi
  ciò che vedresti se l' avessi scosso.   90
Tu non se' in terra, sì come tu credi;
  ma folgore, fuggendo il proprio sito,
  non corse come tu ch' ad esso riedi".   93

and suddenly the light of day I found
  increased twofold, as though the Omnipotent
  had with a second sun the welkin crowned.
Stood Beatrice with gaze still wholly bent
  upon the eternal wheels; and I on her
  fixed mine, withdrawn now from the firmament.
So gazing did I feel in me the stir
  that Glaucus felt, when he consumed of yore
  the herb which made him as the sea-gods were.
Since words may tell not what it means to outsoar
  the human, let the example satisfy
  him for whom grace hath fuller proof in store.
O love, the lord of heaven, if nought was I
  of self save what in man thou new-createst
  is known to thee, whose light I raised me by.
What time the wheel whose love thou never satest
  though thence eternal made, had charmed my ear
  with tones which thou, its tuner, modulatest,
I saw such vast fields of the atmosphere
  lit by the solar flames, that neither flood
  nor deluge ever formed so wide a mere.
The unwonted sound, the light's great magnitude
  such craving roused in me to realise
  their cause, as ne'er till then had fired my blood.
Then she, who saw me as with my own eyes,
  opened her mouth to calm my troubled mind,
  ere I to frame a question, and thus-wise
began: "Thine own false fancies make thee blind;
  hence unperceived are things thou wouldst perceive,
  hadst thou but left thy vain conceits behind.
Thou'rt not on earth still, as thou dost believe,
  but back to thy true home dost swiftlier soar
  than lightning falls, when thence a fugitive".

S' io fui del primo dubbio disvestito
   per le sorrise parolette brevi,
   dentro ad un nuovo più fu' inretito,   96
e dissi: "Già contento requievi
   di grande ammirazion, ma ora ammiro
   com' io trascenda questi corpi levi".   99
Ond' ella, appresso d' un pio sospiro,
   li occhi drizzò ver me con quel sembiante
   che madre fa sovra figlio deliro,   102
e cominciò: "Le cose tutte quante
   hanno ordine tra loro, e questo è forma
   che l' universo a Dio fa simigliante.   105
Qui veggion l' alte creature l' orma
   de l' etterno valore, il qual è fine
   al quale è fatta la toccata norma.   108
Ne l' ordine ch' io dico sono accline
   tutte nature, per diverse sorti,
   più al principio loro e men vicine;   111
onde si muovono a diversi porti
   per lo gran mar de l' essere, e ciascuna
   con istinto a lei dato che la porti.   114
Questi ne porta il foco inver la luna;
   questi ne' cor mortali è permotore;
   questi la terra in sè stringe e aduna: 117
nè pur le creature che son fore
   d' intelligenza quest' arco saetta,
   ma quelle c' hanno intelletto ed amore.   120
La provedenza, che cotanto assetta,
   del suo lume fa 'l ciel sempre quieto
   nel qual si volge quel c' ha maggior fretta;   123
e ora lì, come a sito decreto,
   cen porta la virtù di quella corda
   che ciò che scocca drizza in segno lieto.   126

Freed of my first doubt by the dulcet lore
   instilled thus briefly by my smiling guide,
   yet in new doubt was I enmeshed the more,
and said: "Awhile I rested, satisfied,
   from my great wonder; but I marvel yet,
   how up through these light bodies I can glide".
My question with a pitying sigh she met,
   then eyed me with a mother's anxious care
   for child whose brain delirious dreams beset,
and thus began: "In all things whatsoe'er
   is order found: order is form, indeed,
   which makes the universe God's image bear.
Herein do the higher beings the impress read
   of that eternal worth, which is the end
   whereto the aforesaid rule has been decreed.
In this same order ranked, all natures bend
   their several ways, through divers lots, as near
   and farther from the source whence all descend;
thus onward unto various ports they steer
   through the great sea of being, each impelled
   by instinct, given to make it persevere.
This to the moon keeps blazing fire upheld;
   this is in brutes the spring that makes them move;
   this doth the earth into one substance weld:
nor only creatures, void of reason, prove
   this bow's impelling force, but every soul
   that is endowed with intellect and love.
The providence, which rules this ordered whole,
   keeps making ever tranquil with its light
   the heaven wherein the swiftest sphere doth roll;
and thither, as to pre-appointed site,
   that bow-string which doth all its arrows shoot
   at happy mark, now speeds us by its might.

Vero è che come forma non s' accorda
 molte fiate a l' intenzion de l' arte,
 perch' a risponder la materia è sorda;   129
così da questo corso si diparte
 talor la creatura, c' ha podere
 di piegar, così pinta, in altra parte   132
(e sì come veder si può cadere
 foco di nube), se l' impeto primo
 l' atterra torto da falso piacere.   135
Non dei più ammirar, se bene stimo,
 lo tuo salir, se non come d' un rivo
 se d' alto monte scende giuso ad imo.   138
Maraviglia sarebbe in te, se, privo
 d' impedimento, giù ti fossi assiso,
 com' a terra quiete in foco vivo ".   141
Quinci rivolse inver lo cielo il viso.

CANTO II

O voi che siete in piccioletta barca,
 disiderosi d' ascoltar, seguiti
 dietro al mio legno che cantando varca,   3
tornate a riveder li vostri liti:
 non vi mettete in pelago, chè, forse,
 perdendo me rimarreste smarriti.   6
L' acqua ch' io prendo già mai non si corse:
 Minerva spira, e conducemi Apollo,
 e nove Muse mi dimostran l' Orse.   9
Voi altri pochi che drizzaste il collo
 per tempo al pan de li angeli, del quale
 vivesi qui ma non sen vien satollo,   12

'Tis true that, as the form may oft ill suit
   with the result which art would fain effect,
   because the matter to its call stays mute;
so from this course the creature may deflect
   itself at whiles; for, though thus urged on high,
   its power to swerve aside remains unchecked
(even as fire may oft be seen to fly
   down from a cloud), should the first impulse bring
   it earthward, by false pleasures wrenched awry.
If I deem right, thou shouldst be wondering
   no more at thine ascent, than at a rill
   for rushing downward from its mountain-spring.
Marvel it were in thee, if, with a will
   unhindered, thou hadst hugged a lower plane,
   as in quick fire on earth, if it kept still".
Therewith she turned her face to heaven again.

CANTO II

ALL ye, that in your little boat, full fain
   to listen, have pursued upon its way
   my gallant ship that singing cleaves the main,
put back to your own shores, while yet ye may:
   tempt not the deep; or, venturing too far,
   ye well might lose me and be left astray.
The seas I sail as yet untravelled are:
   Minerva wafts me, and Apollo steers,
   and all his Nine point me to either Bear.
But ye, the few, who from your earliest years
   have held up eager mouths for angels' bread,
   sole food on earth that cloys not whom it cheers,

metter potete ben per l' alto sale
   vostro navigio, servando mio solco
   dinanzi a l' acqua che ritorna equale.   15
Que' gloriosi che passaro a Colco
   non s' ammiraron come voi farete,
   quando Iason vider fatto bifolco.   18
La concreata e perpetua sete
   del deiforme regno cen portava
   veloci quasi come 'l ciel vedete.   21
Beatrice in suso, e io in lei guardava;
   e forse in tanto in quanto un quadrel posa
   e vola e da la noce si dischiava,   24
giunto mi vidi ove mirabil cosa
   mi torse il viso a sè; e però quella
   cui non potea mia cura essere ascosa,   27
volta ver me, sì lieta come bella,
   "Drizza la mente in Dio grata" mi disse,
   "che n' ha congiunti con la prima stella".   30
Parev' a me che nube ne coprisse
   lucida, spessa, solida e pulita,
   quasi adamante che lo sol ferisse.   33
Per entro sè l' etterna margarita
   ne ricevette, com' acqua recepe
   raggio di luce permanendo unita.   36
S' io era corpo, e qui non si concepe
   com' una dimensione altra patio,
   ch' esser convien se corpo in corpo repe,   39
accender ne dovria più il disio
   di veder quella essenza in che si vede
   come nostra natura e Dio s' unio.   42
Lì si vedrà ciò che tenem per fede,
   non dimostrato, ma fia per sè noto
   a guisa del ver primo che l' uom crede.   45

may safely seaward turn your vessel's head,
   if close upon my furrowed wake ye stand,
   or e'er its ridges back to smoothness fade.
More shall ye marvel than the glorious band
   that voyaged to Colchis, when with wondering eyes
   they stared at Jason toiling plough in hand.
The inborn, never-ceasing thirst to rise
   toward the realm which God's own form makes fair,
   winged us with speed that well-nigh matched the sky's.
My guide was gazing upward, I on her;
   and as a quarrel finds the mark, takes wing,
   and quits the peg, so quick or quicklier
arrived I saw me, where a marvellous thing
   drew to itself my gaze; and therefore she
   who saw full well my secret wondering,
bending, as blithe as fair, her looks on me,
   cried, "'Tis the first star! Turn thee, as thou art bound,
   in thanks to God, that joined therewith are we".
Meseemed as though a cloud had wrapped us round:
   luminous, solid, close and smooth, it best
   were likened unto sunlit diamond.
The ever-gleaming pearl held us encased
   within itself, as water holds a ray
   of light, itself remaining undisplaced.
If I was body—and none here can say
   how mass could suffer mass, as must ensue,
   if body into body steals its way—
so much the rather should we burn to view
   that essence which alone discovereth
   how the divine was yet made human too.
There will be seen that which we hold by faith,
   not proven, nay, but of itself made plain,
   like those first truths which no one questioneth.

Io rispuosi: "Madonna, sì devoto
 com' esser posso più, ringrazio lui
 lo qual dal mortal mondo m' ha remoto. 48
Ma ditemi: che son li segni bui
 di questo corpo, che là giuso in terra
 fan di Cain favoleggiare altrui?" 51
Ella sorrise alquanto, e poi "S' egli erra
 l' oppinion" mi disse "de' mortali
 dove chiave di senso non diserra, 54
certo non ti dovrien punger li strali
 d' ammirazione omai, poi dietro ai sensi
 vedi che la ragione ha corte l' ali. 57
Ma dimmi quel che tu da te ne pensi".
 E io: "Ciò che n' appar qua su diverso
 credo che fanno i corpi rari e densi". 60
Ed ella: "Certo assai vedrai sommerso
 nel falso il creder tuo, se bene ascolti
 l' argomentar ch' io li farò avverso. 63
La spera ottava vi dimostra molti
 lumi, li quali e nel quale e nel quanto
 notar si posson di diversi volti. 66
Se raro e denso ciò facesser tanto,
 una sola virtù sarebbe in tutti,
 più e 'men distributa e altrettanto. 69
Virtù diverse esser convegnon frutti
 di principii formali, e quei, for ch' uno,
 seguiterieno a tua ragion distrutti. 72
Ancor, se raro fosse di quel bruno
 cagion che tu dimandi, od oltre in parte
 fora di sua materia sì digiuno 75
esto pianeta, o sì come comparte
 lo grasso e 'l magro un corpo, così questo
 nel suo volume cangerebbe carte. 78

I answered: "Lady, I with heart as fain,
  as heart can be, pay reverent thanks to him
  who hath removed me from the world of men.
But tell me what the spots are which bedim
  this body's surface and down there on earth
  cause folk to tell of Cain that fable grim".
She smiled: and then, "If, where the key held forth
  by sense unlocks not, man's opinion prove,"
  she answered me, "a guide of little worth,
surely the stab of wonder should not move
  thee now, who sëest that, e'en when following sense,
  the flight of reason falleth short thereof.
But tell me what thyself thou deemest. Whence
  come they?" And I: "This mottled aspect here
  I think is caused by bodies rare and dense".
And she: "Doubt not thy thought shall soon appear
  in error drowned, if to the proofs I bring
  against it thou but lend attentive ear.
In the eighth heaven displayed, past numbering,
  are lights, which differ visibly in size
  as in the colour of the beams they fling.
Did this from rare and dense alone arise,
  one virtue only would in all be found
  in greater, less and equal quantities.
Virtues that differ needs must have their ground
  in formal causes, all of which save one
  would be annulled, suppose thy reasoning sound.
Besides, if rarity produced that dun
  effect whose cause thou'dst fain investigate,
  either, right through, this orb in part would run
short of its matter, or as lean and fat
  are interchanged in bodies, so would this
  the leaves within its volume alternate.

Se 'l primo fosse, fora manifesto
　ne l' eclissi del sol per trasparere
　lo lume come in altro raro ingesto.　　　81
Questo non è: però è da vedere
　de l' altro; e s' elli avvien ch' io l' altro cassi,
　falsificato fia lo tuo parere.　　　84
S' elli è che questo raro non trapassi,
　esser conviene un termine da onde
　lo suo contrario più passar non lassi;　　　87
e indi l' altrui raggio si rifonde
　così come color torna per vetro
　lo qual di retro a sè piombo nasconde.　　　90
Or dirai tu ch' el si dimostra tetro
　ivi lo raggio più che in altre parti,
　per esser lì refratto più a retro.　　　93
Da questa instanza può deliberarti
　esperienza, se già mai la pruovi,
　ch' esser suol fonte ai rivi di vostr' arti.　　　96
Tre specchi prenderai; e i due rimovi
　da te d' un modo, e l' altro, più rimosso,
　tr' ambo li primi li occhi tuoi ritrovi.　　　99
Rivolto ad essi, fa che dopo il dosso
　ti stea un lume che i tre specchi accenda
　e torni a te da tutti ripercosso.　　　102
Ben che nel quanto tanto non si stenda
　la vista più lontana, lì vedrai
　come convien ch' igualmente risplenda.　　　105
Or come ai colpi de li caldi rai
　de la neve riman nudo il suggetto
　e dal colore e dal freddo primai,　　　108
così rimaso te ne l' intelletto
　voglio informar di luce sì vivace,
　che ti tremolerà nel suo aspetto.　　　111

We could accept the first hypothesis,
   if at a sun's-eclipse the light shone through,
   as through all other loose-packed substances.
But 'tis not so: and hence we must review
   the other theory, which if I refute,
   then thy opinion will be proved untrue.
Suppose this rareness not to pass right thro' it,
   the dense must form a barrier beyond which
   it doth its contrary's further path dispute;
and thence reflected are the rays that reach
   it from without, as colours are from glass
   that hides behind it lead they cannot breach.
This reflex radiance (now thou'lt argue) has
   less brilliance than the rest, because it starts
   from deeper down within the lunar mass.
From this demur experiment imparts
   the lore to free thee, wilt thou but essay
   that wonted fountainhead of all your arts.
Three mirrors take; move two of them away
   like distance from thee, and the third be seen
   'twixt both the first, but farther off than they.
Then, facing towards them, have a lamp brought in
   behind thy back to illumine them, that so
   all may return thee its reflected sheen.
Albeit the farther mirror will not show
   so wide a surface, yet thou'lt there behold
   how it must needs with equal brilliance glow.
Now even as some snow-encumbered wold,
   when warm beams strike it, doth dismantled lie
   of that which lately made it white and cold,
so thee, dismantled in thy mind, will I
   inform with light so lively it shall shine
   before thee sparkling like a star on high.

Dentro dal ciel de la divina pace
  si gira un corpo ne la cui virtute
  l' esser di tutto suo contento giace.   114
Lo ciel seguente, c' ha tante vedute,
  quell' esser parte per diverse essenze,
  da lui distinte e da lui contenute.   117
Li altri giron per varie differenze
  le distinzion che dentro da sè hanno
  dispongono a lor fini e lor semenze.   120
Questi organi del mondo così vanno,
  come tu vedi omai, di grado in grado,
  che di su prendono e di sotto fanno.   123
Riguarda bene omai sì com' io vado
  per questo loco al vero che disiri,
  sì che poi sappi sol tener lo guado.   126
Lo moto e la virtù de' santi giri,
  come dal fabbro l' arte del martello,
  da' beati motor convien che spiri;   129
e 'l ciel cui tanti lumi fanno bello,
  de la mente profonda che lui volve
  prende l' image e fassene suggello.   132
E come l' alma dentro a vostra polve
  per differenti membra e conformate
  a diverse potenze si risolve,   135
così l' intelligenza sua bontate
  multiplicata per le stelle spiega,
  girando sè sovra sua unitate.   138
Virtù diversa fa diversa lega
  col prezioso corpo ch' ella avviva,
  nel qual, sì come vita in voi, si lega.   141
Per la natura lieta onde deriva,
  la virtù mista per lo corpo luce
  come letizia per pupilla viva.   144

Poised in the heaven of the peace divine
   revolves an orb within whose influence lies
   the being of all things that its bounds confine.
The heaven that follows, bright with myriad eyes,
   divides that being mid diverse essences,
   from it distinct, but which its terms comprise.
The other whorls in various degrees
   dispose to their due ends their own innate
   distinctions and the germs contained in these.
Thus, as thou sëest now, in grades rotate
   these organs of the world, since, from above
   acted upon, below they actuate.
Now mark me crossing by this ford to prove
   the truth thou lovest: then, no aid required,
   thyself with boldness through the shallows move.
The sacred orbs, with virtue and motion fired,
   like hammer guided by the workman's skill,
   by blessèd movers needs must be inspired;
and the heaven so many lights begem, doth feel
   the stamp of that deep spirit which makes it roll,
   and of this stamp itself becomes the seal.
And as in your material frame the soul,
   through different members fashioned to comply
   with different faculties, informs the whole,
so the intelligence unfolds on high
   its goodness through the stars: thus multiplied,
   revolving still on its own unity.
Virtue diverse is diversely allied
   with the rich mass it quickens, in whose frame,
   as life in yours, its being is closely tied.
True to the joyous nature whence it came,
   this virtue, like the joy in sparkling eyes,
   once blent therewith doth all the mass enflame.

Da essa vien ciò che da luce a luce
  par differente, non da denso e raro:
  essa è il formal principio che produce,   147
conforme a sua bontà, lo turbo e 'l chiaro ".

CANTO III

Quel sol che pria d' amor mi scaldò 'l petto,
  di bella verità m' avea scoverto,
  provando e riprovando, il dolce aspetto;   3
e io, per confessar corretto e certo
  me stesso, tanto quanto si convenne
  levai il capo a proferer più erto;   6
ma visione apparve che ritenne
  a sè me tanto stretto, per vedersi,
  che di mia confession non mi sovvenne.   9
Quali per vetri trasparenti e tersi,
  o ver per acque nitide e tranquille,
  non sì profonde che i fondi sien persi,   12
tornan di nostri visi le postille
  debili sì, che perla in bianca fronte
  non vien men tosto a le nostre pupille;   15
tali vid' io più facce a parlar pronte:
  per ch' io dentro a l' error contrario corsi
  a quel ch' accese amor tra l' omo e 'l fonte.   18
Subito sì com' io di lor m' accorsi,
  quelle stimando specchiati sembianti,
  per veder di cui fosser, li occhi torsi;   21
e nulla vidi, e ritorsili avanti
  dritti nel lume de la dolce guida,
  che, sorridendo, ardea ne li occhi santi.   24

From this, and not from dense and rare, arise
   the differences observed 'twixt light and light:
   this is the formal cause whence spring likewise,
Agreeable to its boon, the dull and bright".

CANTO III

Thus did the sun which warmed my heart of yore,
   to proof and disproof paying equal heed,
   show me fair truth and the sweet look she wore;
and I, to own myself convinced and freed
   from error, for confession raised my head
   more boldly, yet no higher than there was need;
when I beheld a sight which in me bred
   such wonder, that mine eyes stayed fixed thereto,
   and my confession from remembrance fled.
As through transparent sheets of glass, or through
   bright, tranquil water, not so deep withal
   as that its bottom should be lost to view,
come shadows of our features back, yet all
   so faint, that pearl, on a white forehead gleaming,
   would not less quickly for attention call;
such I beheld a group of faces seeming
   eager to speak, and erred in counter-wise
   to that which set the fountain-lover dreaming.
No sooner seen, than I, in swift surmise
   that they were mirrored images, to know
   whose they might be, cast back inquiring eyes,
saw nothing, forward looked again, and so
   gazed full into the light of my sweet guide,
   who smiling stood, her holy eyes aglow.

"Non ti maravigliar perch' io sorrida"
   mi disse "appresso il tuo pueril coto,
   poi sopra 'l vero ancor lo piè non fida,   27
ma te rivolve, come suole, a voto:
   vere sustanze son ciò che tu vedi,
   qui rilegate per manco di voto.   30
Però parla con esse e odi e credi;
   chè la verace luce che li appaga
   da sè non lascia lor torcer li piedi."   33
Ed io a l' ombra che parea più vaga
   di ragionar, drizza'mi, e cominciai,
   quasi com' uom cui troppa voglia smaga: 36
"O ben creato spirito, che a' rai
   di vita etterna la dolcezza senti
   che, non gustata, non s' intende mai,   39
grazioso mi fia se mi contenti
   del nome tuo e de la vostra sorte".
   Ond' ella, pronta e con occhi ridenti: 42
"La nostra carità non serra porte
   a giusta voglia, se non come quella
   che vuol simile a sè tutta sua corte.   45
I' fui nel mondo vergine sorella;
   e se la mente tua ben sè riguarda,
   non mi ti celerà l' esser più bella,   48
ma riconoscerai ch' i' son Piccarda,
   che, posta qui con questi altri beati,
   beata sono in la spera più tarda.   51
Li nostri affetti che solo infiammati
   son nel piacer de lo Spirito Santo,
   letizian del suo ordine formati.   54
E questa sorte che par giù cotanto,
   però n' è data, perchè fuor negletti
   li nostri vóti, e vòti in alcun canto".   57

"Be not astonished that I smile", she cried,
   "after thy childish thought, which, even now
   in solid truth unwilling to confide,
sinks thee in error, as it well knows how:
   true substances are these thou dost perceive,
   consigned here for the failure of some vow.
But speak with them and listen and believe;
   for the true light which fills them with content
   unto itself compels their steps to cleave."
And I unto the shade which seemed most bent
   on converse, turned, and thus began, like one
   so eager that he feels bewilderment:
"O spirit born for bliss, who in the sun
   of life eternal dost the sweetness try
   which, save by taste, is understood of none,
'twould please me well if thou wouldst satisfy
   my wish to know thy name and your estate."
   Whence she with smiling eyes made prompt reply:
"To rightful wish our love unlocks the gate
   freely as his doth, whose own graciousness
   he wills that all his courtiers imitate.
On earth I was a virgin-votaress;
   and, if thou search thy mind, 'twill yet be clear
   to thee, despite my greater loveliness,
that thou behold'st Piccarda, stationed here
   among these other blessèd ones, and blest
   myself too in the slowest-moving sphere.
The Holy Ghost imparts their flaming zest
   to our affections, he alone; and he
   orders our gladness as he judgeth best.
And this allotted place which seems to be
   so low is ours, because the vows we made
   were slighted or performed imperfectly".

Ond' io a lei: "Ne' mirabili aspetti
   vostri risplende non so che divino
   che vi trasmuta da' primi concetti: 60
però non fui a rimembrar festino;
   ma or m' aiuta ciò che tu mi dici,
   sì che raffigurar m' è più latino.   63
Ma dimmi: voi che siete qui felici,
   disiderate voi più alto loco
   per più vedere e per più farvi amici?"   66
Con quelle altr' ombre pria sorrise un poco;
   da indi mi rispuose tanto lieta,
   ch' arder parea d' amor nel primo foco: 69
"Frate, la nostra volontà quieta
   virtù di carità, che fa volerne
   sol quel ch' avemo, e d' altro non ci asseta. 72
Se disiassimo esser più superne,
   foran discordi li nostri disiri
   dal voler di colui che qui ne cerne;   75
che vedrai non capere in questi giri,
   s' essere in carità è qui necesse,
   e se la sua natura ben rimiri.   78
Anzi è formale ad esto beato esse
   tenersi dentro a la divina voglia,
   per ch' una fansi nostre voglie stesse: 81
sì che, come noi sem di soglia in soglia
   per questo regno, a tutto il regno piace
   com' a lo re ch' a suo voler ne invoglia. 84
E 'n la sua volontade è nostra pace:
   ell' è quel mare al qual tutto si move
   ciò ch' ella cria e che natura face".   87
Chiaro mi fu allor come ogni dove
   in cielo è paradiso, etsi la grazia
   del sommo ben d' un modo non vi piove. 90

Whence I to her: "Your faces, thus arrayed,
  glow with I know not what of heavenly sheen,
  making one's former notions of you fade:
hence was my recollection not so keen;
  but now thy words awake old memories,
  so that more clearly I recall thy mien.
But tell me, ye who tarry here in bliss,
  would ye not fain ascend to regions higher,
  to win more friends or to see more than this?"
All smiled at first to hear me thus inquire;
  then with such radiant gladness she replied,
  methought her burning in love's primal fire:
"Brother, our wills are wholly satisfied
  by love, whose virtue makes us will alone
  what we possess, and thirst for nought beside.
Wished we to make a loftier seat our own,
  our wish discordant with his will would be,
  who hath assigned this planet for our throne;
the which these orbs admit not, as thou'lt see,
  if here to be in love must needs befall,
  and thou regard love's nature carefully.
Nay, 'tis essential to the being we call
  blest, that it should the will of God fulfil,
  so making one the very wills of all:
therefore our being thus, from sill to sill
  the whole realm through, alike the realm doth please
  and ruler who in-wills us to his will.
And in his will our souls discover peace:
  it is that ocean whither all things fare
  which it creates and nature bids increase".
Thus learned I how in heaven everywhere
  is paradise, albeit the highest good
  sheds not its dew in one sole measure there.

Ma sì com' elli avvien, s' un cibo sazia
  e d' un altro rimane ancor la gola,
  che quel si chiede e di quel si ringrazia,   93
così fec' io con atto e con parola,
  per apprender da lei qual fu la tela
  onde non trasse infino a co la spuola.   96
"Perfetta vita e alto merto inciela
  donna più su" mi disse "a la cui norma
  nel vostro mondo giù si veste e vela,   99
perchè fino al morir si vegghi e dorma
  con quello sposo ch' ogni voto accetta
  che caritate a suo piacer conforma.   102
Dal mondo, per seguirla, giovinetta
  fuggi'mi, e nel suo abito mi chiusi,
  e promisi la via de la sua setta.   105
Uomini poi, a mal più ch' a bene usi,
  fuor mi rapiron de la dolce chiostra:
  Iddio si sa qual poi mia vita fusi.   108
E quest' altro splendor che ti si mostra
  da la mia destra parte e che s' accende
  di tutto il lume de la spera nostra,   111
ciò ch' io dico di me, di sè intende:
  sorella fu, e così le fu tolta
  di capo l' ombra de le sacre bende.   114
Ma poi che pur al mondo fu rivolta
  contra suo grado e contra buona usanza,
  non fu dal vel del cor già mai disciolta.   117
Quest' è la luce della gran Costanza
  che del secondo vento di Soave
  generò il terzo e l' ultima possanza."   120
Così parlommi, e poi cominciò '*Ave
Maria*' cantando, e cantando vanio
  come per acqua cupa cosa grave.   123

But as may be, if sated with one food
   and greedy for another, we have pled
   for this, declining that with gratitude,
such was my gesture, such the words I said,
   to learn from her what web it was wherethrough
   she had not drawn the shuttle to the head.
"Shines higher enskyed," quoth she, "as guerdon due
   to perfect life and high desert, a dame
   whose rule on earth her veiled ones yet pursue,
that so till death, both day and night the same,
   that spouse they may attend who doth reject
   no vow which his dear love absolves from blame.
Shunning the world, did I in youth elect
   to follow her; and, in her habit wrapt,
   I pledged me to the pathway of her sect.
Thereafter men, for ill than good more apt,
   forth snatched me from the cloister's peaceful ways:
   and God knows on what later life I happed.
And lo, this other lustre who displays
   her beauty on my right and whom our sphere
   lights up with the full splendour of its rays,
knows that my story to her own comes near:
   she too a nun, her brows were forced to part
   with the o'ershadowing coif she held so dear.
Yet, when against her will—and though to thwart
   that will was sin—she found herself out-cast
   upon the world, she stayed still veiled in heart.
This light is the great Constance: from one blast,
   the second Swabian, did she generate
   the third imperial whirlwind, and the last."
Thus she addressed me and, beginning straight
   to sing the *Avë*, passed in song away,
   as through deep water sinks a heavy weight.

La vista mia, che tanto la seguio
  quanto possibil fu, poi che la perse,
  volsesi al segno di maggior disio,   126
e a Beatrice tutta si converse;
  ma quella folgorò ne lo mio sguardo
  sì che da prima il viso non sofferse;   129
e ciò mi fece a dimandar più tardo.

CANTO IV

INTRA due cibi, distanti e moventi
  d' un modo, prima si morria di fame,
  che liber' uomo l' un recasse ai denti;   3
sì si starebbe un agno intra due brame
  di fieri lupi, igualmente temendo;
  sì si starebbe un cane intra due dame: 6
per che, s' i' mi tacea, me non riprendo,
  da li miei dubbi d' un modo sospinto,
  poi ch' era necessario, nè commendo.   9
Io mi tacea, ma 'l mio disir dipinto
  m' era nel viso, e 'l dimandar con ello,
  più caldo assai che per parlar distinto.   12
Fè sì Beatrice qual fè Daniello,
  Nabuccodonosor levando d' ira,
  che l' avea fatto ingiustamente fello;   15
e disse: "Io veggio ben come ti tira
  uno e altro disio, sì che tua cura
  se stessa lega sì che fuor non spira.   18
Tu argomenti: 'Se 'l buon voler dura,
  la violenza altrui per qual ragione
  di meritar mi scema la misura?'   21

So long as possible did I essay
   to keep her form in view: when she was gone,
   a livelier desire resumed its sway,
and Beatrice my whole attention won;
   but for a while my vision lacked the power
   to gaze at her, so dazzling bright she shone;
which made me in my questioning the slower.

CANTO IV

Between two foods, equally tempting, placed
   equally near, a man, tho' free to choose,
   would starve before deciding which to taste;
so would a lamb, fearing alike both foes,
   stand fixed between two ravening wolves; and so
   a hound would hesitate between two does:
urged, then, by equal doubts, I count it no
   reproach to have held my peace, since need compelled,
   nor on myself would praise therefor bestow.
But my desire, tho' silenced, was not quelled;
   limned in my looks, it there set forth my plea
   far warmlier in that utterance was withheld.
Did Beatrice what Daniel did, when he
   Nebuchadnezzar from an anger freed,
   which drave him to unrighteous cruelty.
"Plainly", she said, "thy two desires impede
   each one the other; hence thy troubled thought
   so binds itself as to suppress its need.
Thou arguest: 'If the good will fails in nought,
   why should my merit be accounted less,
   because of violence by others wrought?'

Ancor di dubitar ti dà cagione
   parer tornarsi l' anime a le stelle,
   secondo la sentenza di Platone.   24
Queste son le question che nel tuo velle
   pontano igualmente; e però pria
   tratterò quella che più ha di felle.   27
De' Serafin colui che più s' india,
   Moisè, Samuel, e quel Giovanni
   che prender vuoli, io dico, non Maria,   30
non hanno in altro cielo i loro scanni
   che questi spirti che mo t' appariro,
   nè hanno a l' esser lor più o meno anni;   33
ma tutti fanno bello il primo giro,
   e differentemente han dolce vita
   per sentir più e men l' etterno spiro.   36
Qui si mostraro, non perchè sortita
   sia questa spera lor, ma per far segno
   de la celestial c' ha men salita.   39
Così parlar conviensi al vostro ingegno,
   però che solo da sensato apprende
   ciò che fa poscia d' intelletto degno.   42
Per questo la Scrittura condescende
   a vostra facultate, e piedi e mano
   attribuisce a Dio, ed altro intende;   45
e Santa Chiesa con aspetto umano
   Gabriel e Michel vi rappresenta,
   e l' altro che Tobia rifece sano.   48
Quel che Timeo de l' anime argomenta
   non è simile a ciò che qui si vede,
   però che, come dice, par che senta.   51
Dice che l' alma a la sua stella riede,
   credendo quella quindi esser decisa
   quando natura per forma la diede;   54

It further gives thee cause for doubtfulness
   that seemingly, as Plato fancied, all
   disbodied souls to stars their path retrace.
These are the questions which within thee call
   like urgently for answer, hence will I
   treat first of that which hath the more of gall.
No Seraph—not the one to God most nigh,
   not Moses, Samuel or either John,
   not even Mary are enthroned on high
in other heaven than are the souls just gone
   from hence, nor to their being have they there
   more years or fewer in comparison;
but the first circle each and all make fair,
   breathing a life diversely sweet, as they
   or more or less the eternal spirit share.
Nor did they in this sphere their forms display
   as were it their portion, but to mark them thus
   as least reflective of the heavenly ray.
So to bespeak your wit behoveth us,
   for only sense can make it grasp what then
   to intellect it renders luminous.
This is why Scripture condescends to feign
   for your behoof, though meaning otherwise,
   that God hath hands and feet, like mortal men;
and Holy Church depicts in human guise
   Gabriel and Michael, and that other too,
   who restored vision unto Tobit's eyes.
As for Timaeus touching souls, his view
   resembles not that which one here discerns,
   for what he says he seems to think is true.
He says the soul to its own star returns,
   deeming it cut therefrom, when nature gave
   the body form—a view one rightly spurns;

e forse sua sentenza è d' altra guisa
    che la voce non suona, ed esser puote
    con intenzion da non esser derisa.   57
S' elli intende tornare a queste rote
    l' onor de la influenza e 'l biasmo, forse
    in alcun vero suo arco percuote.   60
Questo principio, male inteso, torse
    già tutto il mondo quasi, sì che Giove,
    Mercurio e Marte a nominar trascorse.   63
L' altra dubitazion che ti commove
    ha men velen, però che sua malizia
    non ti poria menar da me altrove.   66
Parere ingiusta la nostra giustizia
    ne li occhi de' mortali, è argomento
    di fede e non d' eretica nequizia.   69
Ma perchè puote vostro accorgimento
    ben penetrare a questa veritate,
    come disiri, ti farò contento.   72
Se violenza è quando quel che pate
    niente conferisce a quel che sforza,
    non fuor quest' alme per essa scusate;   75
chè volontà, se non vuol, non s' ammorza,
    ma fa come natura face in foco,
    se mille volte violenza il torza.   78
Per che, s' ella si piega assai o poco,
    segue la forza; e così queste fero,
    possendo rifuggir nel santo loco.   81
Se fosse stato lor volere intero,
    come tenne Lorenzo in su la grada,
    e fece Muzio a la sua man severo,   84
così l' avria ripinte per la strada
    ond' eran tratte, come fuoro sciolte;
    ma così salda voglia è troppo rada.   87

but haply his opinion he might save
   from mere derision, could his language claim
   a meaning other than it seems to have.
If to these orbs he means return the blame
   and honour of their influence, then maybe
   some truth he strikes, at which his bow took aim.
This lore, mis-learned, perverted formerly
   well nigh the whole world, causing it to err
   by invoking Jove and Mars and Mercury.
The other doubt thou feelst within thee stir
   is less envenomed, for it could not blind
   thine eyes to me nor lead thee otherwhere.
Theirs is no wicked heresy who find
   seeming injustice in our justice—nay,
   it should but make them more to faith inclined.
But seeing that to this truth there leads a way
   which by your intellect might well be used,
   all thou wouldst have me tell I now will say.
If it be force when he which is abused
   in nothing aideth him which doth the ill,
   then not for this these spirits stood excused;
for nought can quench the unconsenting will:
   'tis like to fire which, beaten from its track
   a thousand times, by nature seeks it still.
Hence, if it yields at all through growing slack,
   will abets force, as these did, who, with power
   to turn back to the cloister, turned not back.
Had but their will been whole, like that which o'er
   the grate held Laurence and made Mutius stern
   to his own hand, they would, when free once more,
have been compelled by it to make return
   thither, whence they were dragged by violence;
   but in too few doth will so steadfast burn.

E per queste parole, se ricolte
  l' hai come dei, è l' argomento casso
  che t' avria fatto noia ancor più volte.   90
Ma or ti s' attraversa un altro passo
  dinanzi a li occhi, tal, che per te stesso
  non usciresti, pria saresti lasso.   93
Io t' ho per certo ne la mente messo
  ch' alma beata non poria mentire,
  però ch' è sempre al primo vero appresso;   96
e poi potesti da Piccarda udire
  che l' affezion del vel Costanza tenne;
  sì ch' ella par qui meco contradire.   99
Molte fiate già, frate, addivenne
  che, per fuggir periglio, contra grato
  si fè di quel che far non si convenne;   102
come Almeone, che, di ciò pregato
  dal padre suo, la propria madre spense,
  per non perder pietà, si fè spietato.   105
A questo punto voglio che tu pense
  che la forza al voler si mischia, e fanno
  sì che scusar non si posson l' offense.   108
Voglia assoluta non consente al danno;
  ma consentevi in tanto, in quanto teme,
  se si ritrae, cadere in più affanno.   111
Però, quando Piccarda quello spreme,
  de la voglia assoluta intende, e io
  de l' altra; sì che ver diciamo insieme".   114
Cotal fu l' ondeggiar del santo rio
  ch' uscì del fonte ond' ogni ver deriva;
  tal puose in pace uno e altro disio.   117
"O amanza del primo amante, o diva"
  diss' io appresso "il cui parlar m' inonda
  e scalda sì, che più e più m' avviva,   120

And thus, if thou hast duly gleaned their sense,
　my words refute the reasoning which might yet
　full many a time have caused thee grave offence.
But now before thee winds another strait,
　such that to issue thence would sorely try
　thine own unaided skill, however great.
Firmly impressed it on thy mind have I,
　that, since to primal truth 'tis alway near,
　no soul that dwells in bliss could ever lie;
whereas Piccarda made it no less clear,
　that Constance for the veil her love retained,
　so that she seems to contradict me here.
Brother, ofttimes 'twill hap, that to forfend
　a danger, what men should not, men will do,
　e'en while they hate the means which serve their end;
thus, being by his father urged thereto,
　Alcmaeon, not to fail in filial love,
　hardened his heart and his own mother slew.
Bethink thee that such actions clearly prove
　that force with will combines, annulling so
　all pleas which might the taint of guilt remove.
Tempted to sin, will of itself says 'no',
　but in so far consents, as it may dread,
　through drawing back, to incur some greater woe.
Now, in Piccarda's speech the reference made
　to will was to will absolute, in mine
　to the other; hence in both the truth was said."
Thus rippling from the fountainhead divine
　of every truth, the holy rill supplied
　to both my doubts the longed-for anodyne.
"O loved of the first lover," then I cried,
　"O deity whose speech doth more and more
　refresh me with its warm, full-flowing tide,

non è l' affezion mia sì profonda,
  che basti a render voi grazia per grazia;
  ma quei che vede e puote a ciò risponda.   123
Io veggio ben che già mai non si sazia
  nostro intelletto, se 'l ver non lo illustra
  di fuor dal qual nessun vero si spazia.   126
Posasi in esso come fera in lustra,
  tosto che giunto l' ha; e giugner puollo:
  se non, ciascun disio sarebbe frustra.   129
Nasce per quello, a guisa di rampollo,
  a piè del vero il dubbio; ed è natura
  ch' al sommo pinge noi di collo in collo.   132
Questo m' invita, questo m' assicura
  con reverenza, donna, a dimandarvi
  d' un' altra verità che m' è oscura.   135
Io vo' saper se l' uom può sodisfarvi
  ai voti manchi sì con altri beni,
  ch' a la vostra statera non sien parvi."   138
Beatrice mi guardò con li occhi pieni
  di faville d' amor così divini,
  che, vinta, mia virtute diè le reni,   141
e quasi mi perdei con li occhi chini.

CANTO V

"S' io ti fiammeggio nel caldo d' amore
  di là dal modo che 'n terra si vede,
  sì che de li occhi tuoi vinco il valore,   3
non ti maravigliar; chè ciò procede
  da perfetto veder, che, come apprende,
  così nel bene appreso move il piede.   6

to render grace for grace my own poor store
  of love will reach not; but may he requite
  your bounty, who both sees and hath the power.
I see well that apart from that true light
  which comprehends all truth, the minds of men
  can never glut themselves with full insight.
They rest in truth as wild beast in its den,
  when once they have attained it; and they may
  attain it: else were all desires in vain.
Whence from the bole of truth there buds the spray
  of doubt; and we are urged, thus peak by peak,
  toward the summit in the natural way.
This bids me, this emboldens me to seek
  with reverence, lady, for your aid anent
  another truth of which my grasp is weak.
Fain would I know if man can supplement
  his broken vows by other deeds well done,
  which in your scales may be equivalent."
Beatrice gazed at me with eyes which shone
  love-sparkling, so divine, that it was past
  my power to bear them, and I stood like one
well-nigh bereft of sense, with eyes downcast.

CANTO V

"If that I flame upon thee in ardent love
  surpassing aught beheld in mortal mien,
  so that thine eyes bear not the blaze thereof,
marvel thou not; for such hath ever been
  the effect of perfect sight, which, as it sees,
  so draweth nearer to the blessing seen.

Io veggio ben sì come già resplende
  ne l' intelletto tuo l' etterna luce,
  che, vista, sola e sempre amore accende;   9
e s' altra cosa vostro amor seduce,
  non è se non di quella alcun vestigio,
  mal conosciuto, che quivi traluce.   12
Tu vuo' saper se con altro servigio,
  per manco voto, si può render tanto
  che l' anima sicuri di letigio."   15
Sì cominciò Beatrice questo canto;
  e sì com' uom che suo parlar non spezza,
  continuò così 'l processo santo: 18
"Lo maggior don che Dio per sua larghezza
  fesse creando ed a la sua bontate
  più conformato e quel ch' e' più apprezza,   21
fu de la volontà la libertate;
  di che le creature intelligenti,
  e tutte e sole, fuoro e son dotate.   24
Or ti parrà, se tu quinci argomenti,
  l' alto valor del voto, s' è sì fatto
  che Dio consenta quando tu consenti;   27
chè, nel fermar tra Dio e l' uomo il patto,
  vittima fassi di questo tesoro,
  tal quale io dico; e fassi col suo atto.   30
Dunque che render puossi per ristoro?
  Se credi bene usar quel c' hai offerto,
  di mal tolletto vuo' far buon lavoro.   33
Tu se' omai del maggior punto certo;
  ma perchè Santa Chiesa in ciò dispensa,
  che par contra lo ver ch' i' t' ho scoverto,   36
convienti ancor sedere un poco a mensa,
  però che 'l cibo rigido c' hai preso,
  richiede ancora aiuto a tua dispensa.   39

The eternal light—and this alone it is,
   which, once beheld, enkindles love alway—
   now visibly thy mind from darkness frees;
and if aught else doth lead your love astray,
   'tis only that some trace therein you see,
   albeit ill-marked, of that celestial ray.
Thou askest if for broken vows may be
   with other service such requital made,
   as may secure the soul from further plea."
So Beatrice this canto preluded;
   and, like some fluent speaker's, onward flowed
   her sacred argument, as thus she said:
"Of all the gifts a bounteous God bestowed
   at the creation, that which made appeal
   most to himself and most his goodness showed,
and hence the best, was freedom of the will;
   which to all thinking creatures, and alone
   to them, was granted and is granted still.
By argument, thus based, is clearly shown
   the vow's high value, if thou so contract
   with God, that his approval crowns thy own;
for, in the very sealing of the pact
   between God and the man, this precious thing
   is made a victim, and by its own act.
What compensation, therefore, canst thou bring?
   Free wouldst thou be of stolen wealth, if thou
   to good use think to turn thine offering.
So the main point is clear; but since it now
   seems counter to the truth as just expressed
   that Holy Church dispenses from a vow,
thou must at table keep thy seat as guest
   a little longer, for this solid meal
   needs further help to make it well digest.

Apri la mente a quel ch' io ti paleso
  e fermalvi entro; chè non fa scienza,
  sanza lo ritenere, avere inteso.   42
Due cose si convegnono a l' essenza
  di questo sacrificio: l' una è quella
  di che si fa; l' altr' è la convenenza.   45
Quest' ultima già mai non si cancella
  se non servata; ed intorno di lei
  sì preciso di sopra si favella: 48
però necessità fu a li Ebrei
  pur l' offerere, ancor ch' alcuna offerta
  si permutasse, come saver dei.   51
L' altra, che per materia t' è aperta,
  puote ben esser tal, che non si falla
  se con altra materia si converta.   54
Ma non trasmuti carco a la sua spalla
  per suo arbitrio alcun, sanza la volta
  e de la chiave bianca e de la gialla;   57
e ogni permutanza credi stolta,
  se la cosa dimessa in la sorpresa
  come 'l quattro nel sei non è raccolta.   60
Però qualunque cosa tanto pesa
  per suo valor che tragga ogni bilancia,
  sodisfar non si può con altra spesa.   63
Non prendan li mortali il voto a ciancia:
  siate fedeli, e a ciò far non bieci,
  come Ieptè a la sua prima mancia;   66
cui più si convenia dicer 'Mal feci',
  che, servando, far peggio; e così stolto
  ritrovar puoi il gran duca de' Greci,   69
onde pianse Ifigenia il suo bel volto,
  e fè pianger di sè i folli e i savi
  ch' udir parlar di così fatto colto.   72

Open thy mind to what I now reveal:
  there store it closely; for to have understood,
  but not retained, as knowledge counts for nil.
This sacrifice in essence doth include
  two things, of which the service vowed is one,
  and one the vow that is thereby made good.
This last, concerning which a moment gone
  I uttered language so precise, may ne'er
  be cancelled; all it purposed must be done:
hence were the Hebrews still obliged to bear
  an offering, though some offered things allowed
  of commutation, as thou'rt well aware.
The other, which I called 'the service vowed',
  can well be such as without fault may be
  exchanged for service other than is owed.
E'en so, let none regard himself as free
  to shift his shoulder's burden, ere the door
  be unlocked by both the white and the yellow key;
and let him every thought of change give o'er,
  unless the burden taken up comprise
  the one laid down, as 'six' containeth 'four'.
Hence there can be no charge which satisfies
  the claim of thing so precious, that its weight
  must still o'erbalance every counterpoise.
Then, mortals, vow not lightly: pay your debt,
  but with clear eyes, not with the bisson look
  of Jephthah pledged to kill what first he met;
who should have cried, 'Wrong was the vow I took',
  and not sinned worse by keeping it; no less
  insensate wilt thou find the Greeks' great duke,
whence Iphigénia rued her lovely face,
  and made both wise and simple share her teen,
  to think that rite so foul should e'er take place.

Siate, Cristiani, a muovervi più gravi:
  non siate come penna ad ogni vento,
  e non crediate ch' ogni acqua vi lavi.   75
Avete il novo e 'l vecchio Testamento,
  e 'l pastor de la Chiesa che vi guida:
  questo vi basti a vostro salvamento.   78
Se mala cupidigia altro vi grida,
  uomini siate, e non pecore matte,
  sì che 'l Giudeo di voi tra voi non rida!   81
Non fate com' agnel che lascia il latte
  de la sua madre, e semplice e lascivo
  seco medesmo a suo piacer combatte!"   84
Così Beatrice a me com' io scrivo;
  poi si rivolse tutta disiante
  a quella parte ove 'l mondo è più vivo.   87
Lo suo tacere e 'l trasmutar sembiante
  puoser silenzio al mio cupido ingegno,
  che già nuove questioni avea davante;   90
e sì come saetta, che nel segno
  percuote pria che sia la corda queta,
  così corremmo nel secondo regno.   93
Quivi la donna mia vid' io sì lieta,
  come nel lume di quel ciel si mise,
  che più lucente se ne fè 'l pianeta.   96
E se la stella si cambiò e rise,
  qual mi fec' io che pur da mia natura
  trasmutabile son per tutte guise!   99
Come 'n peschiera ch' è tranquilla e pura
  traggonsi i pesci a ciò che vien di fori
  per modo che lo stimin lor pastura,   102
sì vid' io ben più di mille splendori
  trarsi ver noi, ed in ciascun s' udia:
  "Ecco chi crescerà li nostri amori".   105

Christians, be firmer in resisting sin:
   be not like feather, sport of every breeze,
   nor think that every water laves you clean.
The Testaments are yours, whiche'er ye please;
   the Church's shepherd leaves you not forlorn:
   for your salvation rest content with these.
If e'er by evil lust your souls be torn,
   be men, and not like silly sheep, that so
   the Jew among you laugh you not to scorn!
Do not as doth the lamb, which will forgo
   its mother's milk to enjoy the empty bliss
   of fighting with itself, a wanton foe!"
Such were the very words of Beatrice;
   then, all consumed with keen desire, she turned
   to where the world with life most quickened is.
Her silence and the change which I discerned
   upon her face my eager mind forbade
   to ask the further things it fain had learned;
and swift as shaft which strikes the quarry dead,
   before the bow-string ceases to vibrate,
   so to the second kingdom on we sped.
Here I beheld the dame so radiate
   joy, as within that shining heaven she passed,
   that the bright planet grew thence brighter yet.
And if the star was moved to smile, how was't
   with me, who am obnoxious, of my mere
   nature, to change of every shade and cast!
As in a fish-pond that is calm and clear,
   to aught that enters seeming like to prove
   good for their nourishment the fish draw near,
so did I see a swarm of splendours move
   to usward, and in each was heard the cry:
   "Lo, here is one who will increase our love!"

E sì come ciascuno a noi venia,
   vedeasi l' ombra piena di letizia
   nel fulgor chiaro che di lei uscia.   108
Pensa, lettor, se quel che qui s' inizia
   non procedesse, come tu avresti
   di più savere angosciosa carizia;   111
e per te vederai come da questi
   m' era in disio d' udir lor condizioni,
   sì come a li occhi mi fur manifesti.   114
"O bene nato a cui veder li troni
   del triunfo etternal concede grazia
   prima che la milizia s' abbandoni,   117
del lume che per tutto il ciel si spazia,
   noi semo accesi; e però, se disii
   di noi chiarirti, a tuo piacer ti sazia."   120
Così da un di quelli spirti pii
   detto mi fu; e da Beatrice: "Dì dì
   sicuramente, e credi come a dii".   123
"Io veggio ben sì come tu t' annidi
   nel proprio lume, e che de li occhi il traggi,
   perch' e' corusca sì come tu ridi;   126
ma non so chi tu se', nè perchè aggi,
   anima degna, il grado de la spera
   che si vela a' mortai con altrui raggi."   129
Questo diss' io diritto a la lumera
   che pria m' avea parlato; ond' ella fessi
   lucente più assai di quel ch' ell' era.   132
Sì come il sol che si cela elli stessi
   per troppa luce, come 'l caldo ha rose
   le temperanze di vapori spessi;   135
per più letizia sì mi si nascose
   dentro al suo raggio la figura santa;
   e così chiusa chiusa mi rispuose   138
nel modo che 'l seguente canto canta.

And e'en as towards us each of them drew nigh,
   the brilliance of the beams with which it shone
   expressed the fullness of the spirit's joy.
Think, reader, if the tale I've here begun
   were not continued, with what anxious prayer
   you would forthwith implore me to go on;
and hence imagine what my feelings were,
   who longed to ask them how and what they did,
   the moment that mine eyes beheld them there.
"O happy-born, to whom grace doth concede
   vision of the thrones of endless victory,
   ere from thine earthly warfare thou art freed,
lit by the light that floods all heaven are we;
   if, therefore, thou wouldst have thy need supplied,
   ask freely, and thou shalt enlightened be."
One of those gracious souls it was that cried
   these words to me; then Beatrice: "Fear nought,
   speak to them, speak, and as in gods confide!"
"I see the nest of light thou hast round thee wrought;
   and since thine eyes, whene'er thou smilest, blaze,
   this light is drawn from them, I may not doubt;
but who thou art, O spirit all-worthy praise,
   I know not, nor why stationed in the sphere
   oft veiled from mortals by another's rays."
Unto the light which first had hailed my ear
   I thus addressed me; whereupon it grew
   far brighter than I'd seen it erst appear.
Like as the sun who hides himself from view
   thro' excess of light, when the heat has gnawed away
   the mantle which thick vapours round him drew;
so was that holy form in its own ray
   through mere increase of gladness quite concealed;
   and, thus enveloped, did it say its say,
more fit in fytte ensuing to be revealed.

CANTO VI

"Poscia che Costantin l' aquila volse
    contro al corso del ciel, ch' ella seguio
    dietro a l' antico che Lavina tolse,   3
cento e cent' anni e più l' uccel di Dio
    ne lo stremo d' Europa si ritenne,
    vicino a' monti de' quai prima uscio;   6
e sotto l' ombra de le sacre penne
    governò 'l mondo lì di mano in mano,
    e, sì cangiando, in su la mia pervenne.   9
Cesare fui e son Giustiniano,
    che, per voler del primo amor ch' i' sento,
    d' entro le leggi trassi il troppo e 'l vano.   12
E prima ch' io a l' ovra fossi attento,
    una natura in Cristo esser, non piue,
    credea, e di tal fede era contento;   15
ma il benedetto Agapito, che fue
    sommo pastore, a la fede sincera
    mi dirizzò con le parole sue.   18
Io li credetti; e ciò che 'n sua fede era,
    vegg' io or chiaro sì, come tu vedi
    ogni contradizione e falsa e vera.   21
Tosto che con la Chiesa mossi i piedi,
    a Dio per grazia piacque di spirarmi
    l' alto lavoro, e tutto 'n lui mi diedi;   24
e al mio Belisar commendai l' armi,
    cui la destra del ciel fu sì congiunta,
    che segno fu ch' i' dovessi posarmi.   27
Or qui a la question prima s' appunta
    la mia risposta; ma sua condizione
    mi stringe a seguitare alcuna giunta,   30

CANTO VI

"After that Constantine the eagle had driven
    back on the course which it pursued of yore
    behind Lavinia's lord, who marched with heaven,
the bird of God two hundred years and more
    on Europe's utmost verge its seat maintained
    nigh to the mountains where it learned to soar;
there, shadowed by the sacred plumes, it reigned
    over the world from hand to hand, and then,
    thus changing, did at last on mine descend.
Caesar I was, Justinian I remain,
    whom that prime love, which fires me now, impelled
    to rid the laws of what was gross and vain.
And ere this labour summoned me, I held
    that Christ of but one nature was possessed—
    a faith wherein I long contented dwelled;
but Agapetus—name for ever blest—
    who was chief shepherd, by his reasoning drew
    me on, till I the untainted faith confessed.
Him I believed and now as clearly view
    the inward of his faith, as in thy sight
    all contradictions are both false and true.
Soon as the Church had found and set me right,
    God's grace to that high task my heart inclined,
    which I pursued thenceforth with all my might;
arms to my Belisarius I resigned:
    and heaven to him proved such a staunch ally,
    'twas token I might rest in peace of mind.
Here, then, to thy first question my reply
    were ended, did its tenor not disclose
    a sequel, which I needs must amplify,

perchè tu veggi con quanta ragione
  si move contr' al sacrosanto segno
  e chi 'l s' appropria e chi a lui s' oppone.   33
Vedi quanta virtù l' ha fatto degno
  di reverenza; e cominciò da l' ora
  che Pallante morì per darli regno.   36
Tu sai ch' el fece in Alba sua dimora
  per trecento anni e oltre, infino al fine
  che i tre e tre pugnar per lui ancora.   39
E sai ch' el fè dal mal de le Sabine
  al dolor di Lucrezia in sette regi,
  vincendo intorno le genti vicine.   42
Sai quel che fè, portato da li egregi
  Romani incontro a Brenno, incontro a Pirro,
  incontro a gli altri principi e collegi;   45
onde Torquato e Quinzio che dal cirro
  negletto fu nomato, i Deci e' Fabi
  ebber la fama che volontier mirro.   48
Esso atterrò l' orgoglio de li Arabi
  che di retro ad Annibale passaro
  l' alpestre rocce, Po, di che tu labi.   51
Sott' esso giovanetti triunfaro
  Scipione e Pompeo; ed a quel colle
  sotto 'l qual tu nascesti parve amaro.   54
Poi, presso al tempo che tutto 'l ciel volle
  redur lo mondo a suo modo sereno,
  Cesare per voler di Roma il tolle.   57
E quel che fè da Varo infino al Reno,
  Isara vide ed Era e vide Senna
  e ogne valle onde 'l Rodano è pieno.   60
Quel che fè poi ch' elli uscì di Ravenna
  e saltò Rubicon, fu di tal volo,
  che nol seguiteria lingua nè penna.   63

that thou mayst see what right men have to oppose
   the sacred standard, be they what they may,
   its jealous claimants or its bitter foes.
Behold the power for which all ought to pay
   it homage; and thereof began the tale
   from the hour when Pallas died to give it sway.
Thou knowest that Alba was its citadel
   three hundred years and more, until were found
   three matched for it with three in combat fell:
and knowest what exploits made its name resound,
   from the rape o' the Sabines down to Lucrece' woe,
   'neath seven kings subduing the tribes around:
knowest how it did with Roman champions go
   forth to meet Brennus, Pyrrhus and a throng
   of others, single prince or leaguéd foe;
whence won Torquatus, Quinctius of the long
   rough locks, the Decii, Fabii far and wide
   the fame which I rejoice to embalm in song.
It struck to earth the Arabs in their pride
   who followed Hannibal what time he scaled
   the Alpine crags, whence, Po, thy waters glide.
Under it in their glorious youth prevailed
   Scipio and Pompey; and the self-same hill
   that crests thy home, it bitterly assailed.
Then, nigh the time when heaven did wholly will
   that the world's calm should emulate its own,
   Caesar laid hold of it on Rome's appeal.
And what it wrought from Var to the Rhine did Saône
   and Isère witness, witnessed likewise Seine
   and every vale whose tribute brims the Rhône.
What then it wrought when, swooping south again,
   it left Ravenna, leaped the Rubicon,
   is flight too swift for any tongue or pen.

Inver la Spagna rivolse lo stuolo,
   poi ver Durazzo, e Farsalia percosse
   sì ch' al Nil caldo si sentì del duolo.   66
Antandro e Simoenta, onde si mosse,
   rivide e là dov' Ettore si cuba;
   e mal per Tolomeo poscia si scosse.   69
Da onde scese folgorando a Iuba;
   onde si volse nel vostro occidente,
   ove sentia la pompeiana tuba.   72
Di quel che fè col baiulo seguente,
   Bruto con Cassio ne l' inferno latra,
   e Modena e Perugia fu dolente.   75
Piangene ancor la trista Cleopatra,
che, fuggendoli innanzi, dal colubro
   la morte prese subitana e atra.   78
Con costui corse infino al lito rubro;
   con costui puose il mondo in tanta pace,
   che fu serrato a Iano il suo delubro.   81
Ma ciò che 'l segno che parlar mi face
   fatto avea prima e poi era fatturo
   per lo regno mortal ch' a lui soggiace,   84
diventa in apparenza poco e scuro,
   se in mano al terzo Cesare si mira
   con occhio chiaro e con affetto puro;   87
chè la viva giustizia che mi spira,
   li concedette, in mano a quel ch' i' dico,
   gloria di far vendetta a la sua ira.   90
Or qui t' ammira in ciò ch' io ti replico:
   poscia con Tito a far vendetta corse
   de la vendetta del peccato antico.   93
E quando il dente longobardo morse
   la Santa Chiesa, sotto le sue ali
   Carlo Magno, vincendo, la soccorse.   96

Towards Spain it wheeled the legions, urged them on
   then towards Dyrrachium, and Pharsalia smote
   so sorely, that it made the warm Nile groan.
Antandros, its own Simois and the spot
   where sleeps great Hector it revisited;
   and shook its wings, with ill for Ptolemy fraught.
From him to Juba lightning-swift it sped;
   and thence, when the Pompeian trumpet blew,
   back to your west it turned, unweariéd.
With him who bore it next, the flight it flew
   Brutus and Cassius howl of, down in hell,
   and Modena, with Perugia, learned to rue.
Still doth the tragic Cleopatra wail
   because thereof, who, fleeing its path before,
   took from the adder death, instant and fell.
With him it swept even to the Red Sea shore;
   with him upon the whole wide world conferred
   such peace that Janus locked his temple-door.
But all yet wrought by this imperial bird,
   all it was yet to achieve by sea or land
   among the nations which obey its word,
seems paltry and obscure, if it be scanned
   with pure affection and unclouded eye
   as it appeared in the third Caesar's hand;
for in that hand it was the means whereby
   the living justice, my life-breath, decreed
   its wrath should be avenged so gloriously.
With Titus next—and do thou here give heed
   to my strange replication—it was sent
   to avenge the avenging of the old misdeed.
And when the Holy Church lay gored and rent
   by the fierce Lombard's tusk, beneath its wings
   Charlemain, in triumph, to her rescue went.

Omai puoi giudicar di quei cotali
   ch' io accusai di sopra e di lor falli,
   che son cagion di tutti vostri mali.   99
L' uno al pubblico segno i gigli gialli
   oppone, e l' altro appropria quello a parte,
   sì ch' è forte a veder chi più si falli.   102
Faccian li Ghibellin, faccian lor arte
   sott' altro segno; chè mal segue quello
   sempre chi la giustizia e lui diparte.   105
E non l' abbatta esto Carlo novello
   coi Guelfi suoi; ma tema de li artigli
   ch' a più alto leon trasser lo vello.   108
Molte fiate già pianser li figli
   per la colpa del padre, e non si creda
   che Dio trasmuti l' armi per suoi gigli!   111
Questa picciola stella si correda
   de' buoni spirti che son stati attivi,
   perchè onore e fama li succeda: 114
e quando li disiri poggian quivi,
   sì disviando, pur convien che i raggi
   del vero amore in su poggin men vivi.   117
Ma nel commensurar di nostri gaggi
   col merto è parte di nostra letizia,
   perchè non li vedem minor nè maggi.   120
Quindi addolcisce la viva giustizia
   in noi l' affetto sì, che non si puote
   torcer già mai ad alcuna nequizia.   123
Diverse voci fanno dolci note;
   così diversi scanni in nostra vita
   rendon dolce armonia tra queste rote.   126
E dentro a la presente margarita
   luce la luce di Romeo, di cui
   fu l' ovra grande e bella mal gradita.   129

Judge now of those my late indictment brings
   before thee, what they are—their sin how great,
   who are the cause of all your sufferings.
Against the general standard some would set
   the yellow lilies: some—no less to blame—
   would to themselves its power appropriate.
Go, play, ye Ghibellines, play your cunning game
   beneath some other standard; who divide
   that one from justice serve it but in name.
Nor with his Guelfs let this young Charles deride
   its power, but fear its talons, lest he be
   stripped, as was prouder lion, of his hide.
Oft wailing for their father's fault we see
   the sons: nor let him madly dream that heaven
   will change its scutcheon for his fleur-de-lis!
Adornment to this little star is given
   by noble souls, who through laborious days
   for honour and undying fame have striven:
and when desires have clomb thereto by ways
   thus errant, the true love must needs have soared
   unto its goal emitting feebler rays.
Yet in the balancing of our reward
   with our desert lies part of our delight,
   because we see them in complete accord.
Hence doth the living justice so make right
   our hearts within us, that we have no fears
   of wishing now aught sinful in God's sight.
As diverse voices make in mortal ears
   sweet music, so our diverse grades combine
   to make sweet harmony among these spheres.
And, closed within this pearl, the sheen doth shine
   of Romeo, whose fair deeds of goodly worth
   were guerdoned with ingratitude malign.

Ma i Provenzai che fecer contra lui
  non hanno riso; e però mal cammina
  qual si fa danno del ben fare altrui.   132
Quattro figlie ebbe, e ciascuna reina,
  Ramondo Beringhieri, e ciò li fece
  Romeo, persona umile e peregrina.   135
E poi il mosser le parole biece
  a dimandar ragione a questo giusto,
  che li assegnò sette e cinque per diece.   138
Indi partissi povero e vetusto:
  e se 'l mondo sapesse il cor ch' elli ebbe
  mendicando sua vita a frusto a frusto,   141
assai lo loda, e più lo loderebbe."

CANTO VII

"Osanna, *sanctus Deus sabaoth,*
  superillustrans claritate tua
  felices ignes horum malacoth!"   3
Così, volgendosi a la nota sua,
  fu viso a me cantare essa sustanza,
  sopra la qual doppio lume s' addua: 6
ed essa e l' altre mossero a sua danza,
  e quasi velocissime faville,
  mi si velar di subita distanza.   9
Io dubitava, e dicea "Dille, dille!"
  fra me: 'dille' dicea, a la mia donna
  che mi disseta con le dolci stille.   12
Ma quella reverenza che s' indonna
  di tutto me, pur per *Be* e per *ice*,
  mi richinava come l' uom ch' assonna.   15

But small cause have the Provençáls for mirth
 who wrought his ruin; ill fares the man, I ween,
 who makes from others' riches his own dearth.
Four daughters, and each one a wedded queen,
 had Raymond Berenger, taught thus to thrive
 by Romeo, a mere stranger poor and mean.
Then at a wicked plot did he connive
 and called to reckoning this just man and good,
 who rendered him full six for every five.
Old and in rags he parted thence: and could
 the world but know the gallant heart he bore,
 as, crust by crust, he begged his livelihood,
much as it lauds him it would laud him more."

CANTO VII

"Osanna sanctus Deus sabaoth!
 Thine are these realms, their blesséd fires are thine,
 for thou it is, whose beams illumine both."
So, as it now resumed its song divine,
 meseemed that spirit carolled, on whose head
 two forms of light with equal glory shine:
and it, and those that with it companied,
 whirled to their dance and, like swift sparks, away
 in sudden distance from my vision fled.
A doubt within me "Say it," whispered, "say,
 Oh, say it to my lady! Be it confessed
 to her whose gentle dews my thirst allay".
But that dumb awe which queens it o'er my breast
 wholly, at the mere sound of *Be* and *ice*,
 still bowed me low as one by sleep possessed.

Poco sofferse me cotal Beatrice,
 e cominciò, raggiandomi d' un riso
 tal, che nel foco faria l' uom felice: 18
"Secondo mio infallibile avviso,
 come giusta vendetta giustamente
 punita fosse, t' ha in pensier miso; 21
ma io ti solverò tosto la mente;
 e tu ascolta, chè le mie parole
 di gran sentenza ti faran presente. 24
Per non soffrire a la virtù che vole
 freno a suo prode, quell' uom che non nacque,
 dannando sè, dannò tutta sua prole; 27
onde l' umana specie inferma giacque
 giù per secoli molti in grande errore,
 fin ch' al Verbo di Dio di scender piacque 30
u' la natura, che dal suo fattore
 s' era allungata, unì a sè in persona
 con l' atto sol del suo etterno amore. 33
Or drizza il viso a quel ch' or si ragiona.
 Questa natura al suo fattore unita,
 qual fu creata, fu sincera e buona; 36
ma per se stessa fu ella sbandita
 di paradiso, però che si torse
 da via di verità e da sua vita. 39
La pena dunque che la croce porse,
 se a la natura assunta si misura,
 nulla già mai sì giustamente morse; 42
e così nulla fu di tanta ingiura,
 guardando a la persona che sofferse,
 in che era contratta tal natura. 45
Però d' un atto uscir cose diverse:
 ch' a Dio ed a' Giudei piacque una morte;
 per lei tremò la terra e 'l ciel s' aperse. 48

Not long was I so left by Beatrice,
   who, flashing at me such a smile as might,
   e'en amid flames, have plunged one's soul in bliss,
began, "If I, who cannot err, deem right,
   how a just vengeance could with justice be
   punished, confounds thee in thine own despite;
but I from doubt thy mind will quickly free;
   and to the words I speak do thou give heed,
   for weighty doctrine shall they impart to thee.
Because his will brooked not a curb decreed
   for his own good, the man no woman bore
   damned in his own damnation all his seed;
whence humankind on earth in error sore
   lay sick for ages, till from heaven above
   God's Word came down the nature to restore,
which from its author stood at far remove,
   and made it with himself in person one
   by the sole act of his eternal love.
Now see what follows now and gaze thereon.
   Joined with its author, fair and undefiled,
   such as it first was made, this nature shone;
although, quâ human, it had been exiled
   from paradise, because it left the way
   of truth and its own life, by self beguiled.
By the adopted nature, then, assay
   the cross as penalty and thou wilt find
   that never doom so justly gripped its prey;
and likewise none to justice was so blind,
   if thou the sufferer's person contemplate,
   in whom this human nature was combined.
Thus issued from one act things disparate:
   God and the Jews with the same death were pleased;
   it made earth shudder and oped heaven's gate.

Non ti dee oramai parer più forte,
   quando si dice che giusta vendetta
   poscia vengiata fu da giusta corte.   51
Ma io veggi' or la tua mente ristretta
   di pensiero in pensier dentro ad un nodo,
   del qual con gran disio solver s' aspetta.   54
Tu dici: 'Ben discerno ciò ch' i' odo;
   ma perchè Dio volesse, m' è occulto,
   a nostra redenzion pur questo modo'.   57
Questo decreto, frate, sta sepulto
   a li occhi di ciascuno il cui ingegno
   ne la fiamma d' amor non è adulto.   60
Veramente, però ch' a questo segno
   molto si mira e poco si discerne,
   dirò perchè tal modo fu più degno.   63
La divina bontà, che da sè sperne
   ogni livore, ardendo in sè, sfavilla
   sì che dispiega le bellezze etterne.   66
Ciò che da lei sanza mezzo distilla
   non ha poi fine, perchè non si move
   la sua imprenta quand' ella sigilla.   69
Ciò che da essa sanza mezzo piove
   libero è tutto, perchè non soggiace
   a la virtute de le cose nove.   72
Più l' è conforme, e però più le piace;
   chè l' ardor santo ch' ogni cosa raggia,
   ne la più somigliante è più vivace.   75
Di tutte queste dote s' avvantaggia
   l' umana creatura; e s' una manca,
   di sua nobilità convien che caggia.   78
Solo il peccato è quel che la disfranca,
   e falla dissimile al sommo bene;
   per che del lume suo poco s' imbianca;   81

In future, then, no more with doubts be teased,
  when hearing that a just tribunal wrought
  vengeance for one whom vengeance justly seized.
But now, thy mind enmeshed by thought on thought,
  I see thee waiting with attentive ear
  for clue from me that shall untie the knot.
Thou sayst: 'I well discern what now I hear;
  but wherefore God ordained this means alone
  for our redemption—that is far from clear'.
Too deeply buried, brother, to be shown
  is this decree, except to those whose wit
  within the flame of love is fully grown.
But, inasmuch as many fain would hit
  this mark, and but few strike it, thou shalt learn
  wherefore the method chosen was most fit.
The divine goodness from itself doth spurn
  all envy, so that, sparkling, it reveals
  the eternal beauties that within it burn.
Whatever thence immediately distils
  endures eternally, for there is no
  impression lost when it is God who seals.
Whate'er from him immediately doth flow
  is wholly free, not subject to the might
  of causes which from other causes grow.
As like him more, it gives him more delight;
  for in what most resembles it, most lives
  the holy flame which maketh all things bright.
Such is the birthright that his maker gives
  to man; who must, if even one should fail,
  lose with it all these high prerogatives.
'Tis sin alone can freedom's loss entail
  and mar man's likeness to the sovereign good,
  causing its light, which lightens him, to pale—

ed in sua dignità mai non rivene,
　se non riempie dove colpa vota,
　contra mal dilettar con giuste pene.　　84
Vostra natura, quando peccò tota
　nel seme suo, da queste dignitadi,
　come di paradiso, fu remota;　　87
nè ricovrar potiensi, se tu badi
　ben sottilmente, per alcuna via,
　sanza passar per un di questi guadi:　　90
o che Dio solo per sua cortesia
　dimesso avesse, o che l' uom per se isso
　avesse sodisfatto a sua follia.　　93
Ficca mo l' occhio per entro l' abisso
　de l' etterno consiglio, quanto puoi
　al mio parlar distrettamente fisso.　　96
Non potea l' uomo ne' termini suoi
　mai sodisfar, per non potere ir giuso
　con umiltate obediendo poi,　　99
quanto disobediendo intese ir suso;
　e questa è la cagion per che l' uom fue
　da poter sodisfar per sè dischiuso.　　102
Dunque a Dio convenia con le vie sue
　riparar l' omo a sua intera vita,
　dico con l' una, o ver con amendue.　　105
Ma perchè l' ovra è tanto più gradita
　da l' operante, quanto più appresenta
　de la bontà del core ond' ell' è uscita,　　108
la divina bontà, che 'l mondo imprenta,
　di proceder per tutte le sue vie
　a rilevarvi suso fu contenta.　　111
Nè tra l' ultima notte e 'l primo die
　sì alto o sì magnifico processo,
　o per l' una o per l' altra, fu o fie:　　114

loss irretrievable, except he should
    refill the void his guilty pleasures made
    by righteous pains of equal magnitude.
Your nature, when it all had disobeyed
    in its first germ, was, as from paradise
    expelled, so of these honours disarrayed;
nor could regain them, if thou scrutinise
    the matter strictly, save by crossing one
    of these two fords—thus, or not other wise:
either that of his clemency alone
    God should bestow a pardon, or that man
    should for his folly of himself atone.
Within the abyss of heaven's eternal plan
    thy gaze now fix, and bid thy subtle mind
    cling to my words as closely as it can.
Never could man, in human bounds confined,
    have paid his debt, because he could not stoop
    low by obeying, after he had sinned,
so far as upward it was erst his hope
    to mount by disobeying: this is why
    man with his debt, unaided, could not cope.
God it behoved, then, his own ways to try
    and thus—I mean, by one or both the same—
    to restore man to his integrity.
But as the doer's deed will more proclaim
    its merit in so far as it displays
    the goodness of the heart from whence it came,
the divine goodness, which its imprint lays
    upon the world, to lift you from your fall
    was minded to proceed by all its ways.
And, 'twixt the last night and first day of all,
    deed so sublime, so glorious, no one yet
    saw done by either way, nor ever shall:

chè più largo fu Dio a dar se stesso
  per far l' uom sufficiente a rilevarsi,
  che s' elli avesse sol da sè dimesso;   117
e tutti li altri modi erano scarsi
  a la giustizia, se 'l Figliuol di Dio
  non fosse umiliato ad incarnarsi.   120
Or per empierti bene ogni disio,
  ritorno a dichiarare in alcun loco,
  perchè tu veggi lì così com' io.   123
Tu dici: 'Io veggio l' acqua, io veggio il foco,
  l' aere e la terra e tutte lor misture
  venire a corruzione, e durar poco;   126
e queste cose pur furon creature;
  per che, se ciò ch' è detto è stato vero,
  esser dovrien da corruzion sicure'.   129
Li angeli, frate, e 'l paese sincero
  nel qual tu se', dir si posson creati,
  sì come sono, in loro essere intero;   132
ma li elementi che tu hai nomati,
  e quelle cose che di lor si fanno
  da creata virtù sono informati.   135
Creata fu la materia ch' elli hanno;
  creata fu la virtù informante
  in queste stelle che 'ntorno a lor vanno.   138
L' anima d' ogne bruto e de le piante
  di complession potenziata tira
  lo raggio e 'l moto de le luci sante;   141
ma vostra vita sanza mezzo spira
  la somma beninanza, e la innamora
  di sè sì che poi sempre la disira.   144
E quinci puoi argomentare ancora
  vostra resurrezion, se tu ripensi
  come l' umana carne fessi allora   147
che li primi parenti intrambo fensi".

for God more richly all requirements met,
   giving himself to give man power to rise,
   than had his simple fiat annulled the debt;
and heav'n no other method could devise
   which squared with justice, save that God's own Son
   himself should stoop to put on mortal guise.
Now to leave nought of all thy wish undone,
   I turn me back to illumine a certain place,
   that therein thou and I may see as one.
Thou sayest: 'I see that air and fire no less
   than water, earth and all their compounds grow
   corrupted, and endure but little space;
yet these were creatures, hence should never know
   corruption, but should bide therefrom secure,
   if what thou saidst was true be really so'.
The angels, brother, and the region pure
   wherein thou art, were framed (as all agree)
   in their whole being, as they still endure;
but those four elements just named by thee,
   and whatsoever thence is born and bred,
   through some created virtue came to be.
Created was the stuff whereof they are made;
   created was the virtue which inspires
   these wheeling constellations round them spread.
Such soul as every brute or plant acquires
   draws in, as by complexion it finds power,
   the ray and movement of the holy fires;
but upon you the sovereign good doth shower
   your life direct, and makes you so to love
   itself, that ye desire it evermore.
And hence thou canst by further reasoning prove
   your resurrection, if thou call to mind
   how human flesh was made, what time thereof
were made the first two parents of mankind".

CANTO VIII

Solea creder lo mondo in suo periclo
    che la bella Ciprigna il folle amore
    raggiasse, volta nel terzo epiciclo;   3
per che non pur a lei faceano onore
    di sacrificio e di votivo grido
    le genti antiche ne l' antico errore;   6
ma Dione onoravano e Cupido,
    questa per madre sua, questo per figlio;
    e dicean ch' el sedette in grembo a Dido;   9
e da costei ond' io principio piglio
    pigliavano il vocabol de la stella
    che 'l sol vagheggia or da coppa or da ciglio. 12
Io non m' accorsi del salire in ella;
    ma d' esservi entro mi fè assai fede
    la donna mia ch' i' vidi far più bella.   15
E come in fiamma favilla si vede,
    e come in voce voce si discerne,
    quand' una è ferma e l' altra va e riede;   18
vid' io in essa luce altre lucerne
    muoversi in giro più e men correnti,
    al modo, credo, di lor viste interne.   21
Di fredda nube non disceser venti,
    o visibili o non, tanto festini,
    che non paressero impediti e lenti   24
a chi avesse quei lumi divini
    veduti a noi venir, lasciando il giro
    pria cominciato in li alti Serafini.   27
E dentro a quei che più innanzi appariro
    sonava 'Osanna' sì, che unque poi
    di riudir non fui sanza disiro.   30

CANTO VIII

'Twas the fair Cyprian, pagans once believed,
  who, whirled in the third epicycle, rayed
  love-frenzy down on mortals; whence, deceived
by the ancient fancy, ancient peoples made
  their offerings, and their votive shouts addressed
  not to her only, but like honours paid
to Cupid and Dione, this confessed
  her mother, that her offspring, and were wont
  to fable how he lay on Dido's breast;
and after her upon whose name I count
  to adorn this proem did they name the star
  which woos the sun, now following, now in front.
That in it now was I the proof was clear,
  because, tho' all unconscious that we rose,
  I saw my lady's face had grown more fair.
And even as in flame a sparkle shows,
  and as in voice a voice is heard, when one
  is steady, and the other comes and goes;
I in that light saw other lamps which shone
  revolving, some with less, some greater speed,
  as urged, I trow, by him they gaze upon.
Never descended whirlwind, seen or hid,
  from chill cloud, but would slow and tardy seem
  to eyes that had beheld, as mine now did,
those heavenly radiances towards us stream,
  quitting the circle where they had till then
  been dancing with the exalted Seraphim.
And from the foremost pealed in loud refrain
  such an 'Hosanna' as thereafter I
  was ne'er without the wish to hear again.

Indi si fece l' un più presso a noi
   e solo incominciò: "Tutti sem presti
   al tuo piacer, perchè di noi ti gioi.   33
Noi ci volgiam coi Principi celesti
   d' un giro e d' un girare e d' una sete,
   ai quali tu del mondo già dicesti: 36
' *Voi che 'ntendendo il terzo ciel movete* ';
   e sem sì pien d' amor, che, per piacerti,
   non fia men dolce un poco di quiete ".   39
Poscia che li occhi miei si fuoro offerti
   a la mia donna reverenti, ed essa
   fatti li avea di sè contenti e certi,   42
rivolsersi a la luce che promessa
   tanto s' avea, e "Deh, chi siete?" fue
   la voce mia di grande affetto impressa.   45
E quanta e quale vid' io lei far piue
   per allegrezza nova che s' accrebbe,
   quand' io parlai, a l' allegrezze sue!   48
Così fatta, mi disse: "Il mondo m' ebbe
   giù poco tempo; e se più fosse stato,
   molto sarà di mal, che non sarebbe.   51
La mia letizia mi ti tien celato
   che mi raggia dintorno e mi nasconde
   quasi animal di sua seta fasciato.   54
Assai m' amasti, e avesti ben onde;
   chè s' io fossi giù stato, io ti mostrava
   di mio amor più oltre che le fronde.   57
Quella sinistra riva che si lava
   di Rodano, poi ch' è misto con Sorga,
   per suo segnore a tempo m' aspettava;   60
e quel corno d' Ausonia che s' imborga
   di Bari, di Gaeta e di Catona,
   da ove Tronto e Verde in mare sgorga.   63

Then one alone, yet closer drawing nigh,
    began: "We all stand ready at thy beck
    to serve thee, that thou mayest of us have joy.
We in one circle roll, one circling make,
    one thirst with those high Princedoms share above,
    whom from the world thyself erewhile bespake
as 'Spirits that by understanding move
    the third heaven', now for thee not less content
    to pause awhile, so full we are of love".
Mine eyes, which first with deep respect were bent
    upon my lady, turned, as soon as she
    had made them glad and sure of her assent,
back to the light, which had on terms so free
    proffered itself, and "Oh, then, tell me", I cried
    in tones of deep affection, "who ye be".
How greatly, from new joy which multiplied
    its joys at my request, I saw it grow
    in bulk, how much in sheen intensified!
So fashioned, it rejoined: "Short while below
    the world retained me; had it longer been,
    much would be spared of fast impending woe.
My happiness envelops me within
    the beams it sheds, concealing me from view,
    like animal in silk itself doth spin.
Thou lovedst me well and with good reason too;
    for had I stayed on earth, thou hadst been shown
    more of my love than to mere leafage grew.
The region watered on his left by Rhône,
    beyond the point where Sorgues blends with him,
    me for its sovereign was prepared to own;
yea, and Ausonia's horn, about whose rim
    Bari, Gaëta and Catona stand,
    whence Verde seaward falls and Tronto's stream.

Fulgiemi già in fronte la corona
    di quella terra che 'l Danubio riga
    poi che le ripe tedesche abbandona.   66
E la bella Trinacria, che caliga
    tra Pachino e Peloro, sopra 'l golfo
    che riceve da Euro maggior briga,   69
non per Tifeo ma per nascente solfo,
    attesi avrebbe li suoi regi ancora,
    nati per me di Carlo e di Ridolfo,   72
se mala segnoria, che sempre accora
    li popoli suggetti, non avesse
    mosso Palermo a gridar: 'Mora, mora!'.   75
E se mio frate questo antivedesse,
    l' avara povertà di Catalogna
    già fuggiria, perchè non li offendesse;   78
chè veramente proveder bisogna
    per lui, o per altrui, sì ch' a sua barca
    carcata più di carco non si pogna.   81
La sua natura, che di larga parca
    discese, avria mestier di tal milizia
    che non curasse di mettere in arca".   84
"Però ch' i' credo che l' alta letizia
    che 'l tuo parlar m' infonde, signor mio,
    là 've ogni ben si termina e s' inizia,   87
per te si veggia come la vegg' io,
    grata m' è più; e anco quest' ho caro
    perchè 'l discerni rimirando in Dio.   90
Fatto m' hai lieto, e così mi fa chiaro,
    poi che, parlando, a dubitar m' hai mosso,
    com' esser può di dolce seme amaro."   93
Questo io a lui; ed elli a me: "S' io posso
    mostrarti un vero, a quel che tu dimandi
    terra' il viso come tieni 'l dosso.   96

Upon my brow the crown of that fair land
   already shone which is by Danube bathed,
   when he hath quitted either German strand.
And beautiful Trinacria, cloud-enswathed
   between Pachynus and Pelore, along
   the bay which Eurus never leaves unscathed
(cloud by up-steaming sulphur round it hung,
   not by Typhoeus), had awaited still
   its kings through me of Charles and Rudolf sprung,
if evil lordship, ever prone to fill
   with fury subject-peoples, had not made
   Palermo clamour fiercely: 'Kill them, kill!'.
And could my brother this foresee, in dread
   lest, through her greedy want, grave ill betide,
   he would be shunning Catalonia's aid;
for truly need there is that he provide,
   or others for him, that with further freight
   his over-freighted vessel be not plied.
Bounteous by birth, but grown degenerate,
   his sordid nature needs in those that fight
   his battles more than lust to accumulate ".
"Thy speech, my lord, fills me with deep delight,
   which from this thought derives an added grace,
   that plainly, as 'tis plain to my own sight,
'tis seen of thee in the goal and starting-place
   of all good things; and this, too, hold I dear,
   that thou discernst it, gazing on God's face.
Thou hast made me glad, now likewise make me clear,
   since thou hast stirred a doubt within my mind,
   how a sweet seed a bitter fruit can bear."
Thus I to him; and he to me: "Thou art blind
   to a truth, which can I show thee, then thine eyes
   will have before them what is now behind.

Lo ben che tutto il regno che tu scandi
 volge e contenta, fa esser virtute
 sua provedenza in questi corpi grandi.   99
E non pur le nature provedute
 sono in la mente ch' è da sè perfetta,
 ma esse insieme con la lor salute: 102
per che quantunque quest' arco saetta,
 disposto cade a proveduto fine,
 sì come cosa in suo segno diretta.   105
Se ciò non fosse, il ciel che tu cammine
 producerebbe sì li suoi effetti,
 che non sarebbero arti, ma ruine;   108
e ciò esser non può, se li 'ntelletti
 che muovon queste stelle non son manchi,
 e manco il primo, che non li ha perfetti.   111
Vuo' tu che questo ver più ti s' imbianchi?"
 E io: "Non già; chè impossibil veggio
 che la natura, in quel ch' è uopo, stanchi".   114
Ond' elli ancora: "Or dì: sarebbe il peggio
 per l' uomo in terra, se non fosse cive?"
 "Sì" rispuos' io; "e qui ragion non cheggio."117
"E può elli esser, se giù non si vive
 diversamente per diversi offici?
 Non, se 'l maestro vostro ben vi scrive."   120
Sì venne deducendo infino a quici;
 poscia conchiuse: "Dunque esser diverse
 convien di vostri effetti le radici: 123
per ch' un nasce Solone e altro Serse,
 altro Melchisedech e altro quello
 che, volando per l' aere, il figlio perse.   126
La circular natura, ch' è suggello
 a la cera mortal, fa ben sua arte,
 ma non distingue l' un da l' altro ostello.   129

The good that moves and wholly satisfies
   the realm thou'rt climbing, makes its foresight be
   virtue within these mighty luminaries.
The all-perfect mind doth in itself foresee
   not the mere natures only, but with them
   all that combines for their security:
thus whatsoe'er this bow lets fly the same
   prevision to a destined mark doth bring,
   like missile loosed with an unerring aim.
Else would the heaven, which thou art traversing,
   chaos produce, not such effects as these
   thou sëest, which from ordered beauty spring.
Happen this cannot, if the intelligences
   who move these stars have no defect, and none
   the first; for, could they fail, the fault were his.
Wilt thou that on this truth more light be thrown?"
   And I: "Not so; for nature, I concede,
   can never weary in what must needs be done".
Straight he rejoined: "On earth, should men not lead
   a social life, would they be worse off so?"
   "Yes" answered I; "and this no proof doth need."
"And could they lead it, but that life below
   for divers functions is diversely suited?
   Consult your master, and he tells you 'no'."
Thus came he, having point by point disputed,
   to his conclusion—"Therefore", did it run,
   "effects in you must needs be divers-rooted:
hence one is Solon born, one Xerxes, one
   Melchizedec, one he who sought to win
   his way by air and, flying, lost his son.
Nature that, as she wheels, hath ever been
   stamp to your wax, plies well her task and yet
   favours not one above another inn.

Quinci addivien ch' Esaù si diparte
   per seme da Iacob; e vien Quirino
   da sì vil padre, che si rende a Marte.   132
Natura generata il suo cammino
   simil farebbe sempre a' generanti,
   se non vincesse il proveder divino.   135
Or quel che t' era dietro t' è davanti:
   ma perchè sappi che di te mi giova,
   un corollario voglio che t' ammanti.   138
Sempre natura, se fortuna trova
   discorde a sè, com' ogni altra semente
   fuor di sua region, fa mala prova.   141
E se 'l mondo là giù ponesse mente
   al fondamento che natura pone,
   seguendo lui, avria buona la gente.   144
Ma voi torcete a la religione
   tal che fia nato a cignersi la spada,
   e fate re di tal ch' è da sermone: 147
onde la traccia vostra è fuor di strada ".

CANTO IX

Da poi che Carlo tuo, bella Clemenza,
   m' ebbe chiarito, mi narrò l' inganni
   che ricever dovea la sua semenza;   3
ma disse: "Taci, e lascia volger li anni";
   sì ch' io non posso dir se non che pianto
   giusto verrà di retro ai vostri danni.   6
E già la vita di quel lume santo
   rivolta s' era al Sol che la riempie,
   come quel ben ch' a ogni cosa è tanto.   9

Hence Esau is by seed made separate
    from Jacob; hence Quirinus comes of blood
    so base, that men from Mars his lineage date.
Without the o'erruling providence of God
    begotten nature would forever tread
    the self-same track that the begetters trod.
What was behind thee fronts thee now instead:
    but for a proof of my affection bind
    this, for corollary, about thine head.
Ever with nature, if she fortune find
    discordant with herself, it goeth hard,
    as with all other seeds in soil unkind.
And if the world below paid due regard
    to the foundation nature lays, content
    to build on that, the race were nobly rear'd.
But ye to monkhood twist from his true bent
    the stripling born to gird himself with sword,
    and make a king of one for preaching meant:
thus with the road your foot-prints ill accord".

CANTO IX

After thy Charles, fair Clemence, thus had freed
    my mind of all obscurity, he spake
    next of the wiles which should defraud his seed;
but "Nought reveal", said he, "and let time take
    its destined course"; so I can say but this—
    just woe will follow in your losses' wake.
Now to the Sun which fills it aye with bliss
    that holy lantern's life had turned again,
    as to that good which all-sufficing is.

Ahi anime ingannate e fatture empie,
   che da sì fatto ben torcete i cori,
   drizzando in vanità le vostre tempie!   12
Ed ecco un altro di quelli splendori
   ver me si fece, e 'l suo voler piacermi
   significava nel chiarir di fori.   15
Li occhi di Beatrice, ch' eran fermi
   sovra me, come pria, di caro assenso
   al mio disio certificato fermi.   18
"Deh metti al mio voler tosto compenso,
   beato spirto," dissi, "e fammi prova
   ch' i' possa in te refletter quel ch' io penso!"   21
Onde la luce che m' era ancor nova,
   del suo profondo, ond' ella pria cantava,
   seguette come a cui di ben far giova: 24
"In quella parte de la terra prava
   italica che siede tra Rialto
   e le fontane di Brenta e di Piava,   27
si leva un colle, e non surge molt' alto,
   là onde scese già una facella
   che fece a la contrada un grande assalto.   30
D' una radice nacqui e io ed ella:
   Cunizza fui chiamata, e qui refulgo
   perchè mi vinse il lume d' esta stella.   33
Ma lietamente a me medesma indulgo
   la cagion di mia sorte, e non mi noia;
   che parria forse forte al vostro vulgo.   36
Di questa luculenta e cara gioia
   del nostro cielo che più m' è propinqua,
   grande fama rimase; e pria che moia,   39
questo centesimo anno ancor s' incinqua:
   vedi se far si dee l' uomo eccellente,
   sì ch' altra vita la prima relinqua.   42

Ah, impious souls, of your own blindness fain,
   ye that from such perfection turn aside,
   setting your hearts on things that are but vain!
And of those splendours lo, another hied
   towards me, and by becoming e'en brighter yet
   its will to please me clearly signified.
The eyes of Beatrice, as erstwhile, set
   firmly on mine, the loved assurance brought
   that my desire with her approval met.
"Ah, blessèd spirit," I cried, "delay thou not,
   but to my wish grant speedy recompense,
   and prove thou canst be mirror to my thought!"
Whereat the light from the deep lustre whence
   it sang before, and still disguised therein,
   went on, as joying in its beneficence:
"Within that region of the land of sin
   called Italy, which 'tween Rialto lies
   and there where Piava and Brenta both begin,
uplifts itself a hill of no great size,
   whence hurtling once a little firebrand came
   which smote the country round with fierce emprise.
One root produced both me and it: my name
   know for Cunizza, and that here I shine
   because o'ermastered by this planet's flame.
Yet that which caused this portion to be mine,
   gladly (though your gross minds may wonder why)
   I allow myself, nor aught thereat repine.
Of this bright, precious jewel of our sky,
   which glitters next to me, is left alive
   a fame on earth so great that, ere it die,
this century shall lengthen into five:
   see then if man should aim not so to excel,
   that in a second life the first survive.

E ciò non pensa la turba presente
    che Tagliamento e Adice richiude,
    nè per esser battuta ancor si pente.   45
Ma tosto fia che Padova al palude
    cangerà l' acqua che Vicenza bagna,
    per essere al dover le genti crude.   48
E dove Sile e Cagnan s' accompagna,
    tal signoreggia e va con la testa alta,
    che già per lui carpir si fa la ragna.   51
Piangerà Feltro ancora la difalta
    de l' empio suo pastor, che sarà sconcia
    sì, che per simil non s' entrò in Malta.   54
Troppo sarebbe larga la bigoncia
    che ricevesse il sangue ferrarese,
    e stanco chi 'l pesasse a oncia a oncia,   57
che donerà questo prete cortese
    per mostrarsi di parte; e cotai doni
    conformi fieno al viver del paese.   60
Su sono specchi, voi dicete Troni,
    onde refulge a noi Dio giudicante;
    sì che questi parlar ne paion buoni".   63
Qui si tacette; e fecemi sembiante
    che fosse ad altro volta, per la rota
    in che si mise com' era davante.   66
L' altra letizia, che m' era già nota
    per cara cosa, mi si fece in vista
    qual fin balasso in che lo sol percuota.   69
Per letiziar là su fulgor s' acquista,
    sì come riso qui; ma giù s' abbuia
    l' ombra di fuor, come la mente è trista.   72
"Dio vede tutto, e tuo veder s' inluia"
    diss' io, "beato spirto, sì che nulla
    voglia di sè a te puot' esser fuia.   75

So think not they, the rabble that now dwell
  'twixt Tagliamento and Adigë, nor rue
  they yet their sins, tho' oft chastiséd well.
But soon shall Padua at the marsh imbrue
  the waves that lap Vicenza, since undone
  its folk still leave the thing they ought to do.
And where Cagnán meets Sile, lords it one
  so haughty, that the weaving of the net
  to catch him in is even now begun.
Its wicked pastor's crime will Feltro yet
  bewail, and such shall be his turpitude,
  that Malta for the like ne'er oped her gate.
The vat which should contain Ferrara's blood
  were broad indeed, and weary he that strove
  to weigh it ounce by ounce—so large the flood,
which this obliging priest will give to prove
  himself a partisan; and gifts like his
  will suit the country and the ways thereof.
Aloft are mirrors—'Thrones' your saying is—
  which unto us God's judgments clearly show;
  so that we all approve these utterances".
With that she ceased, and semblance made as though
  her thoughts had elsewhere turned, by taking flight
  back to the ring where she had wheeled but now.
The other joy, already to my sight
  a glorious object, now the likeness had
  of a fine ruby, which the sun should smite.
Rejoicing doth in heaven to brightness add,
  as here to laughter: but in hell grows dim
  the shade without, e'en as the mind is sad.
"God sees all, and thy seeing is in him,"
  said I, "thou blesséd spirit, so that nought
  escapes thee, not my lightest wish or whim.

Dunque la voce tua, che 'l ciel trastulla
  sempre col canto di quei fuochi pii
  che di sei ali fatt' han la coculla,   78
perchè non satisface a' miei disii?
  già non attendere' io tua dimanda,
  s' io m' intuassi, come tu t' inmii."   81
"La maggior valle in che l' acqua si spanda"
  incominciaro allor le sue parole
  "fuor di quel mar che la terra inghirlanda,   84
tra' discordanti liti, contr' al sole
  tanto sen va, che fa meridiano
  là dove l' orizzonte pria far sole.   87
Di quella valle fu' io litorano
  tra Ebro e Macra, che per cammin corto
  parte lo Genovese dal Toscano.   90
Ad un occaso quasi e ad un orto
  Buggea siede e la terra ond' io fui,
  che fè del sangue suo già caldo il porto.   93
Folco mi disse quella gente a cui
  fu noto il nome mio; e questo cielo
  di me s' imprenta, com' io fe' di lui;   96
chè più non arse la figlia di Belo,
  noiando e a Sicheo ed a Creusa,
  di me, infin che si convenne al pelo;   99
nè quella Rodopea che delusa
  fu da Demofoonte, nè Alcide
  quando Iole nel core ebbe rinchiusa.   102
Non però qui si pente, ma si ride,
  non de la colpa, ch' a mente non torna,
  ma del valor ch' ordinò e provide.   105
Qui si rimira ne l' arte ch' adorna
  cotanto effetto, e discernesi 'l bene
  per che 'l mondo di su quel di giù torna.   108

Thou with those genial fires, whose cowl is wrought
   of wings sixfold, dost charm unceasingly
   the heaven with song; then why, ere thus besought,
dost thou not give contentment to my plea?
   to thine long since my answer had been made,
   if I in thee could read, as thou in me."
"The largest vale where lies the water spread,
   drawn from that sea (he then began to say)
   wherewith the whole earth is engarlanded,
'twixt contrary shores, against the solar ray
   stretches so far, it makes the zenith lie
   where at its outset the horizon lay.
A dweller on that valley's coast was I,
   between the Ebro and where the Magra's short
   descent parts Genoa from Tuscany.
Well nigh the same meridian runs athwart
   Bougiah and the city whence I came,
   which with its own blood once made warm the port.
To those that knew it Folco was my name;
   and now with me are stamped this planet's rays
   in the like manner that I was with them;
for fiercelier did not Belus' daughter blaze,
   wronging Sicheus and Crëusa too,
   than I, when young and given to youthful ways;
nor that fair Rhodopean, doomed to rue
   Demophoon's guile, nor he, Alcides hight,
   when Iole to his fond clasp he drew.
Yet here repent we not, but feel delight,
   not for the sin, which none remembers now,
   but for God's overruling and foresight.
Here we examine the art, which worketh so
   effectually, and here discern the weal
   whereby the world above sways that below.

Ma perchè tutte le tue voglie piene
  ten porti che son nate in questa spera,
  procedere ancor oltre mi convene.   111
Tu vuo' saper chi è in questa lumera
  che qui appresso me così scintilla,
  come raggio di sole in acqua mera.   114
Or sappi che là entro si tranquilla
  Raab; e a nostr' ordine congiunta,
  di lei nel sommo grado si sigilla.   117
Da questo cielo, in cui l' ombra s' appunta
  che 'l vostro mondo face, pria ch' altr' alma
  del triunfo di Cristo fu assunta.   120
Ben si convenne lei lasciar per palma
  in alcun cielo de l' alta vittoria
  che s' acquistò con l' una e l' altra palma,   123
perch' ella favorò la prima gloria
  di Iosuè in su la Terra Santa,
  che poco tocca al papa la memoria.   126
La tua città, che di colui è pianta
  che pria volse le spalle al suo fattore
  e di cui è la 'nvidia tanto pianta,   129
produce e spande il maladetto fiore
  c' ha disviate le pecore e li agni,
  però che fatto ha lupo del pastore.   132
Per questo l' Evangelio e i dottor magni
  son derelitti, e solo ai Decretali
  si studia, sì che pare a' lor vivagni.   135
A questo intende il papa e' cardinali:
  non vanno i lor pensieri a Nazarette,
  là dove Gabriello aperse l' ali.   138
Ma Vaticano e l' altre parti elette
  di Roma che son state cimitero
  a la milizia che Pietro seguette,   141
tosto libere fien de l' adultero."

But that, ere hence thou goest, I may fulfil
   all of thy wishes born within this sphere,
   I must proceed a little farther still.
Fain wouldst thou learn who is it radiant here
   beside me in a glittering splendour dressed,
   like sunbeams glancing on a crystal mere.
Know, then, that in it Rahab findeth rest;
   who being to our order joined, 'tis shown
   as with her seal conspicuously impressed.
Unto this heaven, where the shadow thrown
   by your world ends, the first to rise was she
   of all the souls Christ raised up with his own.
Right meet it was to leave her, so it be
   somewhere in heaven, as palm of victory gained
   by the two palms uplifted on the tree,
because she favoured the first glory obtained
   by Joshua o'er the Holy Land, a place
   whereon the pope but little thought doth spend.
Thy city, sprung from him, of all his race
   the first that turned against his maker's power,
   and from whose envy comes such dire distress,
brings forth and spreads abroad the accurséd flower
   which sheep and lambs alike hath led astray,
   making him wolf that shepherd was before.
For this deserted are the fathers, nay
   the Gospels too, and Canon Law alone
   is studied, as its margins well display.
For this the pope and cardinals disown
   all else, nor ever think on Nazareth,
   there where the wingéd Gabriel flew down.
But Rome and all the tombs in it, by faith
   held sacred, with the Vatican, where lie
   the saints who fought with Peter to the death,
shall soon be freed from the adultery."

CANTO X

Guardando nel suo Figlio con l' Amore
    che l' uno e l' altro etternalmente spira,
    lo primo ed ineffabile Valore,   3
quanto per mente e per loco si gira,
    con tant' ordine fè, ch' esser non puote
    sanza gustar di lui chi ciò rimira.   6
Leva dunque, lettore, a l' alte rote
    meco la vista, dritto a quella parte
    dove l' un moto e l' altro si percuote;   9
e lì comincia a vagheggiar ne l' arte
    di quel maestro che dentro a sè l' ama,
    tanto che mai da lei l' occhio non parte.   12
Vedi come da indi si dirama
    l' oblico cerchio che i pianeti porta,
    per sodisfare al mondo che li chiama.   15
E se la strada lor non fosse torta,
    molta virtù nel ciel sarebbe in vano,
    e quasi ogni potenza qua giù morta;   18
e se dal dritto più o men lontano
    fosse il partire, assai sarebbe manco
    e giù e su de l' ordine mondano.   21
Or ti riman, lettor, sovra 'l tuo banco,
    dietro pensando a ciò che si preliba,
    s' esser vuoi lieto assai prima che stanco.   24
Messo t' ho innanzi: omai per te ti ciba;
    chè a sè torce tutta la mia cura
    quella materia ond' io son fatto scriba.   27
Lo ministro maggior de la natura,
    che del valor del ciel lo mondo imprenta
    e col suo lume il tempo ne misura,   30

CANTO X

THE ineffable and uncreated Worth
    gazing with Love upon his Son's dear face—
    the Love that each eternally breathes forth,
hath all things that revolve in mind or space
    with so much order made, that none can view
    his works and taste not of his graciousness.
Raise, then, your vision, reader, as I do,
    unto the lofty wheels, straight to that part
    where the one motion strikes the other through;
and there with joy begin to admire the art
    of him, whose eye is never turned aside
    from masterpiece framed after his own heart.
See how the circle where the planets glide,
    thence branches off obliquely, with the intent
    that Earth, which calls them, may be satisfied.
And had their pathway not been thus-wise bent,
    vain were much heavenly influence and well nigh
    all agencies down here would pine and faint;
and were it farther or less far to lie
    out of the straight, in either hemisphere
    grave loss of order would be caused thereby.
Now, reader, in the banquet persevere,
    reflecting on this foretaste of the meat,
    if, unfatigued, you would enjoy good cheer.
I've set the board: henceforth 'tis yours to eat;
    since all the care I lavish on my rhyme
    is claimed now by the theme of which I treat.
Of nature's servants, he, the most sublime,
    who stamps with heavenly worth the mundane clay
    and gives us light as means to measure time,

con quella parte che su si rammenta
  congiunto, si girava per le spire
  in che più tosto ognora s' appresenta;   33
e io era con lui; ma del salire
  non m' accors' io, se non com' uom s' accorge,
  anzi 'l primo pensier, del suo venire.   36
È Beatrice quella che sì scorge
  di bene in meglio sì subitamente,
  che l' atto suo per tempo non si sporge.   39
Quant' esser convenia da sè lucente
  quel ch' era dentro al sol dov' io entra'mi,
  non per color, ma per lume parvente!   42
Perch' io lo 'ngegno e l' arte e l' uso chiami,
  sì nol direi, che mai s' imaginasse;
  ma creder puossi e di veder si brami.   45
E se le fantasie nostre son basse
  a tanta altezza, non è maraviglia;
  chè sopra 'l sol non fu occhio ch' andasse.   48
Tal era quivi la quarta famiglia
  de l' alto Padre, che sempre la sazia,
  mostrando come spira e come figlia.   51
E Beatrice cominciò: "Ringrazia,
  ringrazia il sol de li angeli, ch' a questo
  sensibil t' ha levato per sua grazia".   54
Cor di mortal non fu mai sì digesto
  a divozione ed a rendersi a Dio
  con tutto il suo gradir cotanto presto,   57
come a quelle parole mi fec' io;
  e sì tutto il mio amore in lui si mise,
  che Beatrice eclissò ne l' oblio.   60
Non le dispiacque; ma sì se ne rise,
  che lo splendor de li occhi suoi ridenti
  mia mente unita in più cose divise.   63

conjoined with Aries in the aforetold way,
    was mounting upward by the spiral stair,
    on which he shines forth earlier day by day;
and I was with him; yet no more aware
    of my ascension, than a man may know
    the thought within his brain before it's there.
'Tis Beatrice, 'tis she who guideth so
    from good to better by such instant flight,
    that, to record it, time is far too slow.
How needs must that have been itself most bright,
    which in the sun, whose orb I entered, shone
    distinguished, not by colour, but by light!
Art, wit, experience—none, though called upon,
    could aid me paint it for the fancy's eye;
    yet men may trust and yearn to gaze thereon.
Nor wonder, if such heights should prove too high
    to be imagined; since none ever met
    the sun's full blaze who was not quelled thereby.
Thus shines the exalted Sire's fourth household, set
    in that bright heaven, to whom for endless bliss
    he shows how he doth breathe and how beget.
"To him, the angels' sun, who unto this,
    the visible sun, hath raised thee by his grace,
    give thanks, give thanks", commanded Beatrice.
Never was mortal so disposed to place
    his mind on God, and none surrendered e'er
    his heart to God with so much willingness,
as I did, when I heard that call to prayer;
    and so on him was all my longing stayed,
    that Beatrice, eclipsed, seemed no more there.
No whit displeased, she smiled—a smile, which made
    her eyes so glorious, that my mind, compelled
    to quit one object, was distributed

Io vidi più fulgor vivi e vincenti
   far di noi centro e di sè far corona,
   più dolci in voce che in vista lucenti: 66
così cinger la figlia di Latona
   vedem talvolta, quando l' aere è pregno,
   sì che ritenga il fil che fa la zona.   69
Ne la corte del cielo, ond' io rivegno,
   si trovan molte gioie care e belle
   tanto che non si posson trar del regno;   72
e 'l canto di quei lumi era di quelle:
   chi non s' impenna sì che là su voli,
   dal muto aspetti quindi le novelle.   75
Poi, sì cantando, quelli ardenti soli
   si fuor girati intorno a noi tre volte,
   come stelle vicine a' fermi poli,   78
donne mi parver non da ballo sciolte,
   ma che s' arrestin tacite, ascoltando
   fin che le nove note hanno ricolte.   81
E dentro a l' un senti' cominciar: "Quando
   lo raggio de la grazia, onde s' accende
   verace amore e che poi cresce amando,   84
multiplicato in te tanto resplende,
   che ti conduce su per quella scala
   u' sanza risalir nessun discende;   87
qual ti negasse il vin de la sua fiala
   per la tua sete, in libertà non fora
   se non com' acqua ch' al mar non si cala.   90
Tu vuo' saper di quai piante s' infiora
   questa ghirlanda che 'ntorno vagheggia
   la bella donna ch' al ciel t' avvalora.   93
Io fui de li agni de la santa greggia
   che Domenico mena per cammino
   u' ben s' impingua se non si vaneggia.   96

mid many dazzling lights I now beheld
  forming a halo, which encircled us
  with radiance, by their song alone excelled.
The daughter of Latona cinctured thus
  we see at times, when vapour fills the sky
  and makes her girdle's texture luminous.
In the celestial court, where once was I,
  are many jewels so precious, that in vain
  one seeks to pluck them from the realm on high;
and of their number was that heavenly strain:
  who thither soars not on the wings of yearning
  may of a dumb man news from thence obtain.
When, chanting thus melodiously, those burning
  suns had wheeled thrice about us where we stood—
  like stars which round the steady poles keep turning,
ladies they seemed, for dancing still in mood,
  who pause in silence at the measure's close,
  listening, till they have caught the strain renewed.
And, from the depth of one, these accents rose:
  "In that the beam of grace, which lights and tends
  true love and then, by dint of loving, grows,
resplendent now in thee so far extends,
  that it conducts thee upward by that stair,
  which save to re-ascend it none descends,
whoso refused thee, for thy thirst, a share
  of wine from his own vial were no more free
  than water is which doth not seaward fare.
Fain wouldst thou know what blossoms these may be,
  engarlanding and with such joy surveying
  the fair dame, who for heaven doth strengthen thee.
Lamb of the holy flock was I, obeying
  that Dominic, who hath a pathway shown,
  where is good fattening, if there be no straying.

Questi che m' è a destra più vicino,
    frate e maestro fummi, ed esso Alberto
    è di Cologna, e io Thomas d' Aquino.   99
Se sì di tutti li altri esser vuo' certo,
    di rietro al mio parlar ten vien col viso
    girando su per lo beato serto.   102
Quell' altro fiammeggiare esce del riso
    di Grazian, che l' uno e l' altro foro
    aiutò sì che piace in paradiso.   105
L' altro ch' appresso adorna il nostro coro,
    quel Pietro fu che con la poverella
    offerse a Santa Chiesa suo tesoro.   108
La quinta luce, ch' è tra noi più bella,
    spira di tale amor, che tutto 'l mondo
    là giù ne gola di saper novella.   111
Entro v' è l' alta mente u' sì profondo
    saver fu messo, che se 'l vero è vero,
    a veder tanto non surse il secondo.   114
Appresso vedi il lume di quel cero
    che giù, in carne, più a dentro vide
    l' angelica natura e 'l ministero.   117
Ne l' altra piccioletta luce ride
    quello avvocato de' tempi cristiani
    del cui latino Augustin si provide.   120
Or se tu l' occhio de la mente trani
    di luce in luce dietro a le mie lode,
    già de l' ottava con sete rimani.   123
Per vedere ogni ben dentro vi gode
    l' anima santa che 'l mondo fallace
    fa manifesto a chi di lei ben ode.   126
Lo corpo ond' ella fu cacciata giace
    giuso in Cieldauro; ed essa da martiro
    e da essilio venne a questa pace.   129

My brother and my master, of Cologne,
  neighbours me on my right: Albert his name,
  and Thomas, called Aquinas, is my own.
If knowledge of the rest be now thine aim,
  around the blissful garland with thine eyes
  follow my speech, as I their worth proclaim.
That other radiance from the smile doth rise
  of Gratian, who to either forum lent
  such aid as causeth joy in paradise.
Behold in him, our choir's next ornament,
  that Peter who, at Holy Church's need,
  like the poor widow, all his treasure spent.
The rays of the fifth—our fairest light—proceed
  from such a love, that there is none below
  but longs with news of it to sate his greed.
It veils the mind inspired with wisdom so
  profound, that ne'er arose, if truth be true,
  a second who could boast as much to know.
Beside him the bright taper meets thy view,
  who gained, while in the flesh, his deep insight
  into what angels be and what they do.
Smileth within that other tiny light
  the champion of the Christian ages, one
  whose studied discourse helped Augustine write.
Now, an thou let thy mental vision run
  from light to light, as I record their praise,
  thine eager quest hath reached the eighth bright sun.
Within it on all good delights to gaze
  the saintly soul, which unto ears that cease
  mishearing shows the world's deceitful ways.
Down in Cieldauro, where it found release,
  it left its tortured body, thence to soar
  from martyrdom and exile to this peace.

Vedi oltre fiammeggiar l' ardente spiro
   d' Isidoro, di Beda e di Riccardo,
   che a considerar fu più che viro.   132
Questi onde a me ritorna il tuo riguardo,
   è 'l lume d' uno spirto che 'n pensieri
   gravi a morir li parve venir tardo: 135
essa è la luce etterna di Sigieri,
   che, leggendo nel vico de li strami,
   sillogizzò invidiosi veri ".   138
Indi, come orologio che ne chiami
   ne l' ora che la sposa di Dio surge
   a mattinar lo sposo perchè l' ami,   141
che l' una parte l' altra tira e urge,
   tin tin sonando con sì dolce nota,
   che 'l ben disposto spirto d'amor turge;   144
così vid' io la gloriosa rota
   muoversi e render voce a voce in tempra
   ed in dolcezza ch' esser non pò nota   147
se non colà dove gioir s' insempra.

CANTO XI

O INSENSATA cura de' mortali,
   quanto son difettivi sillogismi
   quei che ti fanno in basso batter l' ali!   3
Chi dietro a iura, e chi ad aforismi
   sen giva, e chi seguendo sacerdozio,
   e chi regnar per forza o per sofismi,   6
e chi rubare, e chi civil negozio;
   chi nel diletto de la carne involto
   s' affaticava, e chi si dava a l' ozio,   9

See, blazing yonder, fervent Isidore,
   Bede and that Richard who, as mystic seer,
   was all that a mere man can be, and more.
The flame from which thine eye reverteth here
   shines from a soul who, in deep thinking drowned,
   complained that all too slowly death drew near:
it is Siger's eternal light, once found
   teaching in Straw Street, there intent to prove
   that truths which brought him enmity were sound".
Then, even as a clock at call whereof
   the bride of God is roused to serenade
   the bridegroom and thereby to woo his love,
and which, by parts that push and pull, is made
   to strike 'ding-ding' in such a dulcet tone,
   it thrills all hearts that ever truly prayed;
so unto me the glorious wheel was shown
   revolving, voice to voice attuned, and blending
   in sweet harmonious melody unknown
save yonder where delight is never-ending.

CANTO XI

O WITLESS care of mortals, still the dupe
   of that vain reasoning from false premises,
   which makes thy beating pinions downward droop!
One searched the statutes, one Hippocrates
   his maxims: on the priesthood one was bent,
   and one on rule by force or sophistries:
one was on plundering, and one intent
   on civic business: one was wearily given
   to sensual joys, one lying indolent,

quando, da tutte queste cose sciolto,
  con Beatrice m' era suso in cielo
  cotanto gloriosamente accolto.   12
Poi che ciascuno fu tornato ne lo
  punto del cerchio in che avanti s' era,
  fermossi, come a candellier candelo.   15
E io senti' dentro a quella lumera
  che pria m' avea parlato, sorridendo
  incominciar, faccendosi più mera: 18
"Così com' io del suo raggio resplendo,
  sì, riguardando ne la luce etterna,
  li tuoi pensieri onde cagioni apprendo. 21
Tu dubbi, e hai voler che si ricerna
  in sì aperta e 'n sì distesa lingua
  lo dicer mio, ch' al tuo sentir si sterna, 24
ove dinanzi dissi 'U' ben s' impingua',
  e là u' dissi 'Non surse il secondo';
  e qui è uopo che ben si distingua.   27
La provedenza, che governa il mondo
  con quel consiglio nel quale ogni aspetto
  creato è vinto pria che vada al fondo, 30
però ch' andasse ver lo suo diletto
  la sposa di colui ch' ad alte grida
  disposò lei col sangue benedetto,   33
in sè sicura e anche a lui più fida,
  due principi ordinò in suo favore,
  che quinci e quindi le fosser per guida. 36
L' un fu tutto serafico in ardore;
  l' altro per sapienza in terra fue
  di cherubica luce uno splendore.   39
De l' un dirò, però che d' amendue
  si dice l' un pregiando, quale uom prende,
  perch' ad un fine fuor l' opere sue.   42

while I, from all these cares escaped, was even
    thus gloriously made welcome by a band
    of shining saints, with Beatrice, in heaven.
When round the circle each, on every hand
    returning, had attained his former room,
    he stopped, like candle fixed in candle-stand.
And I perceived the radiancy from whom
    speech had already issued, smiling, grow
    more radiant still, and heard it thus resume:
"As I reflect its glory, even so
    in that eternal light, on which I gaze,
    I know thy thoughts and whence they rise I know.
Thou doubtest, and wouldst have me sift my ways
    of speech and choose large language, adequate
    to thy perception baffled by the phrase,
'Where is good fattening', which I used of late,
    and by that other 'Second ne'er arose':
    here let me, then, a clear distinction state.
The providence, which rules the world and shows
    its ways to none, for they are past descrying
    by any means that mortal vision knows,
in order that the bride of him who, crying
    'with a loud voice', wed her with his dear blood,
    might seek her joy both on herself relying
and also with her faith in him renewed,
    for her behoof ordained two chiefs of might
    on either hand to lead her into good.
The one burned all seraphically bright;
    the other for his wisdom was on earth
    a very splendour of cherubic light.
Of one I'll speak, for whoso tells the worth
    of one, whiche'er he take, is both commending,
    because one purpose to their deeds gave birth.

Intra Tupino e l' acqua che discende
  del colle eletto dal beato Ubaldo,
  fertile costa d' alto monte pende,   45
onde Perugia sente freddo e caldo
  da Porta Sole; e di rietro le piange
  per grave giogo Nocera con Gualdo.   48
Di questa costa, là dov' ella frange
  più sua rattezza, nacque al mondo un sole,
  come fa questo tal volta di Gange.   51
Però chi d' esso loco fa parole,
  non dica Ascesi, chè direbbe corto,
  ma Oriente, se proprio dir vuole.   54
Non era ancor molto lontan da l' orto,
  ch' el cominciò a far sentir la terra
  de la sua gran virtute alcun conforto;   57
chè per tal donna, giovinetto, in guerra
  del padre corse, a cui, come a la morte,
  la porta del piacer nessun diserra;   60
e dinanzi a la sua spirital corte
  et coram patre le si fece unito;
  poscia di dì in dì l' amò più forte.   63
Questa, privata del primo marito,
  millecent' anni e più dispetta e scura
  fino a costui si stette sanza invito;   66
nè valse udir che la trovò sicura
  con Amiclate, al suon de la sua voce,
  colui ch' a tutto 'l mondo fè paura;   69
nè valse esser costante nè feroce,
  sì che, dove Maria rimase giuso,
  ella con Cristo pianse in su la croce.   72
Ma perch' io non proceda troppo chiuso,
  Francesco e Povertà per questi amanti
  prendi oramai nel mio parlar diffuso.   75

'Twixt the Tupino and the brook descending
   the blesséd Ubald's chosen hill one sees
   a fruitful slope from a high mount depending,
whence on Perugia's Eastern Gate the breeze
   blows hot and cold; rearward, her irksome sway
   makes Nocera with Gualdo ill at ease.
From this same slope, just where it breaks away
   most gently, to the world was born a sun,
   as this from Ganges on a summer's day.
Therefore, whene'er the place is named, let none
   call it 'Ascesi'—word of meagre sense;
   but 'Orient' should its title rightly run.
For there he rose, nor far had travelled thence,
   ere he began imparting to mankind
   some comfort from his mighty influence.
Mere boy, and to his father's anger blind,
   he wooed a dame, to whom none opes the door
   of pleasure or to death is less inclined;
but he, full fain, his bishop's court before
   et coram patre took her for his own;
   thereafter day by day he loved her more.
Bereaved of her first husband, scorned, unknown,
   more than a thousand and an hundred years
   she lived unwooed, till sought by him alone.
In vain the story that she felt no fears,
   but with Amyclas unperturbed had stood,
   when the world-shaker's voice assailed her ears;
in vain the loyal, the matchless fortitude,
   with which, while even Mary stayed below,
   she wept with Christ upon the very rood.
But lest too little of my meaning show,
   Francis and Poverty henceforward take
   at large for this fond pair and call them so.

La lor concordia e i lor lieti sembianti,
   amore e maraviglia e dolce sguardo
   facieno esser cagion di pensier santi;   78
tanto che 'l venerabile Bernardo
   si scalzò prima, e dietro a tanta pace
   corse e, correndo, li parve esser tardo.   81
Oh ignota ricchezza, oh ben ferace!
   Scalzasi Egidio, scalzasi Silvestro,
   dietro a lo sposo, sì la sposa piace.   84
Indi sen va quel padre e quel maestro
   con la sua donna e con quella famiglia
   che già legava l' umile capestro.   87
Nè li gravò viltà di cor le ciglia
   per esser fi' di Pietro Bernardone,
   nè per parer dispetto a maraviglia;   90
ma regalmente sua dura intenzione
   ad Innocenzio aperse, e da lui ebbe
   primo sigillo a sua religione.   93
Poi che la gente poverella crebbe
   dietro a costui, la cui mirabil vita
   meglio in gloria del ciel si canterebbe,   96
di seconda corona redimita
   fu per Onorio da l' etterno Spiro
   la santa voglia d' esto archimandrita.   99
E poi che, per la sete del martiro,
   ne la presenza del Soldan superba
   predicò Cristo e gli altri che 'l seguiro,   102
e per trovare a conversione acerba
   troppo la gente, per non stare indarno,
   reddissi al frutto de l' italica erba,   105
nel crudo sasso intra Tevero e Arno
   da Cristo prese l' ultimo sigillo,
   che le sue membra due anni portarno.   108

Their concord and glad looks availed to make
   love, wonderment and contemplation sweet
   cause holy thoughts to blossom in their wake.
First, venerable Bernard bared his feet
   and after peace so perfect ran with a speed
   he deemed o'erslow, yet was his footing fleet.
Oh unimagined wealth, Oh fruitful seed!
   Giles bares his feet, his feet Silvester bares,
   following, for such a bride, the bridegroom's lead.
Thenceforth that lord and father onward fares
   with his dear lady and that household, now
   bound with the cord, which each so humbly wears.
Nor did a sense of shame weigh down his brow,
   that he was Peter Bernardone's son,
   nor could men's wondrous scorn his spirit cow;
but he revealed, as might a king have done,
   his stern resolve to Innocent, who granted
   its first seal to his order thus begun.
As multiplied the humble souls that wanted
   to follow one, whose marvellous life were theme
   in the empyrean heaven more fitly chanted,
the eternal Spirit made Honorius deem
   the moment wise to crown yet once again
   the holy purpose of their head supreme.
Next in the Soldan's haughty presence, fain
   of martyrdom, behold him dauntless stand,
   preaching of Christ and those, his saintly train;
but, loth to waste his labours on a land
   unripe for harvest, he returned to reap
   the Italian crop now ready for his hand,
then took from Christ upon the rocky steep,
   'twixt Arno reared and Tiber, his last seal—
   marks that his limbs were two whole years to keep.

Quando a colui ch' a tanto ben sortillo
  piacque di trarlo suso a la mercede
  ch' el meritò nel suo farsi pusillo,   111
a' frati suoi, sì com' a giuste rede,
  raccomandò la donna sua più cara,
  e comandò che l' amassero a fede;   114
e del suo grembo l' anima preclara
  mover si volse, tornando al suo regno,
  e al suo corpo non volse altra bara.   117
Pensa oramai qual fu colui che degno
  collega fu a mantener la barca
  di Pietro in alto mar per dritto segno;   120
e questo fu il nostro patriarca;
  per che, qual segue lui com' el comanda,
  discerner puoi che buone merce carca.   123
Ma 'l suo peculio di nova vivanda
  è fatto ghiotto, sì ch' esser non puote
  che per diversi salti non si spanda;   126
e quanto le sue pecore remote
  e vagabunde più da esso vanno,
  più tornano a l' ovil di latte vote.   129
Ben son di quelle che temono 'l danno
  e stringonsi al pastor; ma son sì poche,
  che le cappe fornisce poco panno.   132
Or se le mie parole non son fioche
  e se la tua audienza è stata attenta,
  se ciò ch' è detto a la mente rivoche,   135
in parte fia la tua voglia contenta,
  perchè vedrai la pianta onde si scheggia,
  e vedrai il corregger che argomenta   138
'U' ben s' impingua, se non si vaneggia'".

When he who chose him for so great a weal
  was pleased at length to raise him to the height
  which he had earned by his self-humbling zeal,
unto his brethren, as to heirs by right,
  he recommended his own lady dear
  and bade them find in her their sole delight;
and from her bosom to its kingly sphere
  on high his glorious spirit willed to flee,
  and for his corpse would brook no other bier.
Bethink thee now how great a saint was he,
  his worthy colleague found, to hold the boat
  of Peter on a straight course in mid-sea.
Such was our patriarch; and therefore note,
  that whoso doth as he commands must needs
  have with him goodly merchandise afloat.
And yet it lusteth so, the flock he leads,
  for new fare, that it cannot help but stray
  to alien pastures, careless where it feeds,
although the more his sheep forsake the way
  nor heed the shepherd, by so much the more
  devoid of milk they come home day by day.
Some, fearing harm, cleave to him as before;
  yea, but so few in number, that of stuff
  to make them cowls there needs but scanty store.
Now, if my words have been distinct enough,
  and if they've sunk in thine attentive ear,
  if from thy memory they meet no rebuff,
in part thou hast thy wish: for both are clear—
  the stock from which they whittle and the saying
  with its implied rebuke, repeated here:
'Where is good fattening, if there be no straying'".

CANTO XII

Sì tosto come l' ultima parola
　　la benedetta fiamma per dir tolse,
　　a rotar cominciò la santa mola;　　　　　　3
e nel suo giro tutta non si volse
　　prima ch' un' altra di cerchio la chiuse,
　　e moto a moto e canto a canto colse;　　　6
canto che tanto vince nostre muse,
　　nostre serene in quelle dolci tube,
　　quanto primo splendor quel ch'e' refuse.　9
Come si volgon per tenera nube
　　due archi paralleli e concolori,
　　quando Iunone a sua ancella iube,　　　　12
nascendo di quel d' entro quel di fori,
　　a guisa del parlar di quella vaga
　　ch' amor consunse come sol vapori;　　　15
e fanno qui la gente esser presaga,
　　per lo patto che Dio con Noè puose,
　　del mondo che già mai più non s' allaga;　18
così di quelle sempiterne rose
　　volgiensi circa noi le due ghirlande,
　　e sì l' estrema a l' intima rispuose.　　　21
Poi che 'l tripudio e l' altra festa grande
　　sì del cantare e sì del fiammeggiarsi
　　luce con luce gaudiose e blande　　　　　24
insieme a punto e a voler quetarsi,
　　pur come li occhi ch' al piacer che i move
　　conviene insieme chiudere e levarsi;　　　27
del cor de l' una de le luci nove
　　si mosse voce, che l' ago a la stella
　　parer mi fece in volgermi al suo dove;　　30

CANTO XII

So spake the blessèd flame and then was still,
　but, ere its final word had ceased to sound,
　already wheeling was the holy mill,
nor yet had once revolved, when, circling round,
　another compassed it in such a way
　that dance to dance and song to song was bound;
song that in those sweet tubes the loveliest lay
　of earthly muse or siren doth excel
　as much as primary light the reflex ray.
E'en as, both limned alike and parallel,
　two bows are drawn o'er softly clouded skies,
　should Juno's hest her handy-maid impel,
the inner to the outer giving rise,
　like to that errant damsel's voice, who died,
　consumed by love, as sun-kissed vapour dies;
which make men augur that, whate'er betide,
　by reason of God's pact with Noah made,
　the world from flood shall ever safe abide;
so, curving round us, those two wreaths displayed
　their sempiternal roses, and so shone
　the inmost in the outmost re-portrayed.
Dance and sublime festivity went on,
　alike of flame that flashed and song that soared,
　light blent with light in smooth, glad unison,
till both together ceased with one accord,
　as eyes perforce together ope and close
　obedient to the will that is their lord;
then issued from the heart of one of those
　new lights a voice, to which I turned, as sways
　the needle thither where the pole-star glows;

e cominciò: "L' amor che mi fa bella
   mi tragge a ragionar de l' altro duca
   per cui del mio sì ben ci si favella.   33
Degno è che, dov' è l' un, l' altro s' induca;
   sì che, com' elli ad una militaro,
   così la gloria loro insieme luca.   36
L' essercito di Cristo, che sì caro
   costò a riarmar, dietro a la 'nsegna
   si movea tardo, sospeccioso e raro,   39
quando lo 'mperador che sempre regna
   provide a la milizia, ch' era in forse,
   per sola grazia, non per esser degna;   42
e come è detto, a sua sposa soccorse
   con due campioni, al cui fare, al cui dire
   lo popol disviato si raccorse.   45
In quella parte ove surge ad aprire
   Zefiro dolce le novelle fronde
   di che si vede Europa rivestire,   48
non molto lungi al percuoter de l' onde
   dietro a le quali, per la lunga foga,
   lo sol tal volta ad ogni uom si nasconde,   51
siede la fortunata Calaroga
   sotto la protezion del grande scudo
   in che soggiace il leone e soggioga.   54
Dentro vi nacque l' amoroso drudo
   de la fede cristiana, il santo atleta
   benigno a' suoi ed a' nemici crudo.   57
E come fu creata, fu repleta
   sì la sua mente di viva virtute,
   che, ne la madre, lei fece profeta.   60
Poi che le sponsalizie fuor compiute
   al sacro fonte intra lui e la fede,
   u' si dotar di mutua salute,   63

and it began: "The love wherewith I blaze
  bids me the other leader celebrate,
    on whose account my own hath won such praise.
'Tis just, where one is named, to name his mate;
  that, as both waged their warfare to one end,
    so should like glory on their triumph wait.
Christ's army, which at such dear cost obtained
  fresh weapons, moved thin-ranked and slow of pace
    behind the standard, for their faith had waned,
when the ever-ruling emperor, in face
  of their sore peril, sent his soldiers aid,
    not through their merit, but of his pure grace,
and, as thou heardest, for his spouse arrayed
  two champions, by whose words and by whose deeds
    the folk were rallied that had erred and strayed.
Within the region, whence at first proceeds
  Zephyr, at whose sweet breath new leaves are bidden
    clothe Europe, when she casts her winter's weeds,
nigh to the shore that is for ever chidden
  by billows beyond which, in weary mood,
    the sun's far-travelled orb at times is hidden,
fortunate Calaroga long hath stood,
  guarded by the great shield on which appear
    two lions, one subduing and one subdued.
In that same town was born the amorous fere
  of the true faith, the holy athlete, kind
    unto his own and to his foes severe.
And, scarce conceived, so lively was his mind,
  that, through its power, his mother prophesied,
    while he was yet within her womb confined.
When at the hallowed font he took for bride
  the faith, and both had pledged themselves to keep
    each other safe, by vows there ratified,

la donna che per lui l' assenso diede,
  vide nel sonno il mirabile frutto
  ch' uscir dovea di lui e de le rede.　　66
E perchè fosse qual era in costrutto,
  quinci si mosse spirito a nomarlo
  del possessivo di cui era tutto.　　69
Domenico fu detto; e io ne parlo
  sì come de l' agricola che Cristo
  elesse a l' orto suo per aiutarlo.　　72
Ben parve messo e famigliar di Cristo;
  chè 'l primo amor che 'n lui fu manifesto,
  fu al primo consiglio che diè Cristo.　　75
Spesse fiate fu tacito e desto
  trovato in terra da la sua nutrice,
  come dicesse: 'Io son venuto a questo'.　　78
Oh padre suo veramente Felice,
  oh madre sua veramente Giovanna,
  se, interpretata, val come si dice!　　81
Non per lo mondo, per cui mo s' affanna
  diretro ad Ostiense e a Taddeo,
  ma per amor de la verace manna　　84
in picciol tempo gran dottor si feo;
  tal che si mise a circuir la vigna
  che tosto imbianca, se 'l vignaio è reo.　　87
E a la sedia che fu già benigna
  più a' poveri giusti, non per lei,
  ma per colui che siede, che traligna,　　90
non dispensare o due o tre per sei,
  non la fortuna di prima vacante,
  non decimas, que sunt pauperum Dei,　　93
addimandò; ma contro al mondo errante
  licenza di combatter per lo seme
  del qual ti fascian ventiquattro piante.　　96

the dame, who was his surety, saw in sleep
  the marvellous fruit one day to issue forth
  from him and from his great companionship.
And, that he might be known at his true worth,
  a spirit moved hence to give the child a name
  derived from his who owned him from his birth.
Dominic was he called; whom I proclaim
  as fellow-labourer chosen out by Christ
  to dress his garden and to keep the same.
True envoy seemed he, and true friend, of Christ,
  since from the first he loved, and was intent
  to follow, the first counsel given of Christ.
Full many a time his nurse would find him bent
  in silence on the ground, awake all night,
  as who should say: 'For this end was I sent'.
Oh 'happy' father, Felix truly hight,
  Oh truly 'full of grace' his mother Joan,
  if they who thus translate the name be right!
Not like our worldlings toiling for their own
  gain at Thaddeus and the Ostian,
  but, out of love for the true bread alone,
soon grown a mighty doctor, he began
  to make inspection of that goodly vine,
  which, if ill tended, quickly turneth wan.
And from the see, no longer now benign
  to the honest poor (not thro' its own fault, nay,
  to its base occupant all blame assign!)
not power to give mere halves or thirds away,
  not promise of the first rich vacancy,
  not *decimas, que sunt pauperum Dei*,
did he demand; but nought save liberty
  with the erring world to battle for the seed
  whence sprang the twice-twelve scions engirdling thee.

Poi con dottrina e con volere insieme
 con l' officio apostolico si mosse
 quasi torrente ch' alta vena preme;   99
e ne li sterpi eretici percosse
 l' impeto suo, più vivamente quivi
 dove le resistenze eran più grosse.   102
Di lui si fecer poi diversi rivi
 onde l' orto cattolico si riga,
 sì che i suoi arbuscelli stan più vivi.   105
Se tal fu l' una rota de la biga
 in che la Santa Chiesa si difese
 e vinse in campo la sua civil briga,   108
ben ti dovrebbe assai esser palese
 l' eccellenza de l' altra, di cui Tomma
 dinanzi al mio venir fu sì cortese.   111
Ma l' orbita che fè la parte somma
 di sua circunferenza, è derelitta,
 sì ch' è la muffa dov' era la gromma.   114
La sua famiglia, che si mosse dritta
 coi piedi a le sue orme, è tanto volta,
 che quel dinanzi a quel di retro gitta.   117
E tosto si vedrà de la ricolta
 de la mala coltura, quando il loglio
 si lagnerà che l' arca li sia tolta.   120
Ben dico, chi cercasse a foglio a foglio
 nostro volume, ancor troveria carta
 u' leggerebbe 'I' mi son quel ch' i' soglio';   123
ma non fia da Casal nè d' Acquasparta,
 là onde vegnon tali a la scrittura,
 ch' uno la fugge, e altro la coarta.   126
Io son la vita di Bonaventura
 da Bagnoregio, che ne' grandi offici
 sempre pospuosi la sinistra cura.   129

Then forth he fared with mind and will agreed,
　　confirmed apostle, as from its high source
　　a torrent bursts, which nothing can impede,
and mid the stocks of heresy with force
　　o'erwhelming rushed—where chief resistance showed,
　　thither directing first his furious course.
From him thereafter various streamlets flowed,
　　watering the catholic garden near and far,
　　whereby fresh life is on its shrubs bestowed.
If such one wheel of the two-wheeléd car,
　　wherein the Holy Church made her defence,
　　and won in open field her civil war,
thou must admit the other's excellence,
　　of which, before my coming, Thomas told,
　　making thereto such courteous reference.
But, where its felly's topmost portion rolled,
　　the rut thus formed thou wilt deserted find,
　　so that the whilom crust is turned to mould.
His family, at first right well inclined
　　to follow where he trod, so much hath wheeled,
　　that those in front are cast on those behind.
And soon the harvesting clear proof shall yield
　　of the bad tillage, when the tares complain
　　they are left out, what time the barns are filled.
I grant that whoso searched and searched again
　　our volume, still might find some page whereon
　　'twas writ, 'As I was wont, so I remain';
but from Casál and Acquasparta none
　　so minded hails: for the due discipline
　　is shirked by this, by that is overdone.
In me doth Bonavénture's spirit shine,
　　of Bagnoregio, who the temporal end
　　put last in each great office that was mine.

Illuminato e Augustin son quici,
  che fuor de' primi scalzi poverelli
  che nel capestro a Dio si fero amici.   132
Ugo da San Vittore è qui con elli,
  e Pietro Mangiadore e Pietro Ispano,
  lo qual giù luce in dodici libelli;   135
Natan profeta e 'l metropolitano
  Crisostomo e Anselmo e quel Donato
  ch' a la prim' arte degnò porre mano.   138
Rabano è qui, e lucemi da lato
  il calavrese abate Giovacchino,
  di spirito profetico dotato.   141
Ad inveggiar cotanto paladino
  mi mosse l' infiammata cortesia
  di fra Tommaso e 'l discreto latino;   144
e mosse meco questa compagnia"

CANTO XIII

IMAGINI chi bene intender cupe
  quel ch' i' or vidi e ritegna l' image,
  mentre ch' io dico, come ferma rupe,   3
quindici stelle che 'n diverse plage
  lo cielo avvivan di tanto sereno,
  che soperchia de l' aere ogne compage;   6
imagini quel carro a cu' il seno
  basta del nostro cielo e notte e giorno,
  sì ch' al volger del temo non vien meno;   9
imagini la bocca di quel corno
  che si comincia in punta de lo stelo
  a cui la prima rota va dintorno,   12

To Illuminato and Austen next attend;
   among his first bare-footed bedesmen these,
   to win God, in the cord, to be their friend.
Hugh of St Victor here beside them is,
   and Peter Comestor and he of Spain,
   shining on earth from his twelve treatises;
Nathan the prophet, Chrysostom and then
   archbishop Anselm and Donatus, he
   that stooped to teach the first great art to men.
Raban is here, and, shining next to me,
   Calabria's abbot, Joachim, the seer
   who was endowed with gift of prophecy.
To emulous praise of such a valiant peer
   the courteous ardour and discreet address
   of brother Thomas moved me, and hath here
moved with me this fair company no less".

CANTO XIII

IMAGINE, ye that fain would visualise
   what now I saw—and let the image stay
   fixed, while I speak, like rock before your eyes—
the fifteen stars we see in heaven display
   in divers regions such a living light,
   that not the thickest air can quench their ray;
imagine too the wain, which day and night
   doth still the bosom of our skies adorn
   so that its pole wheels ever all in sight;
imagine too the opening of the horn,
   which springs from where the axle-point doth lie,
   round about which the primal wheel is borne,

aver fatto di sè due segni in cielo,
 qual fece la figliuola di Minoi
 allora che sentì di morte il gelo;   15
e l' un ne l' altro aver li raggi suoi,
 e amendue girarsi per maniera,
 che l' uno andasse al prima e l' altro al poi; 18
e avrà quasi l' ombra de la vera
 costellazione e de la doppia danza
 che circulava il punto dov' io era;   21
poi ch' è tanto di là da nostra usanza,
 quanto di là dal mover de la Chiana
 si move il ciel che tutti li altri avanza. 24
Lì si cantò non Bacco, non Peana,
 ma tre persone in divina natura,
 ed in una persona essa e l' umana. 27
Compiè il cantare e volger sua misura;
 e attesersi a noi quei santi lumi,
 felicitando sè di cura in cura.   30
Ruppe il silenzio ne' concordi numi
 poscia la luce in che mirabil vita
 del poverel di Dio narrata fumi,   33
e disse: "Quando l' una paglia è trita,
 quando la sua semenza è già riposta,
 a batter l' altra dolce amor m' invita. 36
Tu credi che nel petto onde la costa
 si trasse per formar la bella guancia
 il cui palato a tutto 'l mondo costa, 39
ed in quel che, forato da la lancia,
 e poscia e prima tanto sodisfece,
 che d' ogni colpa vince la bilancia, 42
quantunque a la natura umana lece
 aver di lume, tutto fosse infuso
 da quel valor che l' uno e l' altro fece; 45

to have fashioned of themselves two signs on high,
    such as the daughter of king Minos made,
    when, seized with mortal chill, she came to die;
one by the other's beams encompasséd,
    and both so whirling as that one should pass
    first, and the other follow where it led;
and you will see, though darkly as in a glass,
    the very constellation and the dance
    two-fold, which circled round me where I was;
for things as much exceed our cognisance
    there, as the sphere, above all spheres supreme
    in speed, outstrips the Chiana's slow advance.
No Paean there they raise, no Bacchic hymn,
    but 'in one God three persons' and 'in one
    person two natures' are their endless theme.
When dance and song had their due measure run,
    to us paid heed those shining ministers,
    winning new joy from each new task begun.
Brake silence then amid the accordant peers
    that luminary in which the wondrous tale
    of God's own bedesman had entranced mine ears,
and thus it spake: "Since I have threshed out well
    one sheaf and stored its grain, on the other too
    sweet charity now bids me ply the flail.
Thou thinkest that the bosom from which God drew
    the rib to form the woman fair of mien
    whose palate all mankind so dearly rue,
And his which, when the spear was thrust therein,
    alike for past and future made the great
    atonement, far outweighing every sin,
were by the power, whose virtue did create
    one and the other, filled with all the light
    that is permitted to man's natural state;

e però miri a ciò ch' io dissi suso,
    quando narrai che non ebbe 'l secondo
    lo ben che ne la quinta luce è chiuso.   48
Or apri li occhi a quel ch' io ti rispondo,
    e vedrai il tuo credere e 'l mio dire
    nel vero farsi come centro in tondo.   51
Ciò che non more e ciò che può morire
    non è se non splendor di quella idea
    che partorisce, amando, il nostro sire: 54
chè quella viva luce che sì mea
    dal suo lucente, che non si disuna
    da lui nè da l' amor ch' a lor s' intrea,   57
per sua bontate il suo raggiare aduna,
    quasi specchiato, in nove sussistenze,
    etternalmente rimanendosi una.   60
Quindi discende a l' ultime potenze
    giù d' atto in atto, tanto divenendo,
    che più non fa che brevi contingenze;   63
e queste contingenze esser intendo
    le cose generate, che produce
    con seme e sanza seme il ciel movendo.   66
La cera di costoro e chi la duce
    non sta d' un modo; e però sotto 'l segno
    ideale poi più e men traluce.   69
Ond' elli avvien ch' un medesimo legno,
    secondo specie, meglio e peggio frutta;
    e voi nascete con diverso ingegno.   72
Se fosse a punto la cera dedutta
    e fosse il cielo in sua virtù suprema,
    la luce del suggel parrebbe tutta;   75
ma la natura la dà sempre scema,
    similemente operando a l' artista
    c' ha l' abito de l' arte e man che trema.   78

hence wonderest thou if lately I was right
   in saying no second e'er so wise was found,
   as he whom the fifth lustre veils from sight.
Now mark my words, and thou wilt soon be bound
   to acknowledge that thy thought and my reply
   meet in the truth, as centre in the round.
That which dies not and that with power to die
   are but the beams of that idea, which owes
   its birth to our great sovereign's love on high:
because that living brightness which so flows
   from its bright source, that one therewith it stays
   and one with the love which maketh three with those,
doth, of its bounty, concentrate its rays,
   as in a glass—itself remaining one
   forever—into nine subsistences.
Thence to the lowest powers it passes down
   ever less actively, and brings about
   at last mere brief contingencies alone;
and these contingencies, I make no doubt,
   are things engendered, caused by the heaven to grow,
   of its own motion, with seed or without.
Their wax, and that which moulds it, varies so,
   that, 'neath the signet of the idea, we find
   this more and less thereafter shining through.
Hence comes it that of trees the same in kind
   one better fruit, another worse, doth bear;
   and men are born with differing powers of mind.
Were the wax moulded perfectly and were
   the heaven its highest influence to exert,
   nothing would then the signet's light impair;
but nature never gives it save in part,
   like skilful artist whose unsteady hand
   betrays him in the practice of his art.

Però se 'l caldo amor la chiara vista
  de la prima virtù dispone e segna,
  tutta la perfezion quivi s' acquista.   81
Così fu fatta già la terra degna
  di tutta l' animal perfezione;
  così fu fatta la Vergine pregna: 84
sì ch' io commendo tua oppinione,
  che l' umana natura mai non fue
  nè fia qual fu in quelle due persone.   87
Or s' i' non procedesse avanti piue,
  'Dunque, come costui fu sanza pare?'
  comincerebber le parole tue.   90
Ma perchè paia ben ciò che non pare,
  pensa chi era, e la cagion che 'l mosse,
  quando fu detto 'Chiedi', a dimandare.   93
Non ho parlato sì, che tu non posse
  ben veder ch' el fu re, che chiese senno
  acciò che re sufficiente fosse;   96
non per sapere il numero in che enno
  li motor di qua su, o se necesse
  con contingente mai necesse fenno;   99
non, si est dare primum motum esse,
  o se del mezzo cerchio far si puote
  triangol sì ch' un retto non avesse.   102
Onde, se ciò ch' io dissi e questo note,
  regal prudenza è quel vedere impari
  in che lo stral di mia intenzion percuote;   105
e se al 'surse' drizzi li occhi chiari,
  vedrai aver solamente rispetto
  ai regi, che son molti, e i buon son rari.   108
Con questa distinzion prendi 'l mio detto;
  e così puote star con quel che credi
  del primo padre e del nostro Diletto.   111

Yet, if the primal power's clear image stand
  by fervent love disposed and sealed thereon,
  the work is flawless, even as it was planned.
Thus moulded once to form that paragon
  of living creatures was 'the dust of the ground';
  thus did the Virgin once conceive a Son:
so that I grant thy opinion to be sound,
  that those two persons' equal among men
  was never yet and never shall be found.
Now if from further speech I should refrain,
  'How was that other, then, without a peer?'
  forthwith thou wouldest urge me to explain.
But that what now is dark be rendered clear,
  bethink thee who he was and wherefore he
  begged what he did, when 'Ask' rang in his ear.
Not so I've argued, that thou canst not see
  clearly, he was a king, who begged good sense
  that he as king might all-sufficient be;
not for to know how many powers dispense
  their motion to these heavens, or whether 'may'
  with 'must' can e'er give 'must' as consequence;
not, if a 'first moved' one can rightly say
  exists, or if in circle, when bisected,
  triangle, not right-angled, ever lay.
Whence, if on all I've said thou'st well reflected,
  royal prudence is that peerless seeing whereto
  the dart of my intention is directed;
and if 'arose' thou clearly keep in view,
  to kings alone thou'lt see 'tis apposite,
  of whom be many, but the good are few.
Draw this distinction, and my words are quite
  consistent, taken thus, with thy conceit
  of the first father and of our Delight.

E questo ti sia sempre piombo a' piedi,
 per farti mover lento com' uom lasso
 e al sì e al no che tu non vedi: 114
chè quelli è tra li stolti bene a basso,
 che sanza distinzione afferma e nega
 così ne l' un come ne l' altro passo;   117
perch' elli 'ncontra che più volte piega
 l' oppinion corrente in falsa parte,
 e poi l' affetto l' intelletto lega.   120
Vie più che 'ndarno da riva si parte,
 perchè non torna tal qual e' si move,
 chi pesca per lo vero e non ha l' arte.   123
E di ciò sono al mondo aperte prove
 Parmenide, Melisso, e Brisso, e molti,
 li quali andavano e non sapean dove: 126
sì fè Sabellio e Arrio e quelli stolti
 che furon come spade a le Scritture
 in render torti li diritti volti.   129
Non sien le genti ancor troppo sicure
 a giudicar, sì come quei che stima
 le biade in campo pria che sien mature: 132
ch' i' ho veduto tutto il verno prima
 lo prun mostrarsi rigido e feroce,
 poscia portar la rosa in su la cima; 135
e legno vidi già dritto e veloce
 correr lo mar per tutto suo cammino,
 perire al fine a l' intrar de la foce.   138
Non creda donna Berta e ser Martino,
 per vedere un furare, altro offerere,
 vederli dentro al consiglio divino; 141
chè quel può surgere, e quel può cadere".

And be this ever clog unto thy feet,
   to make thee like a weary man move slow
   towards both the 'yea' and 'nay' that pose thy wit:
for he among the fools is very low
   in either case, who, not distinguishing,
   asserts 'it is' or else 'it is not so';
since oft-times doth a hasty judgment swing
   to the wrong side, and then doth blind self-will
   about the intellect its fetters fling.
He pushes off from shore far vainlier still,
   since he returns not such as forth he went,
   who angles for the truth and lacketh skill.
This to the world make plainly evident
   Parmenides, Melissus, Bryson—all
   who, travelling, knew not whither they were bent.
Sabellius, too, and Arius I recall
   with other fools, who were to Holy Writ
   as swords that did its comely features maul.
Let not the people too securely sit
   in judgment, like the man who, while it grows,
   values his corn, ere time hath ripened it:
for I have seen the briar no leaves unclose,
   but bristling stand, till spring be well nigh past,
   yet, later, on its summit bear the rose;
and once I saw a ship sail straight and fast
   through all her voyage, across smooth seas and fair,
   to perish in the harbour-mouth at last.
Let gossips, then, and wiseacres beware
   of thinking to see men with God's clear eyes,
   seeing one steal, another offerings bear;
for the saint yet may fall, the sinner rise".

CANTO XIV

Dal centro al cerchio, e sì dal cerchio al centro,
    movesi l' acqua in un ritondo vaso,
    secondo ch' è percossa fuori o dentro.   3
Ne la mia mente fè subito caso
    questo ch' io dico, sì come si tacque
    la gloriosa vita di Tommaso,   6
per la similitudine che nacque
    del suo parlare e di quel di Beatrice,
    a cui sì cominciar, dopo lui, piacque: 9
"A costui fa mestieri, e nol vi dice
    nè con la voce nè pensando ancora,
    d' un altro vero andare a la radice.   12
Diteli se la luce onde s' infiora
    vostra sustanza, rimarrà con voi
    etternalmente sì com' ell' è ora;   15
e se rimane, dite come, poi
    che sarete visibili rifatti,
    esser potrà ch' al veder non vi noi".   18
Come, da più letizia pinti e tratti,
    a la fiata quei che vanno a rota
    levan la voce e rallegrano li atti,   21
così, a l' orazion pronta e divota,
    li santi cerchi mostrar nova gioia
    nel torneare e ne la mira nota.   24
Qual si lamenta perchè qui si moia
    per viver colà su, non vide quive
    lo rifrigerio de l' etterna ploia.   27
Quell' uno e due e tre che sempre vive
    e regna sempre in tre e 'n due e 'n uno,
    non circunscritto, e tutto circunscrive,   30

CANTO XIV

In a round vessel water moves about
    'twixt centre and circumference to or fro,
    as smitten from within or from without.
This thought, as here 'tis imaged, even so
    flashed over me, when from the glorious shade
    of Thomas the last words had ceased to flow,
by reason of the likeness then displayed
    'twixt his discourse and that which, after his,
    flowed graciously from Beatrice, who said:
"Need hath this man, although what need it is
    his voice declares not nor his thoughts as yet,
    to probe one more of heaven's mysteries.
Tell him if these bright beams that emanate
    now from your substance will emblossom you
    as radiantly in your eternal state;
and tell him how their lustre, if they do,
    shall not perforce work injury to your sight,
    when once again ye are disclosed to view".
As, goaded by an access of delight,
    with one accord the partners in a reel
    in louder song and livelier dance unite,
so, at her eager and devout appeal,
    by their gyrations and their wondrous strain
    new gladness did those holy cirques reveal.
Whoso laments that here we die to gain
    the life up there, has lived without attending
    to the refreshment of the eternal rain.
That one and two and three, whose never-ending
    dominion is in three and two and one,
    uncomprehended and all-comprehending,

tre volte era cantato da ciascuno
  di quelli spirti con tal melodia,
  ch' ad ogni merto saria giusto muno.   33
E io udi' ne la luce più dia
  del minor cerchio una voce modesta,
  forse qual fu da l' angelo a Maria,   36
risponder: "Quanto fia lunga la festa
  di paradiso, tanto il nostro amore
  si raggerà dintorno cotal vesta.   39
La sua chiarezza seguita l' ardore;
  l' ardor la visione, e quella è tanta,
  quant' ha di grazia sovra suo valore.   42
Come la carne gloriosa e santa
  fia rivestita, la nostra persona
  più grata fia per esser tutta quanta: 45
per che s' accrescerà ciò che ne dona
  di gratuito lume il sommo bene,
  lume ch' a lui veder ne condiziona;   48
onde la vision crescer convene,
  crescer l' ardor che di quella s' accende,
  crescer lo raggio che da esso vene.   51
Ma sì come carbon che fiamma rende,
  e per vivo candor quella soverchia,
  sì che la sua parvenza si difende,   54
così questo fulgor che già ne cerchia
  fia vinto in apparenza da la carne
  che tutto dì la terra ricoperchia;   57
nè potrà tanta luce affaticarne;
  chè li organi del corpo saran forti
  a tutto ciò che potrà dilettarne".   60
Tanto mi parver subiti e accorti
  e l' uno e l' altro coro a dicer 'Amme!',
  che ben mostrar disio de' corpi morti;   63

was thrice hymned by each spirit in a tone
 so passing sweet, that full reward were found
 for highest merit in that song alone.
And from the goodliest light of the inner round
 I heard a low voice, even such, maybe,
 as the angel's unto Mary, gently sound
in answer: "Long as e'er the festal glee
 of paradise endures, so long a space
 our love shall swathe us round thus gloriously.
Its brightness with the fervour shall keep pace;
 the fervour with the vision, and that is keen
 as, o'er its proper worth, 'tis granted grace.
When the transfigured, saintly flesh has been
 assumed once more, our person, being brought
 to entire perfection, will more favour win:
whereby shall be increased the light, unbought,
 which we receive from God's own excellence,
 light without which we should behold him not;
so that the vision must needs grow more intense,
 warmer the love enkindled by the same,
 brighter the glory which proceedeth thence.
But even as the coal which gives forth flame
 outshines it by a livelier, whiter glow,
 and thus its own clear presence doth proclaim,
so this effulgence which enfolds us now,
 will yield in brightness to the flesh which lies
 these ages covered by the earth below;
nor will excess of glory vex our eyes;
 because our natural organs shall be then
 made strong for all delights that heaven supplies".
So eager and alert to cry 'Amen!'
 seemed either chorus, that their keen desire
 for their dead bodies was thereby made plain;

forse non pur per lor, ma per le mamme,
  per li padri e per li altri che fuor cari
  anzi che fosser sempiterne fiamme.   66
Ed ecco intorno, di chiarezza pari,
  nascere un lustro sopra quel che v' era,
  per guisa d' orizzonte che rischiari.   69
E sì come al salir di prima sera
  comincian per lo ciel nove parvenze,
  sì che la vista pare e non par vera,   72
parvemi lì novelle sussistenze
  cominciare a vedere, e fare un giro
  di fuor da l' altre due circunferenze.   75
Oh vero sfavillar del Santo Spiro!
  come si fece subito e candente
  a li occhi miei che, vinti, non soffriro!   78
Ma Beatrice sì bella e ridente
  mi si mostrò, che tra quelle vedute
  si vuol lasciar che non seguir la mente.   81
Quindi ripreser li occhi miei virtute
  a rilevarsi; e vidimi translato
  sol con mia donna in più alta salute.   84
Ben m' accors' io ch' io era più levato,
  per l' affocato riso de la stella,
  che mi parea più roggio che l' usato.   87
Con tutto il core e con quella favella
  ch' è una in tutti a Dio feci olocausto,
  qual conveniesi a la grazia novella.   90
E non er' anco del mio petto esausto
  l' ardor del sacrificio, ch' io conobbi
  esso litare stato accetto e fausto;   93
chè con tanto lucore e tanto robbi
  m' apparvero splendor dentro a due raggi,
  ch' io dissi: "O Eliòs che sì li addobbi!"   96

nor might mere self-regard that cry inspire,
   but thoughts of fathers, mothers and all those
   they loved, ere yet they flamed with deathless fire.
And lo, a sheen of equal brilliance rose
   o'er that already there, spread round us wide,
   like the horizon when it brighter grows.
And as at fall of early eventide
   new lights begin to twinkle in the blue,
   although at first but doubtfully descried,
methought that I could there distinguish new
   subsistences, who in a shining host
   were wheeling round outside the other two.
Oh very sparkling of the Holy Ghost!
   how sudden and how brilliantly it blazed,
   straining my eyes beyond their uttermost!
But with a smile so fair my lady gazed
   upon me that I needs must reckon this
   with other sights from memory erased.
Anon, their strength renewed by Beatrice,
   I raised my eyes and found myself up-caught
   alone with her to more exalted bliss.
Clear proof to me of my ascent was brought
   by the star's burning smile, which glowed with flame
   more ruddy than of wont, or so I thought.
With full heart and that speech which is the same
   in all, I made the holocaust I owed
   for this last boon, to him from whom it came.
Nor was the heat wherewith the offering glowed
   yet quenched within my bosom, ere I knew
   the rite accepted and the omens good;
for with such mighty sheen, such ruddy hue
   splendours shone forth in twofold rays, that I
   exclaimed, "O Elios, lo, thine offspring true!"

Come distinta da minori e maggi
   lumi biancheggia tra' poli del mondo
   Galassia sì, che fa dubbiar ben saggi;   99
sì costellati facean nel profondo
   Marte quei raggi il venerabil segno
   che fan giunture di quadranti in tondo.   102
Qui vince la memoria mia lo 'ngegno;
   chè 'n quella croce lampeggiava Cristo
   sì, ch' io non so trovare essemplo degno: 105
ma chi prende sua croce e segue Cristo,
   ancor mi scuserà di quel ch' io lasso,
   vedendo in quell' albor balenar Cristo.   108
Di corno in corno e tra la cima e 'l basso
   si movien lumi, scintillando forte
   nel congiugnersi insieme e nel trapasso: 111
così si veggion qui diritte e torte,
   veloci e tarde, rinovando vista,
   le minuzie de' corpi, lunghe e corte,   114
moversi per lo raggio onde si lista
   tal volta l' ombra che, per sua difesa,
   la gente con ingegno e arte acquista.   117
E come giga e arpa, in tempra tesa
   di molte corde, fa dolce tintinno
   a tal da cui la nota non è intesa,   120
così da' lumi che lì m' apparinno
   s' accogliea per la croce una melode
   che mi rapiva, sanza intender l' inno.   123
Ben m' accors' io ch' elli era d' alte lode,
   però ch' a me venia 'Resurgi' e 'Vinci'
   come a colui che non intende e ode.   126
Io m' innamorava tanto quinci,
   che 'nfino a lì non fu alcuna cosa
   che mi legasse con sì dolci vinci.   129

As, stretched from pole to pole, the Galaxy
  gleams white, distinct with less and greater stars,
  making the sagest wonder how and why;
thus constellated in the depth of Mars,
  those rays described the venerable sign
  formed in a round by the four quadrant bars.
Here wit to follow memory must decline;
  for beaconing so upon that cross was Christ,
  no human tongue could paint the vision divine:
but whoso bears his cross and follows Christ,
  will pardon me for that I leave unsaid,
  when flashing in that dawn he beholds Christ.
From arm to arm and 'twixt the foot and head
  moved lights, which sparkled vividly whene'er
  one with another met, or past it sped:
even so on earth do atoms in the air,
  aslant and level, slow and rapid, none
  like-sized, remaining never as they were,
move through the ray of light we notice run
  at times athwart the shade which men devise
  with cunning art to screen them from the sun.
And as, with many strings which harmonise,
  viol and harp chime sweetly on an ear
  too gross to catch their subtle melodies,
so from the lights before me did I hear
  throughout the cross entrancing music swell,
  though what the hymn they carolled was not clear.
'Twas of high praises, for I heard right well
  the words 'Arise' and 'Conquer', even as he
  who hears, but what he heareth cannot tell.
I fell in love so with their minstrelsy,
  that naught whereof this poem yet hath told
  had with so sweet a bondage fettered me.

Forse la mia parola par troppo osa,
   posponendo il piacer de li occhi belli,
   ne' quai mirando, mio disio ha posa: 132
ma chi s' avvede che i vivi suggelli
   d' ogni bellezza più fanno più suso,
   e ch' io non m' era lì rivolto a quelli,   135
escusar puommi di quel ch' io m' accuso
   per escusarmi, e vedermi dir vero;
   chè 'l piacer santo non è qui dischiuso,   138
perchè si fa, montando, più sincero.

CANTO XV

Benigna volontade in che si liqua
   sempre l' amor che drittamente spira,
   come cupidità fa ne la iniqua,   3
silenzio puose a quella dolce lira,
   e fece quietar le sante corde
   che la destra del cielo allenta e tira. 6
Come saranno a' giusti preghi sorde
   quelle sustanze che, per darmi voglia
   ch' io le pregassi, a tacer fur concorde? 9
Bene è che sanza termine si doglia
   chi, per amor di cosa che non duri
   etternalmente, quello amor si spoglia.   12
Quale per li seren tranquilli e puri
   discorre ad ora ad or subito foco,
   movendo li occhi che stavan sicuri,   15
e pare stella che tramuti loco,
   se non che da la parte ond' el s' accende
   nulla sen perde, ed esso dura poco;   18

It may be that my words seem overbold,
   as did they the fair eyes depreciate,
    whose charm it stills my longing to behold:
but since more active with each higher state
   become the quick seals of all loveliness,
    and since I there had turned not to them yet,
the thoughtful may excuse what I confess
   in self-excuse, and note, how verily
    the holy charm is honoured here no less,
for, as it mounts, it grows in purity.

CANTO XV

GOODWILL that issues as it ever must
   from all true love, even as base desire
    resolves itself into the will unjust,
silence imposed on that melodious lyre,
   and hushed the sacred chords, now loose, now taut,
    as heaven's right hand which tunes them may require.
How should those glorious spirits hearken not
   to righteous prayers, who, to will me to pray,
    were thus with one accord to silence wrought?
Well may he mourn for ever and for aye,
   who, for the love of thing which hath nowise
    eternal value, casts that love away.
As through the pure and tranquil evening skies
   there shoots at times a sudden trail of light,
    stirring to movement the late listless eyes,
which well might be a star that takes to flight,
   save that from where it first was kindled none
    is missing, and it quickly fades from sight,

tale dal corno che 'n destro si stende
    a piè di quella croce corse un astro
    de la costellazion che lì resplende.   21
Nè si partì la gemma dal suo nastro,
    ma per la lista radial trascorse,
    che parve foco dietro ad alabastro.   24
Sì pia l' ombra d' Anchise si porse,
    se fede merta nostra maggior musa,
    quando in Eliso del figlio s' accorse.   27
"O sanguis meus, o superinfusa
    gratia Dei, sicut tibi cui
    bis unquam celi ianua reclusa?"   30
Così quel lume: ond' io m' attesi a lui;
    poscia rivolsi a la mia donna il viso,
    e quinci e quindi stupefatto fui;   33
chè dentro a li occhi suoi ardea un riso
    tal, ch' io pensai co' miei toccar lo fondo
    de la mia grazia e del mio paradiso.   36
Indi, a udire ed a veder giocondo,
    giunse lo spirto al suo principio cose,
    ch' io non lo 'ntesi, sì parlò profondo;   39
nè per elezion mi si nascose,
    ma per necessità, chè 'l suo concetto
    al segno de' mortal si soprapuose.   42
E quando l' arco de l' ardente affetto
    fu sì sfogato, che 'l parlar discese
    inver lo segno del nostro intelletto,   45
la prima cosa che per me s' intese,
    "Benedetto sia tu" fu "trino e uno,
    che nel mio seme se' tanto cortese!"   48
E seguì: "Grato e lontano digiuno,
    tratto leggendo del magno volume
    du' non si muta mai bianco nè bruno,   51

so from the arm which to the right doth run,
    darting adown that cross to its foot there came
    a star, of those that cluster bright thereon.
Nor parted from its riband was the gem,
    but, like to fire in alabaster, sped
    along the radial shaft its eager flame.
With equal love reached forth Anchises' shade,
    if we may trust our greater muse, when he
    his son perceived in the Elysian glade.
"O blood of mine, O grace abundantly
    shed o'er thee from on high, to whom was e'er
    heav'n's portal opened twice, as now to thee?"
The light thus: whence I gave it all my care,
    then turned, my lady's face to scrutinise,
    and lo! I stood bemazed both here and there;
for such a smile was flaming in her eyes,
    methought that mine had touched the utmost bound
    both of my grace and of my paradise.
Then, glad alike in aspect and in sound,
    that spirit spake such further things as I
    could understand not, they were too profound;
nor did it veil its thought deliberately,
    but could no other, for its argument
    soared, for the mark of mortal minds, too high.
But when the bow, by warm affection bent,
    was so far slackened that its utterance now
    toward our mental range had made descent,
the first I understood was: "Blest be thou,
    threefold and one, who graciously art pleased
    unto my seed such favours to allow!"
And it pursued: "My son, thou hast appeased
    in him thou hearest speaking from this light
    a dear, long-cherished thirst, which on me seized

soluto hai, figlio, dentro a questo lume
  in ch' io ti parlo, mercè di colei
  ch' a l' alto volo ti vestì le piume.   54
Tu credi che a me tuo pensier mei
  da quel ch' è primo, così come raia
  da l' un, se si conosce, il cinque e 'l sei;   57
e però ch' io mi sia e perch' io paia
  più gaudioso a te, non mi domandi,
  che alcun altro in questa turba gaia.   60
Tu credi 'l vero; chè i minori e i grandi
  di questa vita miran ne lo speglio
  in che, prima che pensi, il pensier pandi.   63
Ma perchè 'l sacro amore in che io veglio
  con perpetua vista e che m' asseta
  di dolce disiar, s' adempia meglio,   66
la voce tua sicura, balda e lieta
  suoni la volontà, suoni 'l disio,
  a che la mia risposta è già decreta!"   69
Io mi volsi a Beatrice, e quella udio
  pria ch' io parlassi, e arrisemi un cenno
  che fece crescer l' ali al voler mio.   72
Poi cominciai così: "L' affetto e 'l senno,
  come la prima equalità v' apparse,
  d' un peso per ciascun di voi si fenno;   75
però che 'l sol che v' allumò e arse
  col caldo e con la luce, è sì iguali,
  che tutte simiglianze sono scarse.   78
Ma voglia e argomento ne' mortali,
  per la cagion ch' a voi è manifesta,
  diversamente son pennuti in ali;   81
ond' io, che son mortal, mi sento in questa
  disagguaglianza, e però non ringrazio
  se non col core a la paterna festa.   84

when reading in the mighty tome, where white
   and dusky never change—and all by grace
   of her who fledged thee for thy lofty flight.
Thou deemest that to me thy thought doth pass
   from primal thought, as 'one', if rightly known,
   is of both 'five' and 'six' the starting-place;
hence askest not my name, nor to be shown
   why in this gladsome concourse of the blest
   the joy of none seems equal to my own.
Thou deemest rightly; for both mightiest
   and humblest here into the mirror gaze
   where thou, ere thinking, hast thy thought expressed.
But, that the sacred love which keeps always
   my vision watchful, causing me to pine
   with sweet desire, may yet more brightly blaze,
securely, frankly, blithely be it thine
   to voice the purpose, voice the wish, whereto
   my answer stands decreed by will divine!"
I turned me to my lady, but she knew
   my thought ere uttered, and a sign bestowed
   whereby the wings of my intention grew.
And I began: "So soon as ye abode
   within the first equality, your wit
   shone in like measure as your feeling glowed;
because the sun by whom ye are warmed and lit
   with light and warmth, so equally doth glow,
   that all resemblances fall short of it.
But in mankind—and well the cause ye know—
   wish and the means to give that wish effect
   have pinions which diversely plumaged grow.
I too by this disparity am checked,
   as man: hence for thy fatherly accost
   no other thanks than of the heart expect.

Ben supplico io a te, vivo topazio
 che questa gioia preziosa ingemmi,
 perchè mi facci del tuo nome sazio".   87
"O fronda mia in che io compiacemmi
 pur aspettando, io fui la tua radice":
 cotal principio, rispondendo, femmi.   90
Poscia mi disse: "Quel da cui si dice
 tua cognazione e che cent' anni e piue
 girato ha il monte in la prima cornice,   93
mio figlio fu e tuo bisavol fue:
 ben si convien che la lunga fatica
 tu li raccorci con l' opere tue.   96
Fiorenza dentro da la cerchia antica,
 ond' ella toglie ancora e terza e nona,
 si stava in pace, sobria e pudica.   99
Non avea catenella, non corona,
 non gonne contigiate, non cintura
 che fosse a veder più che la persona.   102
Non faceva, nascendo, ancor paura
 la figlia al padre; chè 'l tempo e la dote
 non fuggien quinci e quindi la misura.   105
Non avea case di famiglia vote;
 non v' era giunto ancor Sardanapalo
 a mostrar ciò che 'n camera si puote.   108
Non era vinto ancora Montemalo
 dal vostro Uccellatoio, che, com' è vinto
 nel montar su, così sarà nel calo.   111
Bellincion Berti vid' io andar cinto
 di cuoio e d' osso, e venir da lo specchio
 la donna sua sanza il viso dipinto;   114
e vidi quel di Nerli e quel del Vecchio
 esser contenti a la pelle scoperta,
 e le sue donne al fuso e al pennecchio.   117

Yet prithee, living topaz—thou, that dost
   ingem this precious jewel, satisfy
   me with thy name: 'tis that I long for most".
"O branch of mine in whom rejoiced have I
   while but expecting thee, I was thy stem":
   such was the preface to its prompt reply.
Then it said: "He that gave thy clan its name,
   who after more than five-score years doth yet
   toil round the mount's first cornice—even the same
my son was, and thy grandsire did beget:
   well may thy prayers, as it is meet they should,
   the long term of his weariness abate.
Florence within her old enclosure stood,
   whence tierce and nones she still hears daily tolled,
   and dwelt in peace, sober and chaste and good.
No chain she had, no coronet of gold,
   no gaily-sandalled dames, no belt in hue
   more striking than its wearer to behold.
No father yet found reason to beshrew
   a daughter's birth; for dower and age to wed
   'scaped not, on either hand, the measure due.
No houses then stood uninhabited;
   no Sardanapálus yet was come to show
   what gallant hearts by chambering are bred.
Nor yet defeat did Montemalo know
   by your Uccellatoi'—to be acquainted,
   swift tho' it rise, with swifter overthrow.
Bellinción Berti saw I pass, contented
   with belt of bone and leather, and his dame
   leaving the mirror with her face unpainted;
saw Nerli's lord and Vecchio's, chiefs of fame,
   content with plain buff coats, their wives withal
   of handling flax and distaff think no shame.

Oh fortunate! ciascuna era certa
  de la sua sepoltura, e ancor nulla
  era per Francia nel letto diserta.   120
L' una vegghiava a studio de la culla,
  e, consolando, usava l' idioma
  che prima i padri e le madri trastulla;   123
l' altra, traendo a la rocca la chioma,
  favoleggiava con la sua famiglia
  de' Troiani, di Fiesole e di Roma.   126
Saria tenuta allor tal maraviglia
  una Cianghella, un Lapo Salterello,
  qual or saria Cincinnato e Corniglia.   129
A così riposato, a così bello
  viver di cittadini, a così fida
  cittadinanza, a così dolce ostello,   132
Maria mi diè, chiamata in alte grida;
  e ne l' antico vostro Batisteo
  insieme fui cristiano e Cacciaguida.   135
Moronto fu mio frate ed Eliseo:
  mia donna venne a me di val di Pado;
  e quindi il sopranome tuo si feo.   138
Poi seguitai lo 'mperador Currado;
  ed el mi cinse de la sua milizia,
  tanto per bene ovrar li venni in grado.   141
Dietro li andai incontro a la nequizia
  di quella legge il cui popolo usurpa,
  per colpa de' pastor, vostra giustizia.   144
Quivi fu' io da quella gente turpa
  disviluppato dal mondo fallace,
  lo cui amor molt' anime deturpa;   147
e venni dal martiro a questa pace".

Oh happy they! Each sure of burial
   in her own tomb, none fated yet to lie
   deserted in her bed at Frenchman's call.
One, o'er the cradle, crooned a lullaby,
   lisping the words with which in every home
   fathers and mothers soothe their infant's cry.
Another to the youngsters bidden come
   and gather round her spinning-wheel would tell
   tales of the Trojans, Fiesole and Rome.
Cornelia and Cincinnatus might as well
   be found among you now, as then had been
   such as Cianghella and Lapo Salterel.
Me to a life so lovely, so serene,
   of fellowship with citizens so staid,
   a hostelry so good to sojourn in,
did Mary give, when loudly called to aid;
   and, in your ancient Baptistery, there
   was I both Christ's and Cacciaguida made.
Moronto and Eliséo my brothers were:
   my wife I took me from the vale of Po;
   and thence the surname comes which thou dost bear.
Anon with the emperor Conrad did I go
   campaigning; and in time he dubbed me knight,
   my gallant deeds of arms had pleased him so.
With him did I that false religion fight
   whose people, by your shepherds' fault, the place
   have long usurped which should be yours by right.
There was I at the hands of that foul race
   dismantled of the world's deceitful shows,
   the love of which doth many a soul debase;
and came from martyrdom to this repose ".

CANTO XVI

O POCA nostra nobiltà di sangue,
   se gloriar di te la gente fai
   qua giù dove l' affetto nostro langue,   3
mirabil cosa non mi sarà mai;
   chè là dove appetito non si torce,
   dico nel cielo, io me ne gloriai.   6
Ben se' tu manto che tosto raccorce;
   sì che, se non s' appon di dì in die,
   lo tempo va dintorno con le force.   9
Dal 'voi' che prima Roma sofferie,
   in che la sua famiglia men persevra,
   ricominciaron le parole mie;   12
onde Beatrice, ch' era un poco scevra,
   ridendo, parve quella che tossio
   al primo fallo scritto di Ginevra.   15
Io cominciai: "Voi siete il padre mio;
   voi mi date a parlar tutta baldezza;
   voi mi levate sì, ch' i' son più ch' io.   18
Per tanti rivi s' empie d' allegrezza
   la mente mia, che di sè fa letizia
   perchè può sostener che non si spezza.   21
Ditemi dunque, cara mia primizia,
   quai fuor li vostri antichi, e quai fuor li anni
   che si segnaro in vostra puerizia: 24
ditemi de l' ovil di San Giovanni
   quanto era allora, e chi eran le genti
   tra esso degne di più alti scanni".   27
Come s' avviva a lo spirar di venti
   carbone in fiamma, così vid' io quella
   luce risplendere a' miei blandimenti.   30

CANTO XVI

O PALTRY heritage, our noble blood,
   if that to glory in thee thou movest men
   down here where we but feebly will the good,
no marvel shall I deem it ever again;
   for there, where right affection never veers,
   I mean in heaven, myself thereof grew vain.
Truly thou art a cloak one soon outwears;
   so that, save cloth be added day by day,
   time doth go round about thee with his shears.
With plural 'you', in the old courtly way
   permitted first by Rome, whose sons appear
   to use it least now, I resumed my say;
whence Beatrice, who stood aloof though near,
   smiling, resembled her whose cough gave sign
   of the first fault they tell of Guinevere.
I thus began: "You are my father, mine;
   you give me boldness to speak all my thought;
   you adorn me so that I myself outshine.
My spirit through so many rills is fraught
   with gladness, that it joys in its own joy
   at being so filled therewith and bursting not.
Thus, then, my honoured stem, the time employ:
   tell me your ancestry, and what was done
   that marked the years, while you were yet a boy:
and tell me of the sheep-fold of St John—
   its size, and which were then the families
   whose worth the highest seats in it had won".
I saw the lustre glow on hearing these
   my blandishments, as embers to a blaze
   are quickened at the breath of passing breeze.

E come a li occhi miei si fè più bella,
  così con voce più dolce e soave,
    ma non con questa moderna favella,   33
dissemi: "Da quel dì che fu detto 'Ave'
  al parto in che mia madre, ch' è or santa,
    s' alleviò di me ond' era grave,   36
al suo Leon cinquecento cinquanta
  e trenta fiate venne questo foco
    a rinfiammarsi sotto la sua pianta.   39
Li antichi miei e io nacqui nel loco
  dove si truova pria l' ultimo sesto
    da quei che corre il vostro annual gioco.   42
Basti de' miei maggiori udirne questo:
  chi ei si fosser e onde venner quivi,
    più è tacer che ragionare onesto.   45
Tutti color ch' a quel tempo eran ivi
  da poter arme tra Marte e 'l Batista,
    erano il quinto di quei ch' or son vivi.   48
Ma la cittadinanza, ch' è or mista
  di Campi, di Certaldo e di Fegghine,
    pura vediesi ne l' ultimo artista.   51
Oh quanto fora meglio esser vicine
  quelle genti ch' io dico, e al Galluzzo
    e a Trespiano aver vostro confine,   54
che averle dentro e sostener lo puzzo
  del villan d'Aguglion, di quel da Signa,
    che già per barattare ha l' occhio aguzzo! 57
Se la gente ch' al mondo più traligna
  non fosse stata a Cesare noverca,
    ma come madre a suo figlio benigna,   60
tal fatto è fiorentino e cambia e merca,
  che si sarebbe volto a Simifonti,
    là dove andava l' avolo a la cerca;   63

And as it grew yet fairer to my gaze,
   so with a sweeter, gentler voice it made
   reply, but not in this our modern phrase,
with these words: "From the day when 'Hail' was said,
   to that whereon my sainted mother's womb
   was of myself, its burden, lightenéd,
to its own Lion had this planet come
   five hundred, fifty and thirty times, its flame
   beneath his burning paw to re-illume.
My ancestors were born and I, like them,
   there, where encountered first is the last ward
   by him who runneth in your annual game.
Suffice it of my forbears to record
   thus much: their names, and what their origin,
   rather than mentioned here, were best ignored.
All those who at that time were there, between
   Mars and the Baptist, fit for arms were man
   for man the fifth of those to-day there seen.
Yet was the commune—now a mongrel clan
   mixed with Fegghine, with Certaldo mixed
   and Campi—pure to the last artisan.
Oh how much better ye should dwell betwixt
   those folk as neighbours, and your boundary
   have at Galluzzo and at Trespiano fixed,
than have them in and thole the stench thereby
   of Aguglione's boor, of Signa's hind,
   whose eye e'en now is sharp for barratry!
If of all folk the most depraved in mind
   had not the stepdame unto Caesar played,
   but as a mother to her son been kind,
some—newly Florentine—who truck and trade,
   would have been hounded back to Simifonti,
   there where their grandsires used to beg their bread;

sariesi Montemurlo ancor de' Conti;
    sarieno i Cerchi nel piovier d' Acone,
    e forse in Valdigrieve i Bondelmonti.   66
Sempre la confusion de le persone
    principio fu del mal de la cittade,
    come del vostro il cibo che s' appone;   69
e cieco toro più avaccio cade
    che 'l cieco agnello; e molte volte taglia
    più e meglio una che le cinque spade.   72
Se tu riguardi Luni e Urbisaglia
    come sono ite, e come se ne vanno
    di retro ad esse Chiusi e Sinigaglia,   75
udir come le schiatte si disfanno
    non ti parrà nova cosa nè forte,
    poscia che le cittadi termine hanno.   78
Le vostre cose tutte hanno lor morte,
    sì come voi; ma celasi in alcuna
    che dura molto; e le vite son corte.   81
E come 'l volger del ciel de la luna
    cuopre e discuopre i liti sanza posa,
    così fa di Fiorenza la Fortuna: 84
per che non dee parer mirabil cosa
    ciò ch' io dirò de li alti Fiorentini
    onde è la fama nel tempo nascosa.   87
Io vidi li Ughi, e vidi i Catellini,
    Filippi, Greci, Ormanni e Alberichi,
    già nel calare, illustri cittadini;   90
e vidi così grandi come antichi,
    con quel de la Sannella, quel de l' Arca,
    e Soldanieri e Ardinghi e Bostichi.   93
Sovra la porta ch' al presente è carca
    di nova fellonia di tanto peso
    che tosto fia iattura de la barca,   96

held yet were Montemurlo by the Conti;
   the Cerchi would Acone's parish hold,
   and Valdigrieve, chance, the Buondelmonti.
Source of the public ill was, from of old,
   in the confusion of the persons found,
   as food makes sick, if greed be uncontrolled.
And the blind bull more headlong falls to the ground
   than the blind lamb, and than five swords doth one
   ofttimes inflict more cuts and deeplier wound.
Consider Luni, how she is past and gone,
   and Urbisaglia; and after them how go
   Chiusi and Sinigaglia: think thereon,
and, inasmuch as cities perish so,
   not hard thou'lt deem it or a strange report
   to hear that families enfeebled grow.
All your belongings in the last resort
   die, as do ye; but some their death conceal
   by enduring long; and human lives are short.
And as the turning of the lunar wheel
   in ceaseless rhythm veils and unveils the shore,
   even so with Florence too doth Fortune deal:
hence should it not be thing to marvel o'er,
   what I of those great Florentines shall say,
   whose fame lies hidden in the days of yore.
The Ughi, Ormanni, and Alberichi, yea,
   Greci, Filippi, and Catellini there
   I saw, yet glorious, even in decay;
and saw as mighty as they ancient were,
   both him of la Sannella, of l' Arca him,
   Bostichi too, Ardinghi and Soldanier.
Still o'er the gateway, laden with such grim,
   unheard-of treachery in these days, that soon
   the ship will 'neath it rather sink than swim,

erano i Ravignani, ond' è disceso
il conte Guido e qualunque del nome
de l' alto Bellincione ha poscia preso.   99

Quel de la Pressa sapeva già come
regger si vuole, e avea Galigaio
dorata in casa sua già l' elsa e 'l pome.   102

Grand' era già la colonna del Vaio,
Sacchetti, Giuochi, Fifanti e Barucci
e Galli e quei ch' arrossan per lo staio.   105

Lo ceppo di che nacquero i Calfucci
era già grande, e già eran tratti
a le curule Sizii e Arrigucci.   108

Oh quali io vidi quei che son disfatti
per lor superbia! e le palle de l' oro
fiorian Fiorenza in tutti suoi gran fatti.   111

Così facieno i padri di coloro
che, sempre che la vostra chiesa vaca,
si fanno grassi stando a consistoro.   114

L' oltracotata schiatta che s' indraca
dietro a chi fugge, e a chi mostra 'l dente
o ver la borsa, com' agnel si placa,   117

già venia su, ma di picciola gente;
sì che non piacque ad Ubertin Donato
che poi il suocero il fè lor parente.   120

Già era il Caponsacco nel mercato
disceso giù da Fiesole, e già era
buon cittadino Giuda ed Infangato.   123

Io dirò cosa incredibile e vera:
nel picciol cerchio s' entrava per porta
che si nomava da quei de la Pera.   126

Ciascun che de la bella insegna porta
del gran barone il cui nome e 'l cui pregio
la festa di Tommaso riconforta,   129

were Ravignani, whom as forbears own
   count Guido and whosoe'er, from then till now,
   his title takes from the great Bellincion.
He of la Pressa knew already how
   to rule, and Galigaio's house yet claimed
   by gilded hilt and pommel its worth to show.
Mighty was yet the column Vair, yet famed
   were Galli, Giuochi, Fifanti, Barucci,
   Sacchetti and those the bushel makes ashamed.
The stock which had for scions the Calfucci
   was still great: to the curule chairs the hour
   was calling still the Sizii and Arrigucci.
Oh, how I saw those mighty who from power
   through pride have fallen! and the balls of gold
   in all their doughty deeds made Florence flower.
Such sires had they, who now consistory hold
   whene'er your church is vacant, and there stay
   and make them fat—such sires were theirs of old.
The o'erweening tribe that will the dragon play
   to him that flees, but doth he turn and show
   his teeth, or purse, no lamb so mild as they,
were on the rise, but still of blood so low,
   that Ubertín Donato grudged it, when
   his father-in-law had made him kin thereto.
The Caponsacchi had come down by then
   from Fiesole to the market; Giuda too,
   with Infangato, was good citizen.
Named of la Pera was a port wherethrough
   one entered the small circuit—of all things
   I've told thee yet, least credible, but true!
Each one who bears the brilliant quarterings
   of the great peer whose name and whose renown
   the feast of Thomas to your memory brings,

da esso ebbe milizia e privilegio;
  avvegna che con popol si rauni
  oggi colui che la fascia col fregio.   132
Già eran Gualterotti ed Importuni;
  e ancor saria Borgo più quieto,
  se di novi vicin fosser digiuni.   135
La casa di che nacque il vostro fleto,
  per lo giusto disdegno che v' ha morti,
  e puose fine al vostro viver lieto,   138
era onorata, essa e suoi consorti:
  o Buondelmonte, quanto mal fuggisti
  le nozze sue per li altrui conforti!   141
Molti sarebber lieti, che son tristi,
  se Dio t' avesse conceduto ad Ema
  la prima volta ch' a città venisti.   144
Ma conveniesi a quella pietra scema
  che guarda il ponte che Fiorenza fesse
  vittima ne la sua pace postrema.   147
Con queste genti e con altre con esse,
  vid' io Fiorenza in sì fatto riposo,
  che non avea cagione onde piangesse: 150
con queste genti vid' io glorioso
  e giusto il popol suo, tanto che 'l giglio
  non era ad asta mai posto a ritroso,   153
nè per division fatto vermiglio ".

CANTO XVII

Qual venne a Climenè, per accertarsi
  di ciò ch' avea incontro a sè udito,
  quei ch' ancor fa i padri ai figli scarsi;   3

was for his knight and for his liegeman known;
   though he that with a bordure rings them round
   to-day has made the people's cause his own.
In Borgo yet were the Importuni found,
   and Gualterotti—a more tranquil place
   now, did it with new neighbours less abound.
The proud house that gave birth to your distress,
   through the just anger which hath been your bane,
   and put a period to your happiness,
itself was honoured, and its consorts, then:
   O Buondelmonte, when by others' rede
   thou fledst its nuptials, little didst thou gain!
Many would have rejoiced, whose hearts now bleed,
   if God in Ema's flood had let thee drown,
   when to the city thou didst first proceed.
But Florence by that mutilated stone
   which guards the bridge was doomed in those, the last
   days of her peace, to strike some victim down.
With these and other houses in times past,
   beheld I Florence live days so serene,
   that she no reason had to be downcast:
with these beheld her folk such glory win,
   that, as befitting those whom justice rules,
   the lily on the lance was never seen
reversed, nor through division tinctured gules".

CANTO XVII

As came to Clymene, intent to clear
   his name of slander, he who still doth make,
   when sons entreat them, fathers slow to hear;

tal era io, e tal era sentito
  e da Beatrice e da la santa lampa
  che pria per me avea mutato sito.   6
Per che mia donna "Manda fuor la vampa
  del tuo disio" mi disse, "sì ch' ella esca
  segnata bene de la interna stampa;   9
non perchè nostra conoscenza cresca
  per tuo parlare, ma perchè t' ausi
  a dir la sete, sì che l' uom ti mesca".   12
"O cara piota mia che sì t' insusi,
  che come veggion le terrene menti
  non capere in triangol due ottusi,   15
così vedi le cose contingenti
  anzi che sieno in sè, mirando il punto
  a cui tutti li tempi son presenti;   18
mentre ch' io era a Virgilio congiunto
  su per lo monte che l' anime cura
  e discendendo nel mondo defunto,   21
dette mi fuor di mia vita futura
  parole gravi, avvegna ch' io mi senta
  ben tetragono ai colpi di ventura.   24
Per che la voglia mia saria contenta
  d' intender qual fortuna mi s' appressa;
  chè saetta prevista vien più lenta."   27
Così diss' io a quella luce stessa
  che pria m' avea parlato; e come volle
  Beatrice, fu la mia voglia confessa.   30
Nè per ambage, in che la gente folle
  già s' inviscava pria che fosse anciso
  l' Agnel di Dio che le peccata tolle,   33
ma per chiare parole e con preciso
  latin rispuose quello amor paterno,
  chiuso e parvente del suo proprio riso: 36

e'en such was I, and such did Beatrice take
  note that I was, as did the holy lamp
  who late had changed his station for my sake.
Wherefore my lady thus: "In nowise damp
  the flame of thy desire, but send it out
  imprinted clearly by the inward stamp;
not that thy speech may banish any doubt
  of ours, but that thou train thyself thereby
  to tell thy need, that men may slake thy drought".
"Dear turf from which I sprang, now raised so high,
  that as to earthly minds 'tis clear that two
  obtuse in one triangle cannot lie,
so unto thee, who hast the point in view
  which sees all times as present, are displayed
  contingent things ere they in fact come true;
while I, with Virgil as companion, made
  my way up o'er the mount that souls doth heal
  and downwards in the world that lieth dead,
pronounced were grave words, tending to reveal
  my future life, albeit I feel me now
  right four-square to the blows that chance may deal.
Wherefore my wish were granted, wouldst thou show
  what lot is drawing nigh me, and from where;
  since bolt foreseen strikes with less sudden blow."
Thus spake I to the light which had whilere
  addressed me, and did thus the will obey
  of Beatrice, and my strong wish declare.
Nor in ambiguous terms, that led astray
  the foolish folk in times ere yet was slain
  the Lamb of God who taketh sins away,
but in clear words and language no less plain
  did that paternal love, which veiled, yet show'd,
  itself in its own smile, thus speak again:

"La contingenza, che fuor del quaderno
  de la vostra matera non si stende,
  tutta è dipinta nel cospetto etterno: 39
necessità però quindi non prende
  se non come dal viso in che si specchia
  nave che per corrente giù discende.   42
Da indi sì come viene ad orecchia
  dolce armonia da organo, mi vene
  a vista il tempo che ti s' apparecchia.   45
Qual si partio Ippolito d'Atene
  per la spietata e perfida noverca,
  tal di Fiorenza partir ti convene.   48
Questo si vuole e questo già si cerca,
  e tosto verrà fatto a chi ciò pensa
  là dove Cristo tutto dì si merca.   51
La colpa seguirà la parte offensa
  in grido, come suol; ma la vendetta
  fia testimonio al ver che la dispensa.   54
Tu lascerai ogni cosa diletta
  più caramente; e questo è quello strale
  che l' arco de lo essilio pria saetta.   57
Tu proverai sì come sa di sale
  lo pane altrui, e come è duro calle
  lo scendere e 'l salir per l' altrui scale. 60
E quel che più ti graverà le spalle,
  sarà la compagnia malvagia e scempia
  con la qual tu cadrai in questa valle;   63
che tutta ingrata, tutta matta ed empia
  si farà contr' a te; ma, poco appresso,
  ella, non tu, n' avrà rossa la tempia.   66
Di sua bestialità il suo processo
  farà la prova; sì ch' a te fia bello
  averti fatta parte per te stesso.   69

"Contingency, which stretches not its mode
   past the brief page where mortal lives are writ,
   is all depicted in the face of God:
yet thence derives necessity no whit
   more than the motion of a ship that fares
   downstream depends on the eye that mirrors it.
From thence, e'en as there stealeth on the ears
   sweet harmony from organ, comes to me
   a vision of thy life in future years.
As his stepmother's wiles and cruelty
   from Athens drave Hippolytus, likewise
   thyself from Florence driven forth must be.
This would they, this already they devise,
   and soon will do it he that plots it there
   where Christ is daily hawked as merchandise.
The side wronged will, as wont, in rumour bear
   the blame; yet shall the vengeance testify
   unto the truth, whereof 'tis minister.
Thou shalt leave each thing that most tenderly
   thou lov'st; and this, of arrows from the bow
   of exile, is the first that it lets fly.
Thou shalt make proof how salt the taste doth grow
   of others' bread, and how it tires the feet
   still up, still down, by others' stairs to go.
And what shall gall thee most, will be to meet
   the company, stupid and evil swine,
   with whom thou shalt be cast into this pit;
who, all mad, all as thankless as malign,
   will turn 'gainst thee; but, ere much time hath flown,
   theirs shall the crimsoned forehead be, not thine.
So shall their brutishness in deeds be shown,
   that 'twill become thee well to have preferred
   to form a party to thyself alone.

Lo primo tuo refugio, il primo ostello
  sarà la cortesia del gran Lombardo
  che 'n su la scala porta il santo uccello;   72
ch' in te avrà sì benigno riguardo,
  che del fare e del chieder, tra voi due,
  fia primo quel che, tra gli altri, è più tardo.   75
Con lui vedrai colui che 'mpresso fue,
  nascendo, sì da questa stella forte,
  che notabili fien l' opere sue.   78
Non se ne son le genti ancora accorte
  per la novella età, chè pur nove anni
  son queste rote intorno di lui torte: 81
ma pria che 'l Guasco l' alto Arrigo inganni,
  parran faville de la sua virtute
  in non curar d' argento nè d' affanni.   84
Le sue magnificenze conosciute
  saranno ancora sì che' suoi nemici
  non ne potran tener le lingue mute.   87
A lui t' aspetta ed a' suoi benefici;
  per lui fia trasmutata molta gente,
  cambiando condizion ricchi e mendici.   90
E portera'ne scritto ne la mente
  di lui, e nol dirai"; e disse cose
  incredibili a quei che fien presente.   93
Poi giunse: "Figlio, queste son le chiose
  di quel che ti fu detto; ecco le 'nsidie
  che dietro a pochi giri son nascose.   96
Non vo' però ch' a' tuoi vicini invidie,
  poscia che s' infutura la tua vita
  vie più là che 'l punir di lor perfidie".   99
Poi che, tacendo, si mostrò spedita
  l' anima santa di metter la trama
  in quella tela ch' io le porsi ordita,   102

First refuge and first inn for thee prepared
    shall be the mighty Lombard's courtesy,
    who on the ladder bears the sacred bird,
who shall have such benign regard for thee,
    that, counter to men's wont, betwixt ye two
    the granting shall before the asking be.
With him shalt thou behold the mortal, who
    at birth was so impressed by this strong star,
    that signal are the deeds which he shall do.
Still unobserved of men his merits are,
    by reason of his youth; for this bright coil
    has round him wheeled but nine brief years so far:
but ere the Gascon the great Harry foil,
    some sparkles of his temper will he show
    in caring not for money or for toil.
Hereafter shall his deeds be bruited so
    for their magnificence, that they shall let
    no tongue be silent, even of his foe.
Him look to, and upon his favours wait;
    through him shall many be transformed in kind,
    rich men and poor, exchanging their estate.
And thou shalt bear hence, written in thy mind
    of him, and tell it not"; and he told things
    which those, who see them, past belief shall find.
He added: "Son, these on the happenings
    foretold thee are the glosses: lo, concealed
    by a few turns o' the year, what ambushings.
Yet to no envy of thy neighbours yield;
    in that thy future life shall far outlast
    the doom by which their treachery shall be sealed".
When, having now from speech to silence pass'd,
    that saintly soul thus showed the web, whereof
    I'd stretched the warp, with woof inwoven fast,

io cominciai, come colui che brama,
    dubitando, consiglio da persona
    che vede e vuol dirittamente e ama: 105
"Ben veggio, padre mio, sì come sprona
    lo tempo verso me, per colpo darmi
    tal, ch' è più grave a chi più s' abbandona;   108
per che di provedenza è buon ch' io m' armi,
    sì che, se 'l loco m' è tolto più caro,
    io non perdessi li altri per miei carmi.   111
Giù per lo mondo sanza fine amaro,
    e per lo monte del cui bel cacume
    li occhi de la mia donna mi levaro,   114
e poscia per lo ciel di lume in lume,
    ho io appreso quel che s' io ridico,
    a molti fia sapor di forte agrume;   117
e s' io al vero son timido amico,
    temo di perder viver tra coloro
    che questo tempo chiameranno antico".   120
La luce in che rideva il mio tesoro
    ch' io trovai lì, si fè prima corusca,
    quale a raggio di sole specchio d' oro;   123
indi rispuose: "Coscienza fusca
    o de la propria o de l' altrui vergogna
    pur sentirà la tua parola brusca.   126
Ma nondimen, rimossa ogni menzogna,
    tutta tua vision fa manifesta;
    e lascia pur grattar dov' è la rogna.   129
Chè se la voce tua sarà molesta
    nel primo gusto, vital nutrimento
    lascerà poi, quando sarà digesta.   132
Questo tuo grido farà come vento,
    che le più alte cime più percuote;
    e ciò non fa d' onor poco argomento.   135

I spake as one who, doubting, fain would prove
   the wisdom of some friend and such doth seek
   as sees and wills uprightly and doth love:
"Father, 'tis clear indeed, how time doth prick
   toward me, that keen arrow to let fly
   which woundeth sorest him of eye least quick;
'tis good to be armed with foresight, then, that I,
   if robbed of the place wherein I most delight,
   lose not the others through my poetry.
Down in the world of sorrows infinite,
   and on the mountain from whose lovely crest
   my lady's eyes upbore me by their might,
and, later, through this heaven, as on I pressed
   from light to light, I've learned what, if retold,
   would have for many a most bitter taste.
And if to truth my friendship turneth cold,
   I fear that I may perish among those
   who will describe these as 'the days of old'".
The light that by its smile I knew to enclose
   my late-found treasure, flashed with such a beam
   as back to the sun a golden mirror throws,
and then replied: "To conscience rendered dim
   by its own or others' shame (no matter which)
   'tis true that sharp will much thou sayest seem;
but, notwithstanding, see there be no breach
   with truth, but publish thou thy vision whole;
   which done, e'en let them scratch who feel the itch.
For though thy voice may cause the palate dole
   at the first taste, 'twill later leave behind,
   when well digested, that which feeds the soul.
This cry of thine shall do as doth the wind,
   which hardest strikes upon the loftiest hills;
   and that is no small proof of noble mind.

Però ti son mostrate in queste rote,
   nel monte e ne la valle dolorosa
   pur l' anime che son di fama note,   138
che l' animo di quel ch' ode, non posa
   nè ferma fede per essemplo ch' aia
   la sua radice incognita e nascosa,   141
nè per altro argomento che non paia ".

CANTO XVIII

Già si godea solo del suo verbo
   quello specchio beato, e io gustava
   lo mio, temprando col dolce l' acerbo.   3
E quella donna ch' a Dio mi menava
   disse: "Muta pensier: pensa ch' i' sono
   presso a colui ch' ogni torto disgrava ".   6
Io mi rivolsi a l' amoroso suono
   del mio conforto; e qual io allor vidi
   ne li occhi santi amor, qui l' abbandono;   9
non perch' io pur del mio parlar diffidi,
   ma per la mente che non può reddire
   sovra sè tanto, s' altri non la guidi.   12
Tanto poss' io di quel punto ridire,
   che, rimirando lei, lo mio affetto
   libero fu da ogni altro disire,   15
fin che il piacere etterno, che diretto
   raggiava in Beatrice, dal bel viso
   mi contentava col secondo aspetto.   18
Vincendo me col lume d' un sorriso,
   ella mi disse: "Volgiti ed ascolta;
   chè non pur ne' miei occhi è paradiso ".   21

Hence have no souls been shown thee in these wheels,
   or on the mount, or in the dolorous vale,
   save those whose names the trump of fame yet peals,
because the hearer's mind can never dwell
   content, or fix its faith, on instance ta'en
   from root unknown or else invisible,
nor yet on other proof which is not plain".

CANTO XVIII

THAT mirror of true bliss enjoyed alone
   his musings for a while, and I too fed,
   tempering with sweet the bitter, on my own.
And she by whom my steps were Godward led
   cried: "Change thy thought: bethink thee that I dwell
   with one by whom all wrongs are lightenéd".
I turned me, as those loving accents fell,
   unto my comfort; and how blazed with love
   her holy eyes just then, I may not tell;
not only that I trust not speech thereof,
   but mortal mind cannot so much retain
   of its own bliss, unaided from above.
This only in my memory lives again,
   that my affection, as I gazed on her,
   was freed from every other longing then.
While the eternal joy, whose beams fell fair
   on Beatrice, still held me entranced—her eyes
   reflecting it, I seeing it mirrored there—
she bade me turn and, smiling in such wise
   that I was dazzled, said: "Give heed; and know,
   not in my eyes alone is paradise".

Come si vede qui alcuna volta
    l' affetto ne la vista, s' elli è tanto
    che da lui sia tutta l' anima tolta,   24
così nel fiammeggiar del fulgor santo,
    a ch' io mi volsi, conobbi la voglia
    in lui di ragionarmi ancora alquanto.   27
El cominciò: "In questa quinta soglia
    de l' albero che vive de la cima
    e frutta sempre e mai non perde foglia,   30
spiriti son beati, che giù, prima
    che venissero al ciel, fuor di gran voce,
    sì ch' ogni musa ne sarebbe opima.   33
Però mira ne' corni de la croce:
    quello ch' io nomerò, lì farà l' atto
    che fa in nube il suo foco veloce".   36
Io vidi per la croce un lume tratto
    dal nomar Iosuè com' el si feo;
    nè mi fu noto il dir prima che 'l fatto.   39
E al nome de l' alto Maccabeo
    vidi moversi un altro roteando,
    e letizia era ferza del paleo.   42
Così per Carlo Magno e per Orlando
    due ne seguì lo mio attento sguardo,
    com' occhio segue suo falcon volando.   45
Poscia trasse Guiglielmo, e Renoardo,
    e 'l duca Gottifredi la mia vista
    per quella croce, e Ruberto Guiscardo.   48
Indi, tra l' altre luci mota e mista,
    mostrommi l' alma che m' avea parlato
    qual era tra i cantor del cielo artista.   51
Io mi rivolsi dal mio destro lato
    per vedere in Beatrice il mio dovere
    o per parlare o per atto segnato;   54

As here at times we see the features show
   the affection, if so mightily this fill
   the spirit as to set it all aglow,
so did the holy light reveal its will,
   whose flame, to which I turned, now made me see
   that it desired some converse with me still.
And it began: "This fifth tier of the tree,
   which draws life from its summit and ne'er knows dearth
   of fruitage nor shall ever leafless be,
holds blesséd spirits, who while down on earth,
   or e'er they came to heaven, had won such fame
   that every muse would grow rich by their worth.
Look, therefore, on the arms of the cross: the flame
   that darts in cloud doth not so swiftly dart
   as there the soul will, whom I now shall name".
Straight I beheld a lustre drawn athwart
   the cross by Joshua's name: he spake, 'twas done;
   nor could I tell the word and deed apart.
He called great Maccabeus, and thereupon
   I saw shoot by another whirling light;
   joy was the whip that made the top spin on.
Two more I thus pursued with eager sight,
   answering to Roland and to Charlëmain,
   as falconer's eye pursues its bird in flight.
Thereafter William and Rainouart, and then
   duke Godfrey to the cross compelled mine eye;
   last, Robert Guiscard flashed upon my ken.
The soul who spake with me then passed on high,
   where mingled with the other lights he plied
   his art among the minstrels of the sky.
I turned me round unto the right-hand side
   to see in Beatrice what I ought to do,
   whether by word or gesture signified;

e vidi le sue luci tanto mere,
  tanto gioconde, che la sua sembianza
  vinceva li altri e l' ultimo solere.   57
E come, per sentir più dilettanza
  bene operando, l' uom di giorno in giorno
  s' accorge che la sua virtute avanza,   60
sì m' accors' io che 'l mio girar dintorno
  col cielo insieme avea cresciuto l' arco,
  veggendo quel miracol più adorno.   63
E qual è il trasmutare in picciol varco
  di tempo in bianca donna, quando il volto
  suo si discarchi di vergogna il carco,   66
tal fu ne li occhi miei, quando fui volto,
  per lo candor de la temprata stella
  sesta, che dentro a sè m' avea ricolto.   69
Io vidi in quella giovial facella
  lo sfavillar de l' amor che lì era,
  segnare a li occhi miei nostra favella.   72
E come augelli surti di rivera
  quasi congratulando a lor pasture,
  fanno di sè or tonda or altra schiera,   75
sì dentro ai lumi sante creature
  volitando cantavano, e faciensi
  or *D*, or *I*, or *L* in sue figure.   78
Prima, cantando, a sua nota moviensi;
  poi, diventando l' un di questi segni,
  un poco s' arrestavano e taciensi.   81
O diva Pegasea che li 'ngegni
  fai gloriosi e rendili longevi,
  ed essi teco le cittadi e' regni,   84
illustrami di te, sì ch' io rilevi
  le lor figure com' io l' ho concette:
  paia tua possa in questi versi brevi!   87

and in her eyes beheld new radiance, new
   delight, so pure that she in this array
   surpassed her former wont, her latest too.
And as a man, through feeling day by day
   more joy in doing good, will thence suspect
   the measure of his advance on virtue's way;
so, wheeling with the heaven, did I detect
   a widening of the arc we swept through space,
   on seeing that miracle more brightly decked.
And such a change as quickly taketh place
   in fair-complexioned lady, when its load
   of bashfulness is put from off her face,
now, as I turned, in all the prospect showed,
   by reason of the mild sixth star, whose white
   radiance it was, that round us softly glowed.
I saw within that jovial cresset bright
   the sparkling of the love that in it lies,
   trace out our human language clear to sight.
And even as birds, when from a bank they rise
   and o'er their pasture join in blithe ado,
   group themselves now in rings, now otherwise,
so, light-enveloped, holy creatures flew
   hither and thither, singing, and now *D*,
   now *I*, now *L* in their own figures drew.
First, chanting, moved they to their measured glee;
   then at each letter, when 'twas wholly writ,
   they paused awhile and hushed their psalmody.
O Pegasea divine, who to the wit
   of men giv'st glory and length of years, as they
   to cities and to realms, an thou permit,
lighten me with thyself, that so I may
   carve out their shapes according to my thought:
   in these scant verses all thy power display!

Mostrarsi dunque in cinque volte sette
    vocali e consonanti; ed io notai
    le parti sì, come mi parver dette.   90
'*DILIGITE IUSTITIAM*' primai
    fur verbo e nome di tutto 'l dipinto;
    '*QUI IUDICATIS TERRAM*' fur sezzai.   93
Poscia ne l' emme del vocabol quinto
    rimasero ordinate; sì che Giove
    pareva argento lì d' oro distinto.   96
E vidi scendere altre luci dove
    era il colmo de l' emme, e lì quetarsi
    cantando, credo, il ben ch' a sè le move.   99
Poi come nel percuoter de' ciocchi arsi
    surgono innumerabili faville,
    onde li stolti sogliono augurarsi;   102
resurger parver quindi più di mille
    luci, e salir, qual assai e qual poco
    sì come il sol che l' accende sortille;   105
e quietata ciascuna in suo loco,
    la testa e 'l collo d' un' aguglia vidi
    rappresentare a quel distinto foco.   108
Quei che dipinge lì, non ha chi 'l guidi;
    ma esso guida, e da lui si rammenta
    quella virtù ch' è forma per li nidi.   111
L' altra beatitudo che contenta
    pareva prima d' ingigliarsi a l' emme,
    con poco moto seguitò la 'mprenta.   114
O dolce stella, quali e quante gemme
    mi dimostraro che nostra giustizia
    effetto sia del ciel che tu ingemme!   117
Per ch' io prego la mente in che s' inizia
    tuo moto e tua virtute, che rimiri
    ond' esce il fummo che 'l tuo raggio vizia;   120

Thirty and five, then, were the signs they wrought,
  both consonants and vowels; as each passed,
  I noted well what every portion taught.
' *DILIGITE IUSTITIAM* ', these, cast
  together, verb and noun, were the first told;
  ' *QUI IUDICATIS TERRAM* ' were the last.
Next, in the em of the fifth word enscrolled,
  awhile they lingered; so that Jupiter
  seemed silver at that point inlaid with gold.
And on the em's crest descend, and settling there,
  more lights I saw that, chanting, seemed to sing
  the good which bids them to itself repair.
Then as from lighted logs, when beaten, spring
  sparkles innumerable, which oft do lend
  excuse to fools for fortune-mongering;
more than a thousand lights saw I ascend
  from thence again and mount, some lower, some higher,
  e'en as the sun who kindles them ordained;
and each alighting where it did require,
  the head and neck of an eagle I descried
  distinctly pictured by that inlaid fire.
Who painteth there hath none to guide him; guide
  himself is, and by him that power of mind
  known as the nesting instinct is supplied.
The other saintly band which seemed inclined
  at first to form a lily of the em,
  by moving slightly, with the print combined.
O lovely star, how many a glorious gem
  showed me that 'tis the heaven whose jewel thou art
  which dowers the just with all that honours them!
Therefore I pray the mind whence issuing start
  thy power and motion, that it look whence blows
  the fog thy radiance fails to cleave apart;

sì ch' un' altra fiata omai s' adiri
    del comperare e vender dentro al templo
    che si murò di segni e di martiri.   123
O milizia del ciel cu' io contemplo,
    adora per color che sono in terra
    tutti sviati dietro al malo essemplo!   126
Già si solea con le spade far guerra;
    ma or si fa togliendo or qui or quivi
    lo pan che 'l pio Padre a nessun serra.   129
Ma tu che sol per cancellare scrivi,
    pensa che Pietro e Paulo, che moriro
    per la vigna che guasti, ancor son vivi.   132
Ben puoi tu dire: "I' ho fermo 'l disiro
    sì a colui che volle viver solo
    e che per salti fu tratto al martiro,   135
ch' io non conosco il pescator nè Polo".

CANTO XIX

Parea dinanzi a me con l' ali aperte
    la bella image che nel dolce frui
    liete facevan l' anime conserte.   3
Parea ciascuna rubinetto in cui
    raggio di sole ardesse sì acceso,
    che ne' miei occhi rifrangesse lui.   6
E quel che mi convien ritrar testeso,
    non portò voce mai, nè scrisse inchiostro,
    nè fu per fantasia già mai compreso: 9
ch' io vidi e anche udi' parlar lo rostro,
    e sonar ne la voce e 'io' e 'mio',
    quand' era nel concetto 'noi' e 'nostro'.   12

so that once more it may be wroth with those
   who buy and sell within the temple-gate—
   that temple built with signs and martyrs' throes.
O soldiery of the heaven I contemplate,
   pray thou for those on earth who all misled
   by evil ensample love what they should hate!
Aforetime waged with swords, war now is made
   by banning, as man listeth, what the kind
   Father locks up from none—his gift of bread.
But thou who writest but to erase, shalt find
   that Paul and Peter, for the vineyard slain
   which thou dost spoil, live yet: bear that in mind.
Well mayst thou argue: "I so yearn and strain
   after the hermit, at a dancer's call
   dragged off to martyrdom, that I disdain
all truck with either fisherman or Poll".

CANTO XIX

BEFORE me with its wings wide open stood
   the lovely shape those banded spirits made
   as they rejoiced in their beatitude.
Seemed each a little ruby, so displayed
   as to reflect into mine eyes the ray
   of twinkling flame by sunlight on it shed.
And what it now behoves me to portray
   voice never spake, nor pen writ, nor did power
   of fancy ever grasp until this day:
for the beak clearly spoke and, furthermore,
   it uttered with its voice both 'I' and 'my',
   when in conception it was 'we' and 'our';

E cominciò: "Per esser giusto e pio
  son io qui esaltato a quella gloria
  che non si lascia vincere a disio;   15
ed in terra lasciai la mia memoria
  sì fatta, che le genti lì malvage
  commendan lei, ma non seguon la storia".   18
Così un sol calor di molte brage
  si fa sentir, come di molti amori
  usciva solo un suon di quella image.   21
Ond' io appresso: "O perpetui fiori
  de l' etterna letizia, che pur uno
  parer mi fate tutti vostri odori,   24
solvetemi, spirando, il gran digiuno
  che lungamente m' ha tenuto in fame,
  non trovandoli in terra cibo alcuno.   27
Ben so io che se 'n cielo altro reame
  la divina giustizia fa suo specchio,
  che 'l vostro non l' apprende con velame. 30
Sapete come attento io m' apparecchio
  ad ascoltar; sapete qual è quello
  dubbio che m' è digiun cotanto vecchio". 33
Quasi falcone ch' esce del cappello,
  move la testa e con l' ali si plaude,
  voglia mostrando e faccendosi bello,   36
vid' io farsi quel segno, che di laude
  de la divina grazia era contesto,
  con canti quai si sa chi là su gaude.   39
Poi cominciò: "Colui che volse il sesto
  a lo stremo del mondo, e dentro ad esso
  distinse tanto occulto e manifesto,   42
non potè suo valor sì fare impresso
  in tutto l' universo, che 'l suo verbo
  non rimanesse in infinito eccesso.   45

beginning: "Just and merciful was I;
   hence am I here exalted to that glory
   which past ambition's utmost reach doth lie;
and there, on earth, I left no transitory
   record, but such as e'en the bad think fit
   to honour, though they follow not the story".
Thus do we feel from many coals one heat,
   as from that image one sole utterance came,
   though many were the loves that spake from it.
Then cried I: "O perpetual flowers, aflame
   with the eternal joy, who to my sense
   cause all your perfumes to appear the same,
break with your breath the stubborn abstinence,
   which, finding no relief on earth, hath held
   my hungry spirit in such long suspense.
Your kingdom, well I know, hath never failed,
   e'en if the mirror of God's justice shine
   elsewhere in heaven, to see its light unveiled.
Ye know how eagerly I now incline
   to listen; and the doubt which hath for years
   been gnawing at my heart ye well divine".
As, when the hood is slipped, a falcon rears
   his head and claps his wings, eager to fly,
   and vaunts himself as a bird that hath no peers,
so moved that figure, woven of revelry
   in the divine grace and with praises fraught
   such as they sing who there rejoice on high.
Then, "He whose compass", were the words I caught,
   "marked out the world, and who within that space
   so much in open and in secret wrought,
could not his power after suchwise impress
   on all the universe, but that his word
   should not remain in infinite excess.

E ciò fa certo che 'l primo superbo,
   che fu la somma d' ogni creatura,
   per non aspettar lume, cadde acerbo;   48
e quinci appar ch' ogni minor natura
   è corto recettacolo a quel bene
   che non ha fine e sè con sè misura.   51
Dunque nostra veduta, che convene
   essere alcun de' raggi de la mente
   di che tutte le cose son ripiene,   54
non pò da sua natura esser possente
   tanto, che suo principio non discerna
   molto di là da quel che l' è parvente.   57
Però ne la giustizia sempiterna
   la vista che riceve il vostro mondo,
   com' occhio per lo mare, entro s' interna;   60
che, ben che da la proda veggia il fondo,
   in pelago nol vede; e nondimeno
   ègli, ma cela lui l' esser profondo.   63
Lume non è, se non vien dal sereno
   che non si turba mai; anzi è tenebra,
   od ombra de la carne, o suo veleno.   66
Assai t' è mo aperta la latebra
   che t' ascondeva la giustizia viva,
   di che facei question cotanto crebra.   69
Chè tu dicevi: 'Un uom nasce a la riva
   de l' Indo, e quivi non è chi ragioni
   di Cristo nè chi legga nè chi scriva;   72
e tutti suoi voleri e atti buoni
   sono, quanto ragione umana vede,
   sanza peccato in vita o in sermoni.   75
Muore non battezzato e sanza fede:
   ov' è questa giustizia che 'l condanna?
   ov' è la colpa sua, se ei non crede?'   78

In proof whereof, he who through pride first erred
  fell immature, through waiting not for light,
  though, once, above all creatures else preferred;
hence, clearly, lesser natures are but slight
  containers for that good, which is alone
  with itself measured, being infinite.
And thus our vision, which must needs be one
  or other of the rays shed by the mind
  which fills all things that know or may be known,
can never be so strong, of its own kind,
  but that, compared with its great origin,
  it should not seem in countless matters blind.
Therefore the sight your world receives, within
  the eternal justice penetrates no more
  than into ocean's depths the eye may win;
which, though it mark the bottom from the shore,
  on the high seas will look for it in vain;
  nathless it is, but the deep veils it o'er.
Light is not, save from that serene domain
  which none may vex; rather 'tis darkness all,
  or shadow of the flesh, or else its bane.
Enough now have I drawn aside the pall
  that hid the living justice from thy sight,
  which thou so often wouldst in question call.
For thou wouldst say: 'A man first sees the light
  beside the Indus, where is none who could
  discourse of Christ or read of him or write;
all his volitions and his acts are good,
  so far as human reason sees, nor fail,
  in life or speech, of perfect rectitude.
He dies unchristened and an infidel:
  where is this justice that condemns the man?
  where, if without faith, is he culpable?'

Or tu chi se' che vuo' sedere a scranna,
    per giudicar di lungi mille miglia
    con la veduta corta d' una spanna?   81
Certo a colui che meco s' assottiglia,
    se la Scrittura sovra voi non fosse,
    da dubitar sarebbe a maraviglia.   84
Oh terreni animali, oh menti grosse!
    La prima volontà, ch' è da sè buona,
    da sè, ch' è sommo ben, mai non si mosse.   87
Cotanto è giusto quanto a lei consuona:
    nullo creato bene a sè la tira,
    ma essa, radiando, lui cagiona".   90
Quale sovresso il nido si rigira,
    poi c' ha pasciuti la cicogna i figli,
    e come quel ch' è pasto, la rimira;   93
cotal si fece, e sì levai i cigli,
    la benedetta imagine, che l' ali
    movea sospinte da tanti consigli.   96
Roteando cantava, e dicea: "Quali
    son le mie note a te, che non le 'ntendi,
    tal è il giudicio etterno a voi mortali".   99
Poi si quetaron quei lucenti incendi
    de lo Spirito Santo ancor nel segno
    che fè i Romani al mondo reverendi,   102
esso ricominciò: "A questo regno
    non salì mai chi non credette 'n Cristo,
    vel pria vel poi ch' el si chiavasse al legno.   105
Ma vedi: molti gridan 'Cristo, Cristo!',
    che saranno in giudicio assai men prope
    a lui, che tal che non conosce Cristo;   108
e tai Cristiani dannerà l' Etiope,
    quando si partiranno i due collegi,
    l' uno in etterno ricco, e l' altro inope.   111

Now who art thou, to assume the chair and scan
    for judgment things a thousand miles away
    with sight restricted to a single span?
The man whose thoughts with me so subtly play,
    truly would wondrous cause for doubting find,
    if over you the Scripture held not sway.
Oh animals of earth, oh dull of mind!
    Good in itself, the primal will hath never
    from its own self, the highest good, declined.
What chimes with it alone is just: nor ever
    aught to created goodness doth it owe,
    but, by its beams, itself thereof is giver".
As o'er her nest the stork doth circling go,
    when she hath fed her brood, and as the one
    just fed doth look up towards her from below,
thus moved the blesséd image, and thereon
    thus looked I, as above me it swept round,
    urged by so many wills in unison.
And, wheeling, thus it sang: "E'en as beyond
    thy grasp my notes are, so for mortal ken
    the eternal judgment is too deep to sound".
Those bright flames of the Holy Spirit then
    ceased movement, forming still the sign whereby
    Rome made the world submissive to her reign,
and it continued: "To this realm on high
    none ever rose without belief in Christ,
    either before, or after, Calvary.
But look you: many now exclaim 'Christ, Christ!',
    who shall at judgment find themselves far more
    estranged from him, than such as knows not Christ;
Christians like these shall the Ethiop triumph o'er
    then, when the two assemblies separate,
    the one forever rich, and the other poor.

Che potran dir li Perse a' vostri regi,
  come vedranno quel volume aperto
  nel qual si scrivon tutti suoi dispregi?   114
Lì si vedrà, tra l' opere d' Alberto,
  quella che tosto moverà la penna,
  per che 'l regno di Praga fia diserto.   117
Lì si vedrà il duol che sovra Senna
  induce, falseggiando la moneta,
  quel che morrà di colpo di cotenna.   120
Lì si vedrà la superbia ch' asseta,
  che fa lo Scotto e l' Inghilese folle,
  sì che non può soffrir dentro a sua meta.   123
Vedrassi la lussuria e 'l viver molle
  di quel di Spagna e di quel di Boemme,
  che mai valor non conobbe nè volle.   126
Vedrassi al Ciotto di Ierusalemme
  segnata con un' I la sua bontate,
  quando 'l contrario segnerà un' emme.   129
Vedrassi l' avarizia e la viltate
  di quei che guarda l' isola del foco,
  ove Anchise finì la lunga etate.   132
E a dare ad intender quanto è poco,
  la sua scrittura fian lettere mozze,
  che noteranno molto in parvo loco.   135
E parranno a ciascun l' opere sozze
  del barba e del fratel, che tanto egregia
  nazione e due corone han fatte bozze.   138
E quel di Portogallo e di Norvegia
  lì si conosceranno, e quel di Rascia
  che male ha visto il conio di Vinegia.   141
Oh beata Ungaria se non si lascia
  più malmenare! e beata Navarra
  se s' armasse del monte che la fascia!   144

What may not Persia say to incriminate
  your kings, when with that open volume faced
  which registers their failings, small and great?
There shall be read, mid deeds that have disgraced
  Albert, the one (now soon to stir the pen)
  through which the realm of Prague shall be laid waste.
There shall be read the woe which on the Seine,
  thro' the false coinage far and wide dispersed,
  he brings, who by a wild-boar shall be slain.
There shall be read the pride that quickens thirst,
  which makes the Scot and Englishman so mad,
  that each would his appointed limit burst.
Be read the luxury and the silken-clad
  life of the Spaniard, the Bohemian's too,
  who virtue never wished and never had.
Be read an I, to the one merit due
  of him, the Cripple of Jerusalem,
  while to his sins an em will give the clue.
Be read the cowardice and the greed which shame
  him in whose keeping is the isle of fire,
  where to his long life's end Anchises came.
Yea, and to set his meanness yet in higher
  relief, the script shall be in letters maimed,
  which for much import little space require.
Yea, and for their foul deeds shall be proclaimed
  his uncle and his brother, who so fair
  a lineage and a double crown have shamed.
Yea, and of Portugal and Norway there
  both kings with him of Rascia shall be shown
  whose coin of Venice loaded him with care.
Oh happy Hungary, if she suffers none
  to ill-treat her further! happy too Navarre,
  made she a rampart of her mountain-zone!

E creder de' ciascun che già, per arra
di questo, Nicosia e Famagosta
per la lor bestia si lamenti e garra,   147
che dal fianco de l' altre non si scosta".

CANTO XX

Quando colui che tutto 'l mondo alluma
de l' emisperio nostro sì discende,
che 'l giorno d' ogne parte si consuma,   3
lo ciel, che sol di lui prima s' accende,
subitamente si rifà parvente
per molte luci, in che una risplende: 6
e questo atto del ciel mi venne a mente,
come 'l segno del mondo e de' suoi duci
nel benedetto rostro fu tacente;   9
però che tutte quelle vive luci,
vie più lucendo, cominciaron canti
da mia memoria labili e caduci.   12
O dolce amor che di riso t' ammanti,
quanto parevi ardente in que' flailli,
ch' avieno spirto sol di pensier santi!   15
Poscia che i cari e lucidi lapilli
ond' io vidi ingemmato il sesto lume,
puoser silenzio a li angelici squilli,   18
udir mi parve un mormorar di fiume
che scende chiaro giù di pietra in pietra,
mostrando l' ubertà del suo cacume.   21
E come suono al collo de la cetra
prende sua forma, e sì com' al pertugio
de la sampogna vento che penetra,   24

Of this see earnest in the times that are,
  when Nicosía with Famagosta weeps,
  by reason of their brutal lord who, far
from parting with the rest, beside them keeps".

CANTO XX

WHEN he who floods the whole, wide world with light
  so far beneath our hemisphere is gone,
  that day on every side melts into night,
the sky, lit up before by him alone,
  suddenly yet again begins to shine
  with many lights, which but reflect the one:
and this sky-change I thought of, when the sign,
  by which the world and the world's lords are sway'd,
  at length was silent in the beak divine;
for all those living lights began to shed
  far brighter radiance and made heaven resound
  with songs which from my memory fall and fade.
Sweet love that with a smile dost wrap thee round,
  how in those holy flutes, whose breathing owns
  their sole inspirer, did thy warmth abound!
After those precious and clear shining stones
  which I beheld encrusting the sixth light,
  had stilled the chime of their angelic tones,
methought I heard a stream that, crystal bright,
  falls murmuring, down from rock to rock, and shows
  how rich the spring that pours it from the height.
And as the sound that from the zither flows
  forms at the neck thereof, and as at vent
  of sackbut doth the wind that through it blows,

così, rimosso d' aspettare indugio,
 quel mormorar de l' aguglia salissi
 su per lo collo, come fosse bugio.   27
Fecesi voce quivi e quindi uscissi
 per lo suo becco in forma di parole,
 quali aspettava il core, ov' io le scrissi.   30
"La parte in me che vede, e pate il sole
 ne l' aguglie mortali" incominciommi,
 "or fisamente riguardar si vole,   33
perchè de' fuochi ond' io figura fommi,
 quelli onde l' occhio in testa mi scintilla,
 e' di tutti lor gradi son li sommi.   36
Colui che luce in mezzo per pupilla,
 fu il cantor de lo Spirito Santo,
 che l' arca traslatò di villa in villa: 39
ora conosce il merto del suo canto,
 in quanto effetto fu del suo consiglio,
 per lo remunerar ch' è altrettanto.   42
Dei cinque che mi fan cerchio per ciglio,
 colui che più al becco mi s' accosta,
 la vedovella consolò del figlio: 45
ora conosce quanto caro costa
 non seguir Cristo, per l' esperienza
 di questa dolce vita e de l' opposta.   48
E quel che segue in la circunferenza
 di che ragiono, per l' arco superno,
 morte indugiò per vera penitenza: 51
ora conosce che 'l giudicio etterno
 non si trasmuta, quando degno preco
 fa crastino là giù de l' odierno.   54
L' altro che segue, con le leggi e meco,
 sotto buona intenzion che fè mal frutto,
 per cedere al pastor si fece greco: 57

so, with no time in tedious waiting spent,
    that murmuring of the eagle, louder grown,
    up through the neck, as it were hollow, went.
There it became a voice and thence was thrown
    from out its beak in words, such in all ways
    as the heart looked for, where I wrote them down.
"The part in me which sees, and bears the rays
    o' the sun in mortal eagles," so it said,
    "must now be noted with a steadfast gaze;
for, of the fires that shape me, in their grade
    those are supreme, those I would have thee mark,
    wherewith the eye doth glitter in my head.
He who as pupil forms the central spark,
    the Holy Spirit's minstrel was on earth,
    who from one town to the other bore the ark:
now knows he, by the guerdon to its worth
    proportioned, the true merit of his song,
    so far as his own counsel gave it birth.
Next, of the five that form the curve along
    mine eyebrow, nearest to the beak is he
    who did the widow justice for her wrong:
now knows he what it costeth not to be
    a Christian, from his own experience
    of this sweet life and of its contrary.
And he who follows in the circumference
    I speak of, on the curve that upward sways,
    put death off by unfeignéd penitencè:
now knows he that the eternal judgment stays
    unaltered, when on earth a worthy prayer
    doth make to-morrow's that which is to-day's.
Who follows next, with good intent which bare
    ill fruit, to leave the shepherd room, transferred
    me and the laws to Greece and settled there:

    ora conosce come il mal dedutto
      dal suo bene operar non li è nocivo,
      avvegna che sia 'l mondo indi distrutto.   60
E quel che vedi ne l' arco declivo,
      Guiglielmo fu, cui quella terra plora
      che piagne Carlo e Federigo vivo: 63
ora conosce come s' innamora
      lo ciel del giusto rege, ed al sembiante
      del suo fulgore il fa vedere ancora.   66
Chi crederebbe giù nel mondo errante,
      che Rifeo Troiano in questo tondo
      fosse la quinta de le luci sante?   69
Ora conosce assai di quel che 'l mondo
      veder non può de la divina grazia,
      ben che sua vista non discerna il fondo."   72
Quale allodetta che 'n aere si spazia
      prima cantando, e poi tace contenta
      de l' ultima dolcezza che la sazia,   75
tal mi sembiò l' imago de la 'mprenta
      de l' etterno piacere, al cui disio
      ciascuna cosa qual ella è diventa.   78
E avvegna ch' io fossi al dubbiar mio
      lì quasi vetro a lo color che 'l veste,
      tempo aspettar tacendo non patio,   81
ma de la bocca "Che cose son queste?"
      mi pinse con la forza del suo peso;
      per ch' io di coruscar vidi gran feste.   84
Poi appresso, con l' occhio più acceso,
      lo benedetto segno mi rispuose,
      per non tenermi in ammirar sospeso: 87
"Io veggio che tu credi queste cose
      perch' io le dico, ma non vedi come;
      sì che, se son credute, sono ascose.   90

now knows he how the evil, first incurred
   through his well-doing, harms him not, although
   the world now lie in ruins because he erred.
And he thou sëest on the downward bow,
   was William, whose decease that land bewails
   which Charles and Frederick, living, plunge in woe:
now knows he how a righteous king compels
   the love of heaven, yea and consciousness
   thereof his glorious semblance yet forthtells.
Who in the erring world below would guess,
   that Trojan Rhipeus should be, in this round,
   the fifth among these lights of holiness?
Now knows he much of what the world hath found
   past understanding in the grace of God,
   e'en though his sight its bottom cannot sound."
Like to the little lark that roameth abroad
   in the air first warbling, and then holds her peace,
   cloyed with the sweets of her last perfect ode,
such seemed to me the image stamped with bliss
   by the eternal pleasure, at whose will
   each thing becomes by nature what it is.
And though my doubting I could there conceal
   scarce more than pane of glass its mantling hue,
   yet bore it not one instant to keep still,
but from my lips "How can these things be true?"
   was forced out by sheer pressure of its weight;
   at which a riot of sparkling met my view.
And thereupon, with eye enkindled yet
   more brightly, the blest emblem made reply,
   to keep my thoughts no longer in debate:
"I see that thou believ'st them, since 'tis I
   who say these things, but thou discernst not how;
   so that, believed, they yet still hidden lie.

Fai come quei che la cosa per nome
  apprende ben, ma la sua quiditate
  veder non può se altri non la prome.   93
Regnum celorum violenza pate
  da caldo amore e da viva speranza,
  che vince la divina volontate;   96
non a guisa che l' omo a l' om sobranza,
  ma vince lei perchè vuole esser vinta,
  e, vinta, vince con sua beninanza.   99
La prima vita del ciglio e la quinta
  ti fa maravigliar, perchè ne vedi
  la region de li angeli dipinta.   102
De' corpi suoi non uscir, come credi,
  gentili, ma cristiani, in ferma fede
  quel de' passuri e quel de' passi piedi.   105
Chè l' una de lo 'nferno, u' non si riede
  già mai a buon voler, tornò a l' ossa;
  e ciò di viva spene fu mercede;   108
di viva spene, che mise la possa
  ne' prieghi fatti a Dio per suscitarla,
  sì che potesse sua voglia esser mossa.   111
L' anima gloriosa onde si parla,
  tornata ne la carne, in che fu poco,
  credette in lui che potea aiutarla;   114
e credendo s' accese in tanto foco
  di vero amor, ch' a la morte seconda
  fu degna di venire a questo gioco.   117
L' altra, per grazia che da sì profonda
  fontana stilla, che mai creatura
  non pinse l' occhio infino a la prima onda,   120
tutto suo amor là giù pose a drittura;
  per che, di grazia in grazia, Dio li aperse
  l' occhio a la nostra redenzion futura: 123

Thou dost as one who something well doth know
  by name, but of its essence nought can see,
  unless another should that essence show.
Heaven's kingdom suffers violence willingly
  from ardent love and lively hope: by these
  alone the will divine may vanquished be;
not like to man's o'er man that victory is,
  but won because the vanquished wills defeat,
  and, vanquished, by its mercy vanquishes.
There are two lives it staggers thee to meet
  decking the angels' realm, to wit the first
  and fifth that in the eyebrow have their seat.
Not Gentiles did they quit the body, as erst
  thou deem'dst, but firm believers in our Lord,
  that after, this before, his feet were pierced.
For one from hell, whence none was e'er restored
  to righteous willing, to his bones returned;
  and that of lively hope was the reward;
of lively hope, inspiring prayers that earned
  the power from God to raise him, and thus made
  him able to will that for which he yearned.
The glorious soul of whom these words are said,
  when re-incarnate a brief while on earth,
  believed in him who had the means to aid;
and, in believing, to such fire gave birth
  of holy love, that, when it died again,
  worthy it was of joining in our mirth.
The other, moved by grace which from a vein
  so deep distils that never yet to sight
  of creature was its primal source made plain,
set all his love below on just and right;
  wherefore from grace to grace God oped his eye
  to see, before it dawned, redemption's light:

ond' ei credette in quella, e non sofferse
  da indi il puzzo più del paganesmo;
  e riprendiene le genti perverse.   126
Quelle tre donne li fur per battesmo
  che tu vedesti da la destra rota,
  dinanzi al battezzar più d' un millesmo.   129
O predestinazion, quanto remota
  è la radice tua da quelli aspetti
  che la prima cagion non veggion tota!   132
E voi, mortali, tenetevi stretti
  a giudicar; chè noi, che Dio vedemo,
  non conosciamo ancor tutti gli eletti;   135
ed enne dolce così fatto scemo,
  perchè il ben nostro in questo ben s' affina,
  che quel che vole Dio, e noi volemo".   138
Così da quella imagine divina,
  per farmi chiara la mia corta vista,
  data mi fu soave medicina.   141
E come a buon cantor buon citarista
  fa seguitar lo guizzo de la corda,
  in che più di piacer lo canto acquista,   144
sì, mentre che parlò, sì mi ricorda
  ch' io vidi le due luci benedette,
  pur come batter d' occhi si concorda,   147
con le parole mover le fiammette.

CANTO XXI

Già eran li occhi miei rifissi al volto
  de la mia donna, e l' animo con essi,
  e da ogni altro intento s' era tolto.   3

whence he believed therein, and the foul sty
   of paganism could no longer bear;
   and 'gainst the froward nations raised his cry.
For baptism, a good millennium ere
   men knew baptising, those three ladies, seen
   of thee at the right wheel, his proxies were.
Predestination, oh what worlds between
   thy root and those doth lie who cannot see
   the primal cause, entire, with mortal een!
Judge, then, you mortals, with restraint; for we,
   to whom the sight of God is granted, still
   know not how many the elect shall be;
and us this very lack with joy doth fill,
   because we find our crowning good herein,
   that what is willed by God we also will".
Thus, by that form divine, sweet medicine
   was giv'n me, from mine eyes to clear the mist,
   that so they might to purer vision win.
And e'en as to good voice good lutanist
   by perfect timing makes the chord vibrate,
   whereby the song's enjoyment is increased,
so, while it spoke, do I remember yet
   that, even as the eyes wink in accord,
   I saw the two enraptured stars equate
their twinkles to its utterance, flame to word.

CANTO XXI

Now on my lady's face again intent
   mine eyes were, and, like them, my thoughts, concerned
   with nothing else, on her alone were bent.

E quella non ridea; ma "S' io ridessi"
 mi cominciò, "tu ti faresti quale
 fu Semelè quando di cener fessi;   6
chè la bellezza mia, che per le scale
 de l' etterno palazzo più s' accende,
 com' hai veduto, quanto più si sale,   9
se non si temperasse, tanto splende,
 che il tuo mortal podere, al suo fulgore,
 sarebbe fronda che trono scoscende.   12
Noi sem levati al settimo splendore,
 che sotto il petto del Leone ardente
 raggia mo misto giù del suo valore.   15
Ficca di retro a li occhi tuoi la mente,
 e fa di quelli specchi a la figura
 che 'n questo specchio ti sarà parvente".   18
Qual savesse qual era la pastura
 del viso mio ne l' aspetto beato
 quand' io mi trasmutai ad altra cura,   21
conoscerebbe quanto m' era a grato
 ubidire a la mia celeste scorta,
 contrapesando l' un con l' altro lato.   24
Dentro al cristallo che 'l vocabol porta,
 cerchiando il mondo, del suo caro duce
 sotto cui giacque ogni malizia morta,   27
di color d' oro in che raggio traluce
 vid' io uno scaleo eretto in suso
 tanto, che nol seguiva la mia luce.   30
Vidi anche per li gradi scender giuso
 tanti splendor, ch' io pensai ch' ogni lume
 che par nel ciel quindi fosse diffuso.   33
E come, per lo natural costume,
 le pole insieme, al cominciar del giorno,
 si muovono a scaldar le fredde piume;   36

And yet no smile upon her visage burned;
    but "Did I smile," quoth she, "thou wouldst be e'en
    as Semele when she to ashes turned;
because my beauty, which, as thou hast seen,
    on this eternal palace-stair, the higher
    it climbs, hath ever more enkindled been,
if not subdued, would prove itself as dire
    (such its effulgence) to thy mortal might,
    as to the branch the thunderbolt's quick fire.
We are exalted to the seventh light,
    which now beneath the burning Lion's breast,
    mixed with his power, sheds down its radiance bright.
Where now thine eyes are, let thy mind be placed,
    and be in turn the image mirrored there
    which in this mirror thou shalt see expressed".
He that should know with what delicious fare
    her saintly look my vision satisfied
    when I transferred me to another care,
would recognise, by weighing the one side
    against the other, how it charmed me still
    to do the bidding of my heavenly guide.
Within the crystal, named, as it doth wheel
    about the world, of him—the world's dear king,
    'neath whom no power could live that worketh ill,
coloured like gold, translucent, glittering,
    saw I a ladder reaching up so high,
    that to my sight it was past following.
I saw, moreover, coming down thereby,
    of glorious beings such a host untold,
    meseemed it shone with every star in the sky.
And as the jackdaws, gathering by an old
    instinctive custom at the break of day,
    flutter about to warm their feathers cold;

poi altre vanno via sanza ritorno,
 altre rivolgon sè onde son mosse,
 e altre roteando fan soggiorno;   39
tal modo parve a me che quivi fosse
 in quello sfavillar che 'nsieme venne,
 sì come in certo grado si percosse.   42
E quel che presso più ci si ritenne,
 si fè sì chiaro, ch' io dicea pensando:
 "Io veggio ben l' amor che tu m' accenne".   45
Ma quella ond' io aspetto il come e 'l quando
 del dire e del tacer, si sta; ond' io,
 contra il disio, fo ben ch' io non dimando.   48
Per ch' ella, che vedea il tacer mio
 nel veder di colui che tutto vede,
 mi disse: "Solvi il tuo caldo disio".   51
E io incominciai: "La mia mercede
 non mi fa degno de la tua risposta;
 ma per colei che 'l chieder mi concede,   54
vita beata che ti stai nascosta
 dentro a la tua letizia, fammi nota
 la cagion che sì presso mi t' ha posta;   57
e dì perchè si tace in questa rota
 la dolce sinfonia di paradiso,
 che giù per l' altre suona sì divota".   60
"Tu hai l' udir mortal sì come il viso"
 rispuose a me; "onde qui non si canta
 per quel che Beatrice non ha riso.   63
Giù per li gradi de la scala santa
 discesi tanto sol per farti festa
 col dire e con la luce che mi ammanta;   66
nè più amor mi fece esser più presta;
 chè più e tanto amor quinci su ferve,
 sì come il fiammeggiar ti manifesta.   69

then some, without returning, fly away,
  some to their starting-point again repair,
  and others wheeling round and round it stay;
even so meseemed the glitterance, gathered there,
  flew off in round or straight or slanting line,
  soon as it struck upon a certain stair.
One, nearest to us, then began to shine
  so brightly, that I said in thought: "'Tis plain
  thou lovest me, for well I see the sign".
But she from whom I await the 'how' and 'when'
  of silence or of speech, is mute; whence I
  do well to ask not, though of asking fain.
She, therefore, when I spake not, seeing why
  in the clear sight of him who all things sees,
  mine ardent longing bade me satisfy.
And I began: "Not mine the merit is,
  which makes me worthy of thine answer; yet,
  if her who allows my question thou wouldst please,
blest spirit that art shrouded in the great
  effulgence of thy joy, do thou make known
  the cause which thee so near to me hath set;
and say why silent in this wheel alone
  is the sweet symphony of paradise,
  chanted with such devotion lower down".
"Thine ears", it answered me, "are, like thine eyes,
  mortal; hence here we sing not for the same
  reason that Beatrice her smile denies.
Down by the steps of the holy stair I came
  thus far, only to greet thee with discourse
  and with the light that wraps me in its flame;
neither in me was greater love the source
  of greater zeal; for love up there doth burn
  (witness the flames) with like and greater force.

Ma l' alta carità, che ci fa serve
   pronte al consiglio che 'l mondo governa,
   sorteggia qui sì come tu osserve."   72
"Io veggio ben" diss' io, "sacra lucerna,
   come libero amore in questa corte
   basta a seguir la provedenza etterna;   75
ma questo è quel ch' a cerner mi par forte,
   perchè predestinata fosti sola
   a questo officio tra le tue consorte."   78
Nè venni prima a l' ultima parola,
   che del suo mezzo fece il lume centro,
   girando sè come veloce mola: 81
poi rispuose l' amor che v' era dentro:
   "Luce divina sopra me s' appunta,
   penetrando per questa in ch' io m' inventro,   84
la cui virtù, col mio veder congiunta,
   mi leva sopra me tanto, ch' i' veggio
   la somma essenza de la quale è munta.   87
Quinci vien l' allegrezza ond' io fiammeggio;
   perch' a la vista mia, quant' ella è chiara,
   la chiarità de la fiamma pareggio.   90
Ma quell' alma nel ciel che più si schiara,
   quel serafin che 'n Dio più l' occhio ha fisso,
   a la dimanda tua non satisfara;   93
però che sì s' innoltra ne lo abisso
   de l' etterno statuto quel che chiedi,
   che da ogni creata vista è scisso.   96
E al mondo mortal, quando tu riedi,
   questo rapporta, sì che non presumma
   a tanto segno più mover li piedi.   99
La mente, che qui luce, in terra fumma;
   onde riguarda come può là giue
   quel che non pote perchè 'l ciel l' assumma". 102

But the high charity, which makes us yearn
    to serve the all-ruling will with instant speed,
    casts the lot here, e'en as thou dost discern."
"O sacred lamp," said I, "'tis clear indeed
    that love, unbidden, in this court will do
    whate'er the eternal foresight hath decreed;
but to this harder knot I find no clue—
    wherefore predestined thou alone shouldst be,
    of all thy peers, this office to pursue."
I had not ended, when, as one may see
    a millstone doing, that which there illumed
    us whirled upon its centre rapidly:
anon, the love within it thus resumed:
    "Focused on me eternal light doth blaze,
    piercing through this whereof I am enwombed,
whose virtue, with my vision blent, doth raise
    me above myself so far, that the divine
    essence it is expressed from meets my gaze.
Hence comes this flaming gladness that is mine;
    for, as my sight is clear, thereto I even
    the clearness of the flame with which I shine.
But by the soul that clearest shines in heaven,
    e'en by the seraph God doth most entrance,
    to thy demand no answer shall be given;
seeing that in the eternal ordinance
    so deeply plunged doth that thou askest lie,
    'tis hid from all created cognisance.
When thou returnest, carry this reply
    back to your world, that none henceforth may dare
    to move his feet unto a goal so high.
The mind, which here is bright, is dim down there;
    how may it, then, on earth do things that pass
    its power to do e'en tho' to heaven it fare?"

Sì mi prescrisser le parole sue,
    ch' io lasciai la quistione, e mi ritrassi
    a dimandarla umilmente chi fue.   105
"Tra' due liti d' Italia surgon sassi,
    e non molto distanti a la tua patria,
    tanto, che' troni assai suonan più bassi,   108
e fanno un gibbo che si chiama Catria,
    di sotto al quale è consecrato un ermo,
    che suole esser disposto a sola latria."   111
Così ricominciommi il terzo sermo;
    e poi, continuando, disse: "Quivi
    al servigio di Dio mi fe' sì fermo,   114
che pur con cibi di liquor d' ulivi
    lievemente passava caldi e geli,
    contento ne' pensier contemplativi.   117
Render solea quel chiostro a questi cieli
    fertilemente; e ora è fatto vano,
    sì che tosto convien che si riveli.   120
In quel loco fu' io Pietro Damiano,
    e Pietro Peccator fu' ne la casa
    di Nostra Donna in sul lito adriano.   123
Poca vita mortal m' era rimasa,
    quando fui chiesto e tratto a quel cappello
    che pur di male in peggio si travasa.   126
Venne Cefàs e venne il gran vasello
    de lo Spirito Santo, magri e scalzi,
    prendendo il cibo da qualunque ostello.   129
Or voglion quinci e quindi chi i rincalzi
    li moderni pastori e chi li meni,
    tanto son gravi!, e chi di rietro li alzi.   132
Cuopron de' manti loro i palafreni,
    sì che.due bestie van sott' una pelle:
    oh pazienza che tanto sostieni!"   135

From further question I refrained, whenas
    it spake these words—they overawed me so—
    and did but ask it humbly who it was.
"'Twixt Italy's two shores a rocky brow,
    not much removed from thine own land, doth rise
    so high, the thunders mutter far below,
and forms a hump, called Catria: 'neath it lies
    a hermitage, which sacred was of yore
    to prayer alone and holy ministries."
A third time thus it spake, then added more
    after this fashion: "There, in service done
    to God, I such a steadfast spirit bore,
that, save for olive juice, with viands none,
    lightly would I endure both heat and cold,
    contented in those things I mused upon.
Rich harvest did that cloister yield of old
    unto these spheres; a harvest grown so rare
    now, that its barrenness must soon be told.
I was entitled Peter Damian there,
    and in Our Lady's house by the Adrian sea
    Peter the Sinner was the name I bare.
When I was nearing death, they summoned me,
    nay, dragged me to the hat, that is from sin
    to greater sin passed on successively.
Came Cephas, came the mighty vessel wherein
    the Holy Spirit dwelt, lean and unshod,
    taking the food of whatsoever inn.
Now on both sides our bloated men of God
    need one to prop them, one to lift their train,
    one to precede them with a verger's rod.
Their mantles drape their palfreys, so that then
    two beasts pace onwards 'neath a single hide:
    oh patience what a load dost thou sustain!"

A questa voce vid' io più fiammelle
  di grado in grado scendere e girarsi,
  e ogni giro le facea più belle.   138
Dintorno a questa vennero e fermarsi,
  e fero un grido di sì alto suono,
  che non potrebbe qui assomigliarsi: 141
nè io lo 'ntesi; sì mi vinse il tuono.

CANTO XXII

Oppresso di stupore, a la mia guida
  mi volsi, come parvol che ricorre
  sempre colà dove più si confida;   3
e quella, come madre che soccorre
  subito al figlio palido e anelo
  con la sua voce, che 'l suol ben disporre,   6
mi disse: "Non sai tu che tu se' in cielo?
  e non sai tu che 'l cielo è tutto santo,
  e ciò che ci si fa vien da buon zelo?   9
Come t' avrebbe trasmutato il canto,
  e io ridendo, mo pensar lo puoi,
  poscia che 'l grido t' ha mosso cotanto;   12
nel qual, se 'nteso avessi i prieghi suoi,
  già ti sarebbe nota la vendetta
  che tu vedrai innanzi che tu muoi.   15
La spada di qua su non taglia in fretta
  nè tardo, ma' ch' al parer di colui
  che disiando o temendo l' aspetta.   18
Ma rivolgiti omai inverso altrui;
  ch' assai illustri spiriti vedrai,
  se com' io dico l' aspetto redui".   21

And at these words more flamelets I espied
   from step to step descending and whirling round,
   and every whirl their beauty intensified.
Round this they thronged, and stayed them, and with
   so loud, so awful shouted, that no wonder   [sound
   if here no likeness for it may be found:
nor grasped I aught; so vanquished me the thunder.

CANTO XXII

Unto my guide, in blank amazement lost
   I turned me, like a child who always there
   for refuge runneth where he trusteth most;
and she, like mother who is quick to bear
   her pale and gasping son the succour given
   by her familiar voice, which soothes his fear,
said to me: "Knowst not thou, thou art in heaven,
   and heaven all holy is, nor doth one aught
   here, save thereto by righteous ardour driven?
How great a change in thee the song had wrought,
   and I by smiling, now right well appears,
   since thou art stirred so deeply by the shout;
wherein, couldst thou have understood its prayers,
   to thee already were the vengeance known
   which thou shalt witness in thy mortal years.
The sword of God, save in their view alone
   who wish or fear his advent, is not slack,
   nor yet in haste, to strike the wicked down.
But turn thee now elsewhither; for no lack
   of very famous spirits wilt thou see,
   if as I say thou cast thy glances back".

Come a lei piacque li occhi ritornai
e vidi cento sperule che 'nsieme
più s' abbellivan con mutui rai.   24
Io stava come quei che 'n sè represe
la punta del disio, e non s' attenta
di domandar, sì del troppo si teme.   27
E la maggiore e la più luculenta
di quelle margherite innanzi fessi,
per far di sè la mia voglia contenta.   30
Poi dentro a lei udi': "Se tu vedessi
com' io la carità che tra noi arde,
li tuoi concetti sarebbero espressi.   33
Ma perchè tu, aspettando, non tarde
a l' alto fine, io ti farò risposta
pur al pensier da che sì ti riguarde.   36
Quel monte a cui Cassino è ne la costa,
fu frequentato già in su la cima
da la gente ingannata e mal disposta;   39
e quel son io che su vi portai prima
lo nome di colui che 'n terra addusse
la verità che tanto ci sublima;   42
e tanta grazia sopra me relusse,
ch' io ritrassi le ville circunstanti
da l' empio colto che 'l mondo sedusse.   45
Questi altri fuochi tutti contemplanti
uomini fuoro, accesi di quel caldo
che fa nascere i fiori e' frutti santi.   48
Qui è Maccario, qui è Romoaldo,
qui son li frati miei che dentro ai chiostri
fermar li piedi e tennero il cor saldo".   51
E io a lui: "L' affetto che dimostri
meco parlando, e la buona sembianza
ch' io veggio e noto in tutti li ardor vostri,   54

My eyes I turned, as she directed me,
  and saw a hundred little globes whose fire
  waxed brighter through their mutual brilliancy.
I stood as one who on his keen desire,
  lest it exceed due limit, such restraint
  imposes, that he dares not to enquire.
And one amid those pearls, pre-eminent
  in size and lustre, drew from out the rest,
  to render of itself my wish content.
Then heard I from within it: "Wert thou blest
  with sight, as I am, of the charity
  we burn with, thy conceits had been expressed.
But that thou wait not and retard thereby
  thy lofty aim, to what thy doubts disguise,
  e'en to thy secret thought, I'll make reply.
The mountain on whose slope Cassino lies,
  was, on its top, much visited of yore
  by folk enslaved to false idolatries;
and it was I that first up thither bore
  the name of him who down to earth conveyed
  the truth which so sublimes us by its power;
and such abundant grace on me was shed,
  that I reclaimed the hamlets scattered round
  from the impious worship that the world misled.
These other fires their happiness all found
  in contemplation, kindled by the heat
  which maketh holy flowers and fruits abound.
Here Romualdus, here Macarius meet
  my brethren, those who in their cells below
  with persevering courage fixed their feet".
And I to him: "The affection thou dost show
  in speaking with me, and the kindly mien
  I see and note in all your ardours glow,

così m' ha dilatata mia fidanza,
   come 'l sol fa la rosa, quando aperta
   tanto divien quant' ell' ha di possanza.   57
Però ti priego, e tu, padre, m' accerta
   s' io posso prender tanta grazia, ch' io
   ti veggia con imagine scoverta ".   60
Ond' elli: " Frate, il tuo alto disio
   s' adempierà in su l' ultima spera,
   ove s' adempion tutti li altri e 'l mio.   63
Ivi è perfetta, matura ed intera
   ciascuna disianza: in quella sola
   è ogni parte là ove sempr' era,   66
perchè non è in loco, e non s' impola;
   e nostra scala infino ad essa varca,
   onde così dal viso ti s' invola.   69
Infin là su la vide il patriarca
   Iacob porgere la superna parte,
   quando li apparve d' angeli sì carca.   72
Ma, per salirla, mo nessun diparte
   da terra i piedi, e la regola mia
   rimasa è per danno de le carte.   75
Le mura che solieno esser badia,
   fatte sono spelonche, e le cocolle
   sacca son piene di farina ria.   78
Ma grave usura tanto non si tolle
   contra 'l piacer di Dio, quanto quel frutto
   che fa il cor de' monaci sì folle;   81
chè quantunque la Chiesa guarda, tutto
   è de la gente che per Dio dimanda;
   non di parenti nè d' altro più brutto.   84
La carne de' mortali è tanto blanda,
   che giù non basta buon cominciamento
   dal nascer de la quercia al far la ghianda.   87

swelling my confidence, have made it e'en
  as the sun makes the rose, when he doth swell
  her calyx till its inmost heart is seen.
Hence I entreat thee, and thou, father, tell
  me truly, if on me such grace can shine,
  that I may see thy shape without a veil".
He therefore: "Like all others and like mine,
  thy lofty wish shall be fulfilled whenas
  thou attainest, brother, to the sphere divine.
There only all we long for comes to pass:
  there only all is perfect, ripe and whole,
  and every part is where it always was,
for it lies not in space, nor has it pole;
  and even thereuntó our stair doth go,
  whence thus thine eyes it cheateth of their goal.
Thither the patriarch Jacob saw it throw
  its upper span, when it appeared to him
  laden with angels passing to and fro.
But now, for climbing it, doth no one dream
  of lifting foot from earth; and, unobeyed,
  my rule does but a waste of paper seem.
The walls that were for monastery made,
  are turned now into dens; the cowls are sacks
  crammed full of flour all worthless and decayed.
But the usurer's greed, however gross it wax,
  doth not so much for God's displeasure call
  as that which makes the monkish heart so lax;
for what the Church in keeping hath, should all
  to those who in the name of God make suit,
  not to one's kin, or viler claimants, fall.
The flesh of man is grown so dissolute,
  that good beginnings with their goodness part,
  before the sapling comes to bearing fruit.

Pier cominciò sanz' oro e sanz' argento,
  e io con orazione e con digiuno,
  e Francesco umilmente il suo convento.   90
E se guardi il principio di ciascuno,
  poscia riguardi là dov' è trascorso,
  tu vederai del bianco fatto bruno.   93
Veramente Iordan volto retrorso
  più fu, e 'l mar fuggir, quando Dio volse
  mirabile a veder che qui 'l soccorso ".   96
Così mi disse, e indi si raccolse
  al suo collegio, e 'l collegio si strinse;
  poi, come turbo, in su tutto s' avvolse.   99
La dolce donna dietro a lor mi pinse
  con un sol cenno su per quella scala,
  sì sua virtù la mia natura vinse;   102
nè mai qua giù dove si monta e cala
  naturalmente, fu sì ratto moto,
  ch' agguagliar si potesse a la mia ala.   105
S' io torni mai, lettore, a quel divoto
  triunfo per lo quale io piango spesso
  le mie peccata e 'l petto mi percuoto,   108
tu non avresti in tanto tratto e messo
  nel foco il dito, in quant' io vidi 'l segno
  che segue il Tauro e fui dentro da esso.   111
O gloriose stelle, o lume pregno
  di gran virtù, dal quale io riconosco
  tutto, qual che si sia, il mio ingegno,   114
con voi nasceva e s' ascondeva vosco
  quegli ch' è padre d' ogni mortal vita,
  quand' io senti' di prima l' aere tosco;   117
e poi, quando mi fu grazia largita
  d' entrar ne l' alta rota che vi gira,
  la vostra region mi fu sortita.   120

With gold and silver none did Peter start
   his convent; I, with prayers and fasting, mine;
   and Francis his, in humbleness of heart.
And if of each thou mark the first design,
   then mark again to where it thence hath strayed,
   thou wilt behold that dim, which used to shine.
And yet the sea, when God so willed it, fled,
   and Jordan was turned backward—both, to view
   more wondrous, than if here his hand should aid ".
Thus spake he to me, and anon withdrew
   to his assembly; they in one their flame
   composed: then all, like whirlwind, upward flew.
And, with a single gesture, my sweet dame
   behind them up the ladder urged me on,
   so much her power my nature overcame;
nor here on earth, where men go up and down
   by natural means, was e'er such rapid flight,
   as with my wing could bear comparison.
So, reader, may I once again have sight
   of the holy triumph, for the which my sin
   ofttimes do I bewail and bosom smite,
you had not dipped your finger out and in
   the fire so quickly, as I saw the sign
   which follows Taurus and was therewithin.
O glorious stars, O radiancy divine
   pregnant with mighty power, to which is due,
   all of whatever genius may be mine,
the father of each mortal life with you
   was born, with you was setting, at the time
   when first on me the Tuscan breezes blew;
and after, when within the wheel sublime
   that whirls you, grace was granted me thuswise
   to enter, yours was my allotted clime.

A voi divotamente ora sospira
   l' anima mia, per acquistar virtute
   al passo forte che a sè la tira.   123
"Tu se' sì presso a l' ultima salute"
   cominciò Beatrice, "che tu dei
   aver le luci tue chiare ed acute.   126
E però, prima che tu più t' inlei,
   rimira in giù, e vedi quanto mondo
   sotto li piedi già esser ti fei;   129
sì che 'l tuo cor, quantunque può, giocondo
   s' appresenti a la turba triunfante
   che lieta vien per questo etera tondo."   132
Col viso ritornai per tutte quante
   le sette spere, e vidi questo globo
   tal, ch' io sorrisi del suo vil sembiante;   135
e quel consiglio per migliore approbo
   che l' ha per meno; e chi ad altro pensa
   chiamar si puote veramente probo.   138
Vidi la figlia di Latona incensa
   sanza quell' ombra che mi fu cagione
   per che già la credetti rara e densa.   141
L' aspetto del tuo nato, Iperione,
   quivi sostenni, e vidi com si move
   circa e vicino a lui, Maia e Dione.   144
Quindi m' apparve il temperar di Giove
   tra 'l padre e 'l figlio; e quindi mi fu chiaro
   il variar che fanno di lor dove.   147
E tutti e sette mi si dimostraro
   quanto son grandi, e quanto son veloci,
   e come sono in distante riparo.   150
L' aiuola che ci fa tanto feroci,
   volgendom' io con li etterni Gemelli,
   tutta m' apparve da' colli a le foci.   153
Poscia rivolsi li occhi a li occhi belli.

Yea, and for strength to meet the hard emprise
   that draws her to itself, my soul no less
   to you now, even now, devoutly sighs.
"Thou art so near the final blessedness"
   thus Beatrice began, "that it is meet
   thine eyes the utmost clearness should possess.
So, ere thou wend yet farther into it,
   look down once more, and the vast world survey,
   by me already placed beneath thy feet;
thus shall thy heart, with all the joy it may,
   greet the triumphant throng which for thy cheer
   now speeds exulting down this starry way."
In vision I re-travelled, sphere by sphere,
   the seven heavens, and saw this globe of ours
   such, that I smiled, so mean did it appear;
and highest I esteem his mental powers
   who rates it least; and him, whose thoughts elsewhere
   are fixed, good sense with truest wisdom dowers.
I saw Latona's daughter shining bare
   of all the shadow which some while agone
   had caused me to suppose her dense and rare.
The aspect of thy child, Hyperion,
   here I endured, and saw Dione move,
   and Maia, round and near him where he shone.
From here I saw the tempering of Jove
   between his sire and son, from here could trace
   their true positions and each change thereof.
Likewise did all the seven, how swift their pace,
   how vast their size, unto my vision show,
   and each from each how far removed in space.
As for this petty floor we boast of so,
   I, rolling with the timeless Twins, discerned
   it all, from the hills to where its streams outflow.
Then to the beauteous eyes mine eyes returned.

CANTO XXIII

Come l' augello, intra l' amate fronde,
    posato al nido de' suoi dolci nati
    la notte che le cose ci nasconde,   3
che, per veder li aspetti disiati
    e per trovar lo cibo onde li pasca,
    in che gravi labor li sono aggrati,   6
previene il tempo in su aperta frasca,
    e con ardente affetto il sole aspetta,
    fiso guardando pur che l' alba nasca;   9
così la donna mia stava eretta
    e attenta, rivolta inver la plaga
    sotto la quale il sol mostra men fretta: 12
sì che, veggendola io sospesa e vaga,
    fecimi qual è quei che disiando
    altro vorria, e sperando s' appaga.   15
Ma poco fu tra uno e altro quando,
    del mio attender, dico, e del vedere
    lo ciel venir più e più rischiarando.   18
E Beatrice disse: "Ecco le schiere
    del triunfo di Cristo e tutto il frutto
    ricolto del girar di queste spere!"   21
Pariemi che 'l suo viso ardesse tutto,
    e li occhi avea di letizia sì pieni,
    che passar men convien sanza costrutto.   24
Quale ne' plenilunii sereni
    Trivia ride tra le ninfe etterne
    che dipingon lo ciel per tutti i seni,   27
vidi sopra migliaia di lucerne
    un sol che tutte quante l' accendea,
    come fa il nostro le viste superne;   30

CANTO XXIII

Even as the bird, who in some sheltered bower
    broods on the nest of her loved progeny
    the long night through, while darkness hath its hour,
but yearning to behold their looks and fly
    in search of food as wherewithal to stay
    their hunger—sweet though weary task to ply—
foreruns the time upon the open spray
    and doth with ardent zeal the sun expect,
    fixedly watching for the break of day;
so stood my lady, heedful and erect,
    facing the region beneath which the sun
    is more than elsewhere in his progress checked:
I, seeing her rapt attention, thereupon
    was like a man whom the sure hope to win
    his heart's desire contents, till it be won.
Yet was the time but short, to wit, between
    my waiting and my seeing the sky o'erspread
    at every moment with a brighter sheen.
Cried Beatrice: "Behold the legions led
    by the triumphant Christ, and all the fruit
    by these revolving spheres safe harvested!"
Her face seemed all on fire, her eyes to shoot
    forth sparkles of a joy so wondrous bright,
    it needs must render all description mute.
As on a calm and full-mooned summer night
    Trivía smiles mid her immortal train
    of nymphs who spangle heaven from depth to height,
outshining myriad lamps beheld I then
    one sun who kindled each and all, as ours
    kindles the stars that throng his high domain;

e per la viva luce trasparea
la lucente sustanza tanto chiara
nel viso mio, che non la sostenea.   33
Oh Beatrice dolce guida e cara!
Ella mi disse: "Quel che ti sobranza
è virtù da cui nulla si ripara.   36
Quivi è la sapienza e la possanza
ch' aprì le strade tra 'l cielo e la terra,
onde fu già sì lunga disianza".   39
Come foco di nube si diserra
per dilatarsi sì che non vi cape,
e fuor di sua natura in giù s' atterra,   42
la mente mia così, tra quelle dape
fatta più grande, di se stessa uscio,
e che si fesse rimembrar non sape.   45
"Apri li occhi e riguarda qual son io:
tu hai vedute cose, che possente
se' fatto a sostener lo riso mio."   48
Io era come quei che si risente
di visione oblita e che s' ingegna
indarno di ridurlasi a la mente,   51
quand' io udi' questa proferta, degna
di tanto grato, che mai non si stingue
del libro che 'l preterito rassegna.   54
Se mo sonasser tutte quelle lingue
che Polimnìa con le suore fero
del latte lor dolcissimo più pingue,   57
per aiutarmi, al millesmo del vero
non si verria, cantando il santo riso
e quanto il santo aspetto facea mero.   60
E così, figurando il paradiso,
convien saltar lo sacrato poema,
come chi trova suo cammin riciso.   63

and through the rays, poured down in living showers,
   the radiant substance, blazing on me, tried
   my mortal vision far beyond its powers.
Oh Beatrice, beloved and loving guide!
   And she: "This power by which thy own are quelled,
   is such as nought created may abide.
Here is the might and wisdom which availed
   'twixt heaven and earth to open every road
   so long from yearning human hearts withheld".
As lightning from a cloud must needs explode
   through room too strait to hold the swelling flame,
   which falls to earth against its natural mode,
even so then did my spirit burst its frame,
   grown greater at those banquets through excess
   of sweets, and it forgets what it became.
"Open thine eyes and mark my loveliness:
   thou hast seen things, from whence thou shalt derive
   the strength to bear the smile upon my face."
I was like one who, eager to revive
   some long-forgotten dream, with all his wit
   strives to recall it, yet doth vainly strive,
when I this invitation heard, so meet
   for largest thanks, that it shall aye be found
   traced in the volume where my past is writ.
Should now to aid me all the tongues resound
   which Polyhymnia and her sisterhood
   have with their sweetest milk made most abound,
when chanting of her holy smile they would
   not even a thousandth of its charm portray,
   nor how therewith her holy visage glow'd.
So too the sacred poem, which would essay
   to picture paradise, must leap, like him
   who finds an interruption to his way.

Ma chi pensasse il ponderoso tema
 e l' omero mortal che se ne carca,
 nol biasmerebbe se sott' esso trema.   66
Non è pileggio da picciola barca
 quel che fendendo va l' ardita prora,
 nè da nocchier ch' a se medesmo parca.   69
"Perchè la faccia mia sì t' innamora,
 che tu non ti rivolgi al bel giardino
 che sotto i raggi di Cristo s' infiora?   72
Quivi è la rosa in che il verbo divino
 carne si fece; quivi son li gigli
 al cui odor si prese il buon cammino."   75
Così Beatrice; e io, che a' suoi consigli
 tutto era pronto, ancora mi rendei
 a la battaglia de' debili cigli.   78
Come a raggio di sol che puro mei
 per fratta nube già prato di fiori
 vider, coverti d' ombra, li occhi miei,   81
vid' io così più turbe di splendori,
 fulgorate di su da raggi ardenti,
 sanza veder principio di fulgori.   84
O benigna vertù che sì li 'mprenti,
 su t' esaltasti, per largirmi loco
 a li occhi lì che non t' eran possenti.   87
Il nome del bel fior ch' io sempre invoco
 e mane e sera, tutto mi ristrinse
 l' animo ad avvisar lo maggior foco.   90
E come ambo le luci mi dipinse
 il quale e il quanto de la viva stella
 che là su vince, come qua giù vinse,   93
per entro il cielo scese una facella,
 formata in cerchio a guisa di corona,
 e cinsela e girossi intorno ad ella.   96

Yet none that ponders on the weighty theme,
  which a mere man sustains, will take amiss
  his staggering under burden so extreme.
No sea-way for a bauble-boat is this
  cut by my daring keel, but one to prove
  the steersman's mettle in extremities.
"Why with my face art thou so much in love,
  that thou dost turn not to the garden rare
  which blossoms beneath Christ who shines above?
The rose which bore the incarnate word is there:
  there are the lilies whose sweet odour gave
  men strength along the narrow way to fare."
Thus Beatrice; and I, the willing slave
  of her injunctions, set myself anew
  to make my frail lids for the contest brave.
As in a sun-ray, slanting undimmed through
  a broken cloud, erewhile a flowery field,
  myself in shadow, I have chanced to view,
so to my gaze were countless lights revealed,
  irradiated by a downward flow
  of brilliant splendour from a source concealed.
O kindly power whose seal doth stamp them so,
  thou rosest higher expressly to afford
  my eyes more scope, else dazzled by thy glow.
The name of that fair flower, by me implored
  morning and evening, made me concentrate
  upon the fire from which most radiance poured.
And as on both my eyes 'twas limned how great
  and glorious is the living star who there
  shines, as she shone on earth, supreme in state,
there fell through heaven a torch, which as it were
  a crown—for, whirling, such the shape it bore—
  straightway encircled and revolved round her.

Qualunque melodia più dolce sona
　　qua giù, e più a sè l' anima tira,
　　parrebbe nube che squarciata tona,　　99
comparata al sonar di quella lira
　　onde si coronava il bel zaffiro
　　del quale il ciel più chiaro s' inzaffira.　　102
"Io sono amore angelico che giro
　　l' alta letizia che spira del ventre
　　che fu albergo del nostro disiro;　　105
e girerommi, donna del ciel, mentre
　　che seguirai tuo figlio, e farai dia
　　più la spera suprema perchè gli entre."　　108
Così la circulata melodia
　　si sigillava, e tutti li altri lumi
　　facean sonare il nome di Maria.　　111
Lo real manto di tutti i volumi
　　del mondo, che più ferve e più s' avviva
　　ne l' alito di Dio e nei costumi,　　114
avea sopra di noi l' interna riva
　　tanto distante, che la sua parvenza,
　　là dov' io era, ancor non appariva:　　117
però non ebber li occhi miei potenza
　　di seguitar la coronata fiamma
　　che si levò appresso sua semenza.　　120
E come fantolin che 'nver la mamma
　　tende le braccia, poi che 'l latte prese,
　　per l' animo che 'nfin di fuor s' infiamma;　　123
ciascun di quei candori in su si stese
　　con la sua fiamma, sì che l' alto affetto
　　ch' elli avieno a Maria mi fu palese.　　126
Indi rimaser lì nel mio cospetto,
　　'Regina celi' cantando sì dolce,
　　che mai da me non si partì 'l diletto.　　129

The sweetest tune that on this earthly shore
    most draws to itself the soul in fond desire,
    would seem a splitting thunder-cloud's harsh roar,
matched with the tones of that melodious lyre
    wherewith I saw the lovely sapphire crowned
    which floods the brightest heaven with azure fire.
"Angelic love am I, who circle round
    the exalted joy breathed from the womb, yea thine,
    in which the world's desire fit lodging found:
and there to circle, lady of heaven, is mine,
    till, following thy son, thou enterest
    the heaven of heavens to make it more divine."
Thus on the circling music was impressed
    its seal, and 'Mary' was the name that rung
    through heaven, by all the other lights confessed.
The mantle royal round all the swathings flung
    that wrap the world, the most intensely bright,
    most godlike in its ways all spheres among,
upreared its inner shore to such a height
    above us, that, where I had chanced to take
    my station, it was still beyond my sight:
hence did the crownéd flame ere long forsake
    the range of my weak vision, as it rose
    on high, while following in its offspring's wake.
And as an infant to its mother throws
    its little arms out, when the breast is drained,
    for thus the love flames forth which in it glows;
each of those starry splendours upward strained
    its flame, whereby they visibly displayed
    how all to Mary yearned with love unfeigned.
Anon, still present to my sight they stayed,
    chanting '*Regina celi*' in a strain
    so sweet, my joy thereat can never fade.

Oh quanta è l' ubertà che si soffolce
in quelle arche ricchissime che fuoro
a seminar qua giù buone bobolce !   132
Quivi si vive e gode del tesoro
che s' acquistò piangendo ne lo essilio
di Babilon, ove si lasciò l' oro.   135
Quivi triunfa, sotto l' alto filio
di Dio e di Maria, di sua vittoria,
e con l' antico e col novo concilio,   138
colui che tien le chiavi di tal gloria.

CANTO XXIV

"O SODALIZIO eletto a la gran cena
del benedetto agnello, il qual vi ciba
sì, che la vostra voglia è sempre piena,   3
se per grazia di Dio questi preliba
di quel che cade de la vostra mensa,
prima che morte tempo li prescriba,   6
ponete mente a l' affezione immensa,
e roratelo alquanto: voi bevete
sempre del fonte onde vien quel ch' ei pensa." 9
Così Beatrice; e quelle anime liete
si fero spere sopra fissi poli,
fiammando, volte, a guisa di comete.   12
E come cerchi in tempra d' oriuoli
si giran sì, che 'l primo a chi pon mente
quieto pare, e l' ultimo che voli;   15
così quelle carole, differente-
mente danzando, de la sua ricchezza
mi facieno stimar, veloci e lente.   18

Oh, how abundant is the garnered grain
   stored in those wealthy coffers which in sowing
   proved themselves here on earth good husbandmen!
There live they and enjoy the overflowing
   treasure which, exiled once in Babylon,
   spurning its gold, they gained beyond their knowing.
There too in triumph, 'neath the exalted son
   of God and Mary, with the saints enrolled
   in both the councils, old and new, sits one
who doth the keys of all this glory hold.

CANTO XXIV

"O company whom the blessèd lamb so feeds
   at the great supper he hath called you to,
   that ever satisfied are all your needs,
if by divine grace, ere his term be due
   prescribed by death, this man foretasteth aught
   spilled from the board so richly spread for you,
mindful of his immeasurable drought,
   shed some few drops upon him: ye for aye
   drink of the fountain whence proceeds his thought."
Thus Beatrice; and those joyful spirits straightway
   made them as spheres on fixèd poles, thereby
   flashing, revolved, with a comet's fiery ray.
And as in clockwork, when with heedful eye
   you watch the wheels, the first seems motionless,
   so slow its movement, and the last to fly;
thus, by the varied measure of their pace-
   enwoven dances, whether swift or slow,
   those carols made me gauge their happiness.

Di quella ch' io notai di più carezza
   vid' io uscire un foco sì felice,
   che nullo vi lasciò di più chiarezza;   21
e tre fiate intorno di Beatrice
   si volse con un canto tanto divo,
   che la mia fantasia nol mi ridice.   24
Però salta la penna e non lo scrivo;
   chè l' imagine nostra a cotai pieghe,
   non che 'l parlare, è troppo color vivo.   27
"O santa suora mia che sì ne prieghe
   divota, per lo tuo ardente affetto
   da quella bella spera mi disleghe."   30
Poscia, fermato, il foco benedetto
   a la mia donna dirizzò lo spiro,
   che favellò così com' i' ho detto.   33
Ed ella: "O luce etterna del gran viro
   a cui Nostro Signor lasciò le chiavi
   ch' ei portò giù di questo gaudio miro,   36
tenta costui di punti lievi e gravi,
   come ti piace, intorno de la fede,
   per la qual tu su per lo mare andavi.   39
S' elli ama bene e bene spera e crede,
   non t' è occulto, perchè 'l viso hai quivi
   dov' ogni cosa dipinta si vede;   42
ma perchè questo regno ha fatto civi
   per la verace fede, a gloriarla,
   di lei parlare è ben ch' a lui arrivi".   45
Sì come il baccellier s' arma e non parla,
   fin che 'l maestro la question propone,
   per approvarla, non per terminarla,   48
così m' armava io d' ogni ragione,
   mentre ch' ella dicea, per esser presto
   a tal querente ed a tal professione.   51

From that which I remarked the fairest, lo,
    a flame emerged of such resplendent bliss,
    that none it left there shone with livelier glow;
and three times it revolved round Beatrice
    with so divine a song, that fancy keeps
    no record of those subtle melodies.
Therefore my pen describes them not, but skips;
    since for such folds no poet's thought could e'er
    limn colours fine enough, far less his lips.
"O saintly sister mine, thine earnest prayer,
    enkindled by thy burning love, hath made
    me unbind myself from yonder circle fair."
Such were the words which, when its course was stayed,
    forthwith the blesséd luminary breathed
    toward my lady; whereupon she said:
"O mighty soul for ever light-enwreathed,
    to whom the keys of paradise which he
    bore down below were by Our Lord bequeathed,
question this man, as seemeth good to thee,
    on points both light and grave, touching the faith,
    by which of old thou walkedst on the sea.
If rightly he loves, and hopeth rightly, and hath
    a sound belief, to thee e'en now is shown
    in him, who all that is discovereth;
but since by the true faith, and that alone,
    this realm hath gained its citizens, 'tis meet
    it fall to him to make its glory known".
As, while the master poseth question fit,
    the bachelor in silence arms his mind,
    not to decide the point, but argue it,
so did I arm myself with every kind
    of reason, while she spake, for such a creed
    and such a querist fitting proofs to find.

"Dì, buon cristiano, fatti manifesto:
  fede che è?" Ond' io levai la fronte
  in quella luce onde spirava questo;   54
poi mi volsi a Beatrice, ed essa pronte
  sembianze femmi perch' io spandessi
  l' acqua di fuor del mio interno fonte.   57
"La Grazia che mi dà ch' io mi confessi"
  comincia' io "da l' alto primopilo,
  faccia li miei concetti bene espressi."   60
E seguitai: "Come 'l verace stilo
  ne scrisse, padre, del tuo caro frate
  che mise teco Roma nel buon filo,   63
fede è sustanza di cose sperate,
  ed argomento de le non parventi;
  e questa pare a me sua quiditate".   66
Allora udi': "Dirittamente senti,
  se bene intendi perchè la ripuose
  tra le sustanze e poi tra li argomenti".   69
E io appresso: "Le profonde cose
  che mi largiscon qui la lor parvenza,
  a li occhi di là giù son sì ascose,   72
che l' esser loro v' è in sola credenza,
  sopra la qual si fonda l' alta spene;
  e però di sustanza prende intenza.   75
E da questa credenza ci convene
  sillogizzar, sanz' avere altra vista;
  però intenza d' argomento tene".   78
Allora udi': "Se quantunque s' acquista
  giù per dottrina, fosse così inteso,
  non li avria loco ingegno di sofista".   81
Così spirò di quello amore acceso;
  indi soggiunse: "Assai ben è trascorsa
  d' esta moneta già la lega e 'l peso: 84

"Good Christian, speak: declare thee such indeed;
  what thing is faith?" Whereat I raised my brow
  unto the light which bade me thus proceed;
then turned to Beatrice, who was quick to show
  clear tokens that from out their secret place
  within me I should let the waters flow.
"May the same Grace which grants me to confess
  before the chief centurion, in my mouth
  put words that shall my notions well express."
Thus I, then added: "Father, as with sooth
  thy brother wrote, who was thy loved ally
  in guiding Rome into the way of truth,
'faith is the substance of things hoped for, ay
  and argument withal of things not seen';
  and this I take to be its quiddity".
Then heard I: "Thou thereof dost rightly ween,
  if, when he terms it first a substance, then
  an argument, thou knowest what he doth mean".
"The deep things," so I answered him again,
  "which to my vision here are freely shown,
  on earth are so concealed from mortal ken,
that they exist there in belief alone,
  to which the intention of substance well applies,
  because exalted hope is based thereon.
And since from faith, as wanting other eyes,
  we needs must make our syllogisms start,
  it holds intention of argument likewise."
Then heard I: "If all lore, in learning's mart
  acquired below, were thuswise understood,
  no room were left there for the sophist's art".
So breathed the flame of love, and then pursued:
  "Right well we have now assayed this coin throughout,
  both in alloy and weight, and found it good:

ma dimmi se tu l' hai ne la tua borsa ".
  Ond' io: "Sì, ho, sì lucida e sì tonda,
  che nel suo conio nulla mi s' inforsa ".   87
Appresso uscì de la luce profonda
  che lì splendeva: "Questa cara gioia
  sopra la quale ogni virtù si fonda,   90
onde ti venne?" E io: "La larga ploia
  de lo Spirito Santo ch' è diffusa
  in su le vecchie e 'n su le nuove cuoia,   93
è sillogismo che la m' ha conchiusa
  acutamente sì, che 'nverso d' ella
  ogni dimostrazion mi pare ottusa ".   96
Io udi' poi: "L' antica e la novella
  proposizion che così ti conchiude
  perchè l' hai tu per divina favella?"   99
E io: "La prova che 'l ver mi dischiude
  son l' opere seguite, a che natura
  non scaldò ferro mai nè battè incude ".   102
Risposto fummi: "Dì, chi t' assicura
  che quell' opere fosser? Quel medesmo
  che vuol provarsi, non altri, il ti giura ".   105
"Se 'l mondo si rivolse al cristianesmo "
  diss' io "sanza miracoli, quest' uno
  è tal, che li altri non sono il centesmo;   108
chè tu intrasti povero e digiuno
  in campo, a seminar la buona pianta
  che fu già vite e ora è fatta pruno."   111
Finito questo, l' alta corte santa
  risonò per le spere un 'Dio laudamo'
  ne la melode che là su si canta.   114
E quel baron che sì di ramo in ramo,
  essaminando, già tratto m' avea,
  che a l' ultime fronde appressavamo,   117

but is it in thy purse?" Quoth I: "Without
   question it is, and that so bright and round,
   that in its stamp there is no shade of doubt"
Forthwith there issued from the light profound
   that shone there: "This inestimable gem
   which is of every virtue the sole ground,
whence came it to thee?" And I: "From him it came,
   the Holy Spirit, whose abundant rain
   flooding the parchments, old and new, in them
is syllogism which by proof so plain
   concludes it for me, that in point and force
   all others, when with that compared, seem vain".
"Why holdest thou", was breathed from the same source,
   "the elder premise, and the new, whose might
   doth so persuade thee, for divine discourse?"
And I: "The proof which brings the truth to light
   are the works consequent, which nature ne'er
   made iron hot for, nor did anvil smite".
Came answer: "That those wonders ever were
   who vouches? Save the writ that seeks thereby
   to prove itself, none else to them doth swear".
"If the world turned to Christianity",
   I answered, "without miracles, this one
   doth all the rest a hundredfold outvie;
for thou, both poor and fasting, wentest down
   into the field to sow the goodly plant,
   which, a vine once, is now a bramble grown."
This ended, straightway such a jubilant
   '*Te Deum*' rang through heaven from star to star,
   as only the redeemed have power to chant.
That baron who from branch to branch so far
   by questioning had led me, that we now
   unto the topmost leaves were drawing near,

ricominciò: "La Grazia, che donnea
 con la tua mente, la bocca t' aperse
 infino a qui come aprir si dovea,   120
sì ch' io approvo ciò che fuori emerse:
 ma or convene esprimer quel che credi,
 e onde a la credenza tua s' offerse".   123
"O santo padre, spirito che vedi
 ciò che credesti sì che tu vincesti
 ver lo sepulcro più giovani piedi,"   126
comincia' io, "tu vuoi ch' io manifesti
 la forma qui del pronto creder mio,
 e anche la cagion di lui chiedesti.   129
E io rispondo: Io credo in uno Dio
 solo ed etterno, che tutto il ciel move,
 non moto, con amore e con disio.   132
E a tal creder non ho io pur prove
 fisice e metafisice, ma dalmi
 anche la verità che quinci piove   135
per Moisè, per profeti e per salmi,
 per l' Evangelio e per voi che scriveste
 poi che l' ardente Spirto vi fè almi.   138
E credo in tre persone etterne, e queste
 credo una essenza sì una e sì trina,
 che soffera congiunto 'sono' ed 'este'.   141
De la profonda condizion divina
 ch' io tocco mo, la mente mi sigilla
 più volte l' evangelica dottrina.   144
Quest' è il principio, quest' è la favilla
 che si dilata in fiamma poi vivace,
 e come stella in cielo in me scintilla."   147
Come 'l segnor ch' ascolta quel che i piace,
 da indi abbraccia il servo, gratulando
 per la novella, tosto ch' el si tace;   150

began once more: "The Grace, which loves to woo
   thy mind, thus far hath oped thy lips and made
   them give the answer it behoved them to;
wherefore I sanction that which they have said:
   but now 'tis meet that thou declare thy creed,
   and whence to such belief thy thoughts were led".
"O holy father, spirit that for thy meed
   here sëest what thou didst so believe, that thou
   didst younger feet to the sepulchre outspeed,"
I thus began, "since here thou'dst have me show
   the essentials of my faith, and tell thee why
   I hold them with full confidence, then know
that I believe in one, sole Deity
   eternal, who, himself unmoved, doth move
   with love and longing all that wheels on high.
Such is my creed, and ample proof thereof
   nature supplies, and reason more, but most
   the truth which raineth down from here above
through Moses, through the psalms and through a host
   of prophets, through the Gospel and through you,
   when ye were quickened of the Holy Ghost.
Three infinite persons I believe in too;
   I believe these an essence, one yet trine,
   so that thereof both 'sunt' and 'est' are true.
Of the mysterious estate divine
   whereof I speak, my mind doth bear the mark,
   impressed on it by many a gospel line.
From this beginning, from this pregnant spark
   the lively flame dilates and, glittering clear
   like to a star in heaven, dispels my dark."
E'en as a lord who from his page doth hear
   good news, when he hath heard it, moved by strong
   delight, embraces him and holds him dear;

così, benedicendomi cantando,
   tre volte cinse me, sì com' io tacqui,
   l' apostolico lume al cui comando   153
io avea detto; sì nel dir li piacqui!

CANTO XXV

SE mai continga che 'l poema sacro
   al quale ha posto mano e cielo e terra,
   sì che m' ha fatto per più anni macro,   3
vinca la crudeltà che fuor mi serra
   del bello ovile ov' io dormi' agnello,
   nimico ai lupi che li danno guerra;   6
con altra voce omai, con altro vello
   ritornerò poeta; ed in sul fonte
   del mio battesmo prenderò 'l cappello;   9
però che ne la fede, che fa conte
   l' anime a Dio, quivi intra' io, e poi
   Pietro per lei sì mi girò la fronte.   12
Indi si mosse un lume verso noi
   di quella spera ond' uscì la primizia
   che lasciò Cristo de' vicari suoi;   15
e la mia donna, piena di letizia,
   mi disse: "Mira, mira: ecco il barone
   per cui là giù si visita Galizia".   18
Sì come quando il colombo si pone
   presso al compagno, l' uno all' altro pande,
   girando e mormorando, l' affezione;   21
così vid' io l' uno da l' altro grande
   principe glorioso essere accolto,
   laudando il cibo che là su li prande.   24

thus, pouring benediction forth with song,
   thrice wheeled about me, as I silent fell,
   the apostolic radiance who my tongue
had prompted; so its utterance pleased him well!

CANTO XXV

If e'er it fortune that the sacred lay,
   at which both heaven and earth have toiled and
   so that it long hath worn my flesh away,   [wrought,
should melt the cruel hearts that bar me out
   from the fair sheepfold where, a lamb, I knew
   sweet sleep, at war with the wolves that rage without,
with other voice and fleece of other hue
   I shall forthwith return, and at my own
   baptismal font receive a laureate's due;
for there the faith, which maketh spirits known
   to God, I first embraced, and Peter then,
   to honour it, thus made himself my crown.
Next moved a lustre towards us, once again
   out of that circle whence had issued forth
   the first fruit of Christ's vicars among men.
"Look, look: behold the baron who on earth
   draws pilgrims to Galicia"—thus, elate,
   my lady made me know that spirit's worth.
As when the ring-dove settles near his mate,
   wheeling and cooing, each the affection shows
   which mutual love doth in their hearts beget;
so welcomed of each other saw I those
   two great and glorious chiefs, the while in praise
   they chanted of the food which heaven bestows.

Ma poi che 'l gratular si fu assolto,
  tacito coram me ciascun s' affisse,
  ignito sì che vincea il mio volto.   27
Ridendo allora Beatrice disse:
  "Inclita vita per cui la larghezza
  de la nostra basilica si scrisse,   30
fa risonar la spene in questa altezza:
  tu sai, che tante fiate la figuri,
  quante Iesù ai tre fè più carezza".   33
"Leva la testa e fa che t' assicuri;
  chè ciò che vien qua su del mortal mondo,
  convien ch' ai nostri raggi si maturi."   36
Questo conforto del foco secondo
  mi venne; ond' io levai li occhi a' monti
  che li 'ncurvaron pria col troppo pondo.   39
"Poi che per grazia vuol che tu t' affronti
  lo nostro imperadore, anzi la morte,
  ne l' aula piu secreta co' suoi conti,   42
sì che, veduto il ver di questa corte,
  la spene, che là giù bene innamora,
  in te ed in altrui di ciò conforte,   45
dì quel che ell' è, e come se ne 'nfiora
  la mente tua, e dì onde a te venne."
  Così seguì 'l secondo lume ancora.   48
E quella pia che guidò le penne
  de le mie ali a così alto volo,
  a la risposta così mi prevenne: 51
"La Chiesa militante alcun figliuolo
  non ha con più speranza, com' è scritto
  nel sol che raggia tutto nostro stuolo: 54
però li è conceduto che d' Egitto
  vegna in Ierusalemme per vedere,
  anzi che 'l militar li sia prescritto.   57

But both, whenas these glad assurances
   were ended, *coram me* in silence glowed,
   so burning bright as to o'ercome my gaze.
Beatrice smiled, then spake after this mode:
   "O spirit renowned, of the gifts called to write
   which by our kingly palace are bestowed,
make hope resound on this celestial height:
   thou knowest that thou as oft its symbol art,
   as dearer were the three in Jesus' sight".
"Lift up thy head and be thou of good heart;
   for that which hither mounts from the world below
   soon mellows in the warmth our beams impart."
Thus strengthened me the second flame; and so
   I lifted up mine eyes unto the hills
   whose weight, till then o'erheavy, had made them bow.
"Seeing that of his grace our emperor wills
   that thou shouldst, living, with his lords consort
   here in the hall which most his presence fills,
so that this vision of our very court
   may strengthen in thyself and others too
   hope, which doth men to a right love exhort,
say what it is, how far it lends its hue
   to thine own mind, and whence to thee it came."
   Thus did the second light its speech pursue.
That gentle one who to such lofty aim
   my wings had guided, with this quick riposte
   prevented me, ere I could answer frame:
"No son of the Church militant can boast
   of having fuller hope, as may be read
   in him whose beams enlighten all our host:
therefore he hath by special grace been led
   from Egypt to Jerusalem, its bliss
   to see, or e'er his fighting days be sped.

Li altri due punti, che non per sapere
  son dimandati, ma perch' ei rapporti
  quanto questa virtù t' è in piacere,   60
a lui lasc' io; chè non li saran forti
  nè di iattanzia; ed elli a ciò risponda,
  e la grazia di Dio ciò li comporti".   63
Come discente ch' a dottor seconda
  pronto e libente in quel ch' egli è esperto,
  perchè la sua bontà si disasconda,   66
"Spene" diss' io "è uno attender certo
  de la gloria futura, il qual produce
  grazia divina e precedente merto.   69
Da molte stelle mi vien questa luce;
  ma quei la distillò nel mio cor pria
  che fu sommo cantor del sommo duce.   72
'Sperino in te' ne la sua teodia
  dice 'color che sanno il nome tuo':
  e chi nol sa, s' elli ha la fede mia?   75
Tu mi stillasti, con lo stillar suo,
  ne la pistola poi; sì ch' io son pieno,
  ed in altrui vostra pioggia repluo".   78
Mentr' io diceva, dentro al vivo seno
  di quello incendio tremolava un lampo
  subito e spesso a guisa di baleno.   81
Indi spirò: "L' amore ond' io avvampo
  ancor ver la virtù che mi seguette
  infin la palma ed a l' uscir del campo,   84
vuol ch' io rispiri a te che ti dilette
  di lei; ed emmi a grato che tu diche
  quello che la speranza ti promette".   87
E io: "Le nove e le scritture antiche
  pongono il segno, ed esso lo mi addita,
  de l' anime che Dio s' ha fatte amiche.   90

The two remaining points, enquired ywis
   not for more knowledge sake, but that he may
   report how dear to thee this virtue is,
I leave to him; not difficult are they,
   nor of self-praise; and he may well reply,
   God helping him, to both in his own way ".
As practised scholar, who would fain thereby
   reveal his worth, displays an eager spirit
   in seconding his teacher, "Hope", said I,
is of the glory that we shall inherit
   a sure expectancy, the fruit withal
   of grace divine and of preceding merit.
On me from many stars this light doth fall;
   but the chief captain's chief musician, he
   instilled it in my heart the first of all.
'Let all who know thy name have hope in thee'—
   so praised be God: and what man knows it not,
   dwells but in him the faith that dwells in me?
Drenching me fell, dew of his dew begot,
   thine own epistle next; and now to pour
   your rain on others is in turn my lot ".
As thus I spake, quick flashes o'er and o'er
   repeated, as of sudden lightning, shone
   within that conflagration's living core.
Then it breathed forth: "The love that still burns on
   within me for the virtue which pursued
   my steps till palm and foughten field were won,
bids me respond to thee as one imbued
   with the same hope, and wills that thou unfold
   what it doth promise thee of future good ".
And I: "The latter scriptures, and the old,
   set forth the mark, and this doth make it clear,
   of souls whom God doth in his friendship hold.

Dice Isaia che ciascuna vestita
  ne la sua terra fia di doppia vesta;
  e la sua terra è questa dolce vita.   93
E 'l tuo fratello assai vie più digesta,
  là dove tratta de le bianche stole,
  questa revelazion ci manifesta ".   96
E prima, appresso al fin d' este parole,
  ' *Sperent in te* ' di sopra noi s' udì;
  a che rispuoser tutte le carole.   99
Poscia tra esse un lume si schiarì
  sì che se 'l Cancro avesse un tal cristallo,
  l' inverno avrebbe un mese d' un sol dì.   102
E come surge e va ed entra in ballo
  vergine lieta, sol per fare onore
  a la novizia, non per alcun fallo,   105
così vid' io lo schiarato splendore
  venire a' due che si volgieno a nota
  qual conveniesi al loro ardente amore.   108
Misesi lì nel canto e ne la rota;
  e la mia donna in lor tenea l' aspetto,
  pur come sposa tacita ed immota.   111
"Questi è colui che giacque sopra 'l petto
  del nostro pellicano; e questi fue
  di su la croce al grande officio eletto."   114
La donna mia così; nè però piue
  mosser la vista sua di stare attenta
  poscia che prima le parole sue.   117
Qual è colui ch' adocchia e s' argomenta
  di vedere eclissar lo sole un poco,
  che, per veder, non vedente diventa;   120
tal mi fec' io a quell' ultimo foco
  mentre che detto fu: "Perchè t' abbagli
  per veder cosa che qui non ha loco?   123

Isaiah says, in their own land they wear
   each one a double robe; and their own land
   is the existence ye delight in here.
Which revelation hath thy brother's hand
   depicted in far clearer imagery
   there where he treateth of the white-robed band".
And when these words were ended, instantly
   '*Sperent in Te*' rang o'er us from the height;
   unto which all the carols made reply.
Then in their midst a star became so bright,
   that if in Cancer sparkled such a gem,
   winter would have a month without a night.
And as a maiden, moved by nought to blame,
   but solely to do honour to the bride,
   where folk are dancing, runs to dance with them,
so saw I that enkindled lustre glide
   toward the other twain, whose whirling pace
   was such as with their ardent love complied.
In song and wheel it took its own due place;
   the while my lady, gazing at them, stood
   as stands the bride, silent and motionless.
"Lo, this is he o'er whom most loved to brood
   our pelican; and this is he who bore
   the mighty charge laid on him from the rood."
My lady thus; nor, for all that, the more
   was she withdrawn from her intent regard
   by that she spake, thereafter than before.
As one who'd fain contrive, by looking hard,
   to see the sun eclipsed in some degree,
   by dint of seeing finds his seeing marred;
so, before that last flame, it happed with me,
   till this was said: "Why dazzlest thou thine eye
   in seeking that which is not here to see?

In terra terra è 'l mio corpo, e saragli
   tanto con li altri, che 'l numero nostro
   con l' etterno proposito s' agguagli.   126
Con le due stole nel beato chiostro
   son le due luci sole che saliro;
   e questo apporterai nel mondo vostro ".   129
A questa voce l' infiammato giro
   si quietò con esso il dolce mischio
   che si facea nel suon del trino spiro,   132
sì come, per cessar fatica o rischio,
   li remi, pria ne l' acqua ripercossi,
   tutti si posano al sonar d' un fischio.   135
Ahi quanto ne la mente mi commossi,
   quando mi volsi per veder Beatrice,
   per non poter veder, ben che io fossi   138
presso di lei, e nel mondo felice !

CANTO XXVI

Mentr' io dubbiava per lo viso spento,
   de la fulgida fiamma che lo spense
   uscì un spiro che mi fece attento,   3
dicendo: "Intanto che tu ti risense
   de la vista che hai in me consunta,
   ben è che ragionando la compense.   6
Comincia dunque; e dì ove s' appunta
   l' anima tua, e fa ragion che sia
   la vista in te smarrita e non defunta;   9
perchè la donna che per questa dia
   region ti conduce, ha ne lo sguardo
   la virtù ch' ebbe la man d'Anania ".   12

Earth is my body, in earth, and there will lie
  with the others, till our number fills the tale
  which shall the eternal purpose satisfy.
With the two vestures in the heavenly pale
  are the two lights alone that have ascended;
  and this report to the world wherein ye dwell".
This utterance checked the fiery reel and ended
  therewith the sweet harmonious rise and fall
  of sound in which the trinal breath was blended,
even as, fatigue or danger to forestall,
  the oars, which smote the waves a moment past,
  stop all together at a whistle's call.
Ah into what a stir my mind was cast,
  whenas I turned me to see Beatrice,
  through lack of power to see, though I was fast
beside her still, and in the world of bliss!

CANTO XXVI

While, blinded thus, I strove to banish fear,
  there issued from the radiancy intense
  which blinded me a breath that held my ear,
as thus it spake: "Till thou regain the sense
  of vision which thou hast consumed on me,
  'tis well that thou in speech find recompense.
Begin then; and declare what is for thee
  thy soul's chief aim, and reckon that not dead,
  but only wildered, is thy power to see;
for in her look the lady who hath led
  thee through this realm divine, hath virtue as great
  as once the hand of Ananias had".

Io dissi: "Al suo piacere e tosto e tardo
　　vegna rimedio a li occhi che fuor porte
　　quand' ella entrò col foco ond' io sempr' ardo. 15
Lo ben che fa contenta questa corte,
　　Alfa ed O è di quanta scrittura
　　mi legge Amore o lievemente o forte". 18
Quella medesma voce che paura
　　tolta m' avea del subito abbarbaglio,
　　di ragionare ancor mi mise in cura; 21
e disse: "Certo a più angusto vaglio
　　ti conviene schiarar: dicer convienti
　　chi drizzò l' arco tuo a tal berzaglio". 24
E io: "Per filosofici argomenti
　　e per l' autorità che quinci scende
　　cotale amor convien che in me s' imprenti. 27
Chè il bene, in quanto ben, come s' intende,
　　così accende amore, e tanto maggio
　　quanto più di bontate in sè comprende. 30
Dunque a l' essenza ov' è tanto avvantaggio,
　　che ciascun ben che fuor di lei si trova
　　altro non è ch' un lume di suo raggio, 33
più che in altra convien che si mova
　　la mente, amando, di ciascun che cerne
　　il vero in che si fonda questa prova. 36
Tal vero a l' intelletto mio sterne
　　colui che mi dimostra il primo amore
　　di tutte le sustanze sempiterne. 39
Sternel la voce del verace autore,
　　che dice a Moisè, di sè parlando:
　　'Io ti farò vedere ogni valore'. 42
Sternilmi tu ancora, incominciando
　　l' alto preconio che grida l' arcano
　　di qui là giù sovra ogni altro bando". 45

I answered: "To the eyes which were the gate
   what time she entered with her quenchless fire,
   come healing, as she wills, or soon or late.
The good which in this court fulfils desire,
   begins and ends all scripture Love is fain
   to read to me in lower tones or higher".
The same voice which had late relieved me when
   oppressed by fear o' the sudden dazzle, now
   inspired me with the wish to speak again;
and said: "In sooth with finer sieve must thou
   make clear this matter: it is meet thou tell
   who caused thee at such mark to aim thy bow".
And I: "Philosophy must needs avail
   to stamp me with such love, and to that end
   authority comes down from here as well.
For good, *quâ* good, even as we apprehend
   it truly, kindles love, and that the more
   as more of goodness is therein contained.
Hence to the essence which contains such store
   of goodness that all good outside it found
   does but reflect the ray itself doth pour,
more than to others must, in love, be bound
   the mind of whosoe'er distinguishes
   the truth which is this demonstration's ground.
He to my understanding well displays
   the truth concerned who shows me the first love
   of all the everlasting substances.
Displays it the true word of one above,
   who, speaking of himself, to Moses saith:
   'I in thy sight will all my goodness prove'.
Displays it further that which preludeth
   thine own great gospel, chief of all to cry
   in mortal ears the mysteries of the faith".

E io udi': "Per intelletto umano
   e per autoritadi a lui concorde
   de' tuoi amori a Dio guarda il sovrano.   48
Ma dì ancor se tu senti altre corde
   tirarti verso lui, sì che tu suone
   con quanti denti questo amor ti morde".   51
Non fu latente la santa intenzione
   de l' aguglia di Cristo, anzi m' accorsi
   dove volea menar mia professione.   54
Però ricominciai: "Tutti quei morsi
   che posson far lo cor volgere a Dio,
   a la mia caritate son concorsi;   57
chè l' essere del mondo e l' esser mio,
   la morte ch' el sostenne perch' io viva,
   e quel che spera ogni fedel com' io,   60
con la predetta conoscenza viva,
   tratto m' hanno del mar de l' amor torto,
   e del diritto m' han posto a la riva.   63
Le fronde onde s' infronda tutto l' orto
   de l' ortolano etterno, am' io cotanto
   quanto da lui a lor di bene è porto".   66
Sì com' io tacqui, un dolcissimo canto
   risonò per lo cielo, e la mia donna
   dicea con gli altri: "Santo, santo, santo!"   69
E come a lume acuto si disonna
   per lo spirto visivo che ricorre
   a lo splendor che va di gonna in gonna,   72
e lo svegliato ciò che vede aborre,
   sì nescia è la subita vigilia
   fin che la stimativa non soccorre;   75
così de li occhi miei ogni quisquilia
   fugò Beatrice col raggio de' suoi,
   che rifulgea da più di mille milia: 78

"The human intellect", so came reply,
  "and consonant authorities unite
  to fix thy sovran love on the Most High.
But say if other cords there be, of might
  to pull thee towards him, that thuswise thou show
  what the teeth are wherewith this love doth bite."
Nor could I not the holy purpose know
  of the eagle of Christ—rather could well divine
  the way which he would have my avowal go.
Hence I resumed: "Joined in this love of mine
  all the sharp bitings that were ever known
  to turn the heart to God, their powers combine;
for that the world's existence and my own,
  the death which he for my redemption bore,
  and the whole Church's hope (not mine alone),
joined to that lively knowledge named before,
  have from the sea of passion men miscall
  love, to the right love drawn me safe to shore.
As for the leaves that render leafy all
  the garden by the eternal gardener tended,
  I love each, as on each his dew doth fall".
A song most sweet, soon as my words were ended,
  made the whole heaven resound, and with the rest
  my lady's voice in the *ter sanctus* blended.
And as, when a light flashes, sleep is chased
  away from the eyes, because their spirit runs
  to meet the glare that spreads from vest to vest,
and the roused sleeper what he sëeth shuns,
  until the power of judgment comes to aid
  the sense which that abrupt awakening stuns;
thus from my eyes drove Beatrice every shred
  of cloud away by radiance which her own
  more than a thousand miles around her spread:

onde mei che dinanzi vidi poi;
  e quasi stupefatto domandai
  d' un quarto lume ch' io vidi con noi.   81
E la mia donna: "Dentro da quei rai
  vagheggia il suo fattor l' anima prima
  che la prima virtù creasse mai".   84
Come la fronda, che flette la cima
  nel transito del vento e poi si lieva
  per la propria virtù che la sublima,   87
fec' io in tanto in quant' ella diceva,
  stupendo, e poi mi rifece sicuro
  un disio di parlare ond' io ardeva.   90
E cominciai: "O pomo che maturo
  solo prodotto fosti, o padre antico
  a cui ciascuna sposa è figlia e nuro,   93
divoto quanto posso a te supplico
  perchè mi parli: tu vedi mia voglia,
  e per udirti tosto, non la dico".   96
Talvolta un animal coverto broglia,
  sì che l' affetto convien che si paia
  per lo seguir che face a lui la 'nvoglia;   99
e similmente l' anima primaia
  mi facea trasparer per la coverta
  quant' ella a compiacermi venia gaia.   102
Indi spirò: "Sanz' essermi proferta
  da te, la voglia tua discerno meglio
  che tu qualunque cosa t' è più certa;   105
perch' io la veggio nel verace speglio
  che fa di sè pareglio a l' altre cose,
  e nulla face lui di sè pareglio.   108
Tu vuogli udir quant' è che Dio mi puose
  ne l' eccelso giardino ove costei
  a così lunga scala ti dispuose,   111

whence I saw better now than I had done
   before, and asked, as though in deep amaze,
   touching a fourth light which among us shone.
Quoth Beatrice: "Concealed in yonder rays
   the first soul ever framed by the first might
   regards its maker with adoring gaze".
Even as a leafy bough, that bends its light
   crest in a passing breeze, then backward swayed
   by its own virtue stands again upright,
so I while she was speaking bowed my head,
   awe-stricken; and then, stronger than my awe,
   these words so burned within me that I said:
"O thou sole fruit that the world ever saw
   produced already ripe, O sire of old
   to whom each bride is daughter and daughter-in-law,
devoutly as I may, I pray thee hold
   converse with me; my wish thou sëest, and I,
   to hear thee sooner, leave it all untold".
An animal which under wraps doth lie,
   whene'er it stirs must make its feelings plain,
   since with it move the folds 'tis covered by;
even so the first of living souls did then
   make clear to me through its integument
   how it to do my pleasure was full fain.
Then breathed it: "That whereon thy mind is bent,
   tho' untold by thee, is clearer to my view
   than unto thine a fact self-evident;
because I see it in the mirror true,
   itself reflecting all things whatsoe'er,
   while reflect it is that which nought can do.
How long is it since God, thou fain wouldst hear,
   in the high garden placed me where yon dame
   rendered thee fit to climb so long a stair,

e quanto fu diletto a li occhi miei,
   e la propria cagion del gran disdegno,
   e l' idioma ch' usai e ch' io fei.   114
Or, figliuol mio, non il gustar del legno
   fu per sè la cagion di tanto essilio,
   ma solamente il trapassar del segno.   117
Quindi onde mosse tua donna Virgilio,
   quattromilia trecento e due volumi
   di sol desiderai questo concilio;   120
e vidi lui tornare a tutt' i lumi
   de la sua strada novecento trenta
   fiate, mentre ch' io in terra fu'mi.   123
La lingua ch' io parlai fu tutta spenta
   innanzi che all' ovra inconsummabile
   fosse la gente di Nembròt attenta;   126
chè nullo effetto mai razionabile,
   per lo piacere uman che rinnovella
   seguendo il cielo, sempre fu durabile.   129
Opera naturale è ch' uom favella;
   ma così o così, natura lascia
   poi fare a voi, secondo che v' abbella.   132
Pria ch' io scendessi a l' infernale ambascia,
   I s' appellava in terra il sommo bene
   onde vien la letizia che mi fascia;   135
e *EL* si chiamò poi: e ciò convene,
   chè l' uso de' mortali è come fronda
   in ramo, che sen va e altra vene.   138
Nel monte che si leva più da l' onda,
   fu' io, con vita pura e disonesta,
   da la prim' ora a quella che seconda,   141
come 'l sol muta quadra, l' ora sesta ".

and how long did mine eyes enjoy the same,
    and the true reason for the mighty wrath,
    and what the speech my lips did use and frame.
Mankind, my son, for its long exile hath
    to blame, not the mere tasting of the tree,
    but the desertion of the appointed path.
I for this council yearned four thousand, three
    hundred and two years in the place below
    whence Virgil set forth at thy lady's plea;
to all the lights that on his pathway glow
    nine hundred times and thirty I saw the sun
    return, whilst I on earth went to and fro.
The language which I spoke was all fordone
    long ere the work they could not consummate
    by Nimrod's progeny was e'en begun;
for nought of reason born was ever yet
    perdurable, since human liking still
    keeps changing with the stars, which rise and set.
In speaking, man doth nature's law fulfil;
    but in this way or that she then doth leave
    to you to do, after your own sweet will.
Ere thither I went down where spirits grieve,
    JAH was the name on earth of the chief good
    which doth this light of gladness round me weave;
and *EL* men called him, as 'tis meet they should,
    thereafter; in that, like to leaves on spray,
    their habits pass and are, like leaves, renewed.
On the world's highest mountain did I stay,
    pure to begin with, then in guiltiness,
    from the first hour to that which, as the day
shifts quadrant, makes the sixth hour yield it place".

CANTO XXVII

"Al Padre, al Figlio, a lo Spirito Santo"
  cominciò "gloria!" tutto il paradiso,
  sì che m' inebriava il dolce canto.   3
Ciò ch' io vedeva mi sembiava un riso
  de l' universo; per che mia ebbrezza
  intrava per l' udire e per lo viso.   6
Oh gioia! oh ineffabile allegrezza!
  oh vita integra d' amore e di pace!
  oh sanza brama sicura ricchezza!   9
Dinanzi a li occhi miei le quattro face
  stavano accese, e quella che pria venne
  incominciò a farsi più vivace,   12
e tal ne la sembianza sua divenne,
  qual diverrebbe Giove, s' elli e Marte
  fossero augelli e cambiassersi penne.   15
La provedenza, che quivi comparte
  vice ed officio, nel beato coro
  silenzio posto avea da ogni parte,   18
quand' io udi': "Se io mi trascoloro,
  non ti maravigliar; chè, dicend' io,
  vedrai trascolorar tutti costoro.   21
Quelli ch' usurpa in terra il luogo mio,
  il luogo mio, il luogo mio, che vaca
  ne la presenza del Figliuol di Dio,   24
fatt' ha del cimiterio mio cloaca
  del sangue e de la puzza; onde 'l perverso
  che cadde di qua su, là giù si placa".   27
Di quel color che per lo sole avverso
  nube dipigne da sera e da mane,
  vid' io allora tutto il ciel cosperso.   30

CANTO XXVII

"Glory to Father, Son and Holy Ghost!"
    all paradise began: and I the while,
    so sweet the song, in ecstasy was lost.
And well the ear its bliss could reconcile
    with that which entrance found by way of sight;
    for, as I gazed, creation seemed to smile.
Oh joy! oh inexpressible delight!
    oh perfect life, fulfilled of love and peace!
    oh wealth unenvious, treasure nought can blight!
Stood the four torches, flaming without cease,
    before me still, and that which first had shone,
    in brilliancy began now to increase.
And such an aspect did it then put on,
    as Jupiter would do, if he and Mars
    were birds and should each other's plumage don.
That providence, which all particulars
    of function here assigns and service due,
    had hushed the song, and silence held the stars,
when thus I heard: "Marvel not, if my hue
    be changed; for, while I'm speaking, thou wilt see
    all my companions changing colour too.
He who usurps the place bestowed on me,
    on me, on me, that place on earth, which now
    the Son of God regards as vacant—he
hath made my cemetery, like sewer, flow
    with blood and filth; whereby the renegade
    who fell from hence, comforts himself below".
With colour of the tint by the sun laid
    on adverse cloud at dawn and close of day,
    beheld I then all heaven overspread.

E come donna onesta che permane
 di sè sicura e per l' altrui fallanza,
 pur ascoltando, timida si fane,   33
così Beatrice trasmutò sembianza;
 e tale eclissi credo che 'n ciel fue,
 quando patì la suprema possanza.   36
Poi procedetter le parole sue
 con voce tanto da sè trasmutata,
 che la sembianza non si mutò piue: 39
"Non fu la sposa di Cristo allevata
 del sangue mio, di Lin, di quel di Cleto,
 per essere ad acquisto d' oro usata;   42
ma, per acquisto d' esto viver lieto,
 e Sisto e Pio e Calisto e Urbano
 sparser lo sangue dopo molto fleto.   45
Non fu nostra intenzion ch' a destra mano
 de' nostri successor parte sedesse,
 parte da l' altra del popol cristiano;   48
nè che le chiavi che mi fuor concesse
 divenisser signaculo in vessillo,
 che contr' a battezzati combattesse;   51
nè ch' io fossi figura di sigillo
 a privilegi venduti e mendaci,
 ond' io sovente arrosso e disfavillo.   54
In vesta di pastor lupi rapaci
 si veggion di qua su per tutti i paschi:
 o difesa di Dio, perchè pur giaci?   57
Del sangue nostro Caorsini e Guaschi
 s' apparecchian di bere: o buon principio,
 a che vil fine convien che tu caschi!   60
Ma l' alta provedenza che con Scipio
 difese a Roma la gloria del mondo,
 soccorrà tosto, sì com' io concipio.   63

And as a modest damsel, in no way
   doubtful of her own virtue, yet at bare
   report of other's fault, reveals dismay,
thus Beatrice was changed in look and air;
   and thus, methinks, what time the Almighty bore
   the pains of death, the heavens eclipséd were.
His voice went on, but not now as before,
   since from itself so great a change it show'd.
   that even his semblance did not alter more:
"The spouse of Christ was never with my blood,
   with that of Linus and of Cletus fed,
   to find in gain of gold her highest good;
but Sextus, Pius and Calixtus bled,
   and Urban, after suffering woes untold,
   to gain thereby this happy life instead.
We purposed no dividing of Christ's fold,
   whereby some sheep on our successors' right,
   and others on the left, their station hold;
nor that upon a banner men should write
   as crest the keys entrusted unto me,
   and bear them against folk baptised, in fight;
nor that I should myself as signet see
   to false and venal privileges set,
   whence oft I redden and glow indignantly.
In every pasture hence our eyes are met
   by ravening wolves that shepherd's clothes do wear:
   O God our strength, why dost thou linger yet?
Sons of Cahors and Gascony prepare
   to drink our blood: oh, that so vile a doom
   must needs await thee, promise once so fair!
But that high providence which saved for Rome
   the glory of the world by Scipio's sword,
   will, if I err not, soon bid succour come.

E tu, figliuol, che per lo mortal pondo
    ancor giù tornerai, apri la bocca,
    e non asconder quel ch' io non ascondo".   66
Sì come di vapor gelati fiocca
    in giuso l' aere nostro, quando il corno
    de la capra del ciel col sol si tocca,   69
in su vid' io così l' etera adorno
    farsi e fioccar di vapor triunfanti
    che fatto avean con noi quivi soggiorno.   72
Lo viso mio seguiva i suoi sembianti,
    e seguì fin che 'l mezzo, per lo molto,
    li tolse il trapassar del più avanti.   75
Onde la donna, che mi vide assolto
    de l' attendere in su, mi disse: "Adima
    il viso, e guarda come tu se' volto".   78
Da l' ora ch' io avea guardato prima
    i' vidi mosso me per tutto l' arco
    che fa dal mezzo al fine il primo clima;   81
sì ch' io vedea di là da Gade il varco
    folle d' Ulisse, e di qua presso il lito
    nel qual si fece Europa dolce carco.   84
E più mi fora discoverto il sito
    di questa aiuola; ma 'l sol procedea
    sotto i mie' piedi un segno e più partito.   87
La mente innamorata, che donnea
    con la mia donna sempre, di ridure
    ad essa li occhi più che mai ardea: 90
e se natura o arte fè pasture
    da pigliare occhi, per aver la mente,
    in carne umana o ne le sue pitture,   93
tutte adunate, parrebber niente
    ver lo piacer divin che mi refulse,
    quando mi volsi al suo viso ridente.   96

And thou, son, who to earth must be restor'd
   by reason of thy mortal burden, hide
   nought that I hide not; tell it, word for word".
As, when the she-goat's horn is so enskied
   that it doth touch the sun, downwards our air
   is flaked with frozen vapours far and wide,
upwards saw I the ether thus made fair
   and flaked thick with triumphal vapours who
   had sojourned for a season with us there.
My sight pursued, and ceased not to pursue,
   their semblances, till height on heights beyond
   of intervenient space obscured its view.
Wherefore the lady, who my visage found
   absolved from gazing up, said: "Downward cast
   thy sight, and see how thou hast circled round".
Since I had looked before, behold we had passed
   all round so much of the first 'climate' as
   extends between its mid-point and its last;
hence saw I, that side Gades, the mad pass
   Ulysses crossed, and, this side, nigh the shore
   where once Europa a sweet burden was.
And further had this little threshing-floor
   been shown me; but the sun beneath my feet
   had onward moved a sign away and more.
My enamoured mind, which ever found it sweet
   to woo my lady, never more her wooer
   than now, burned once again her glance to meet:
and if that nature or art hath fashioned lure
   to catch the eyes, and so the mind possess,
   in human flesh or in its portraiture,
all such combined would nothing seem, or less,
   to the divine delight which on me shone,
   whenas I turned me to her smiling face.

E la virtù che lo sguardo m' indulse,
del bel nido di Leda mi divelse,
e nel ciel velocissimo m' impulse.   99

Le parti sue vicinissime e eccelse
sì uniforme son, ch' i' i' non so dire
qual Beatrice per loco mi scelse.   102

Ma ella, che vedea il mio disire,
incominciò, ridendo tanto lieta,
che Dio parea nel suo volto gioire: 105

"La natura del mondo, che quieta
il mezzo e tutto l' altro intorno move,
quinci comincia come da sua meta.   108

E questo cielo non ha altro dove
che la mente divina, in che s' accende
l' amor che il volge e la virtù ch' ei piove.   111

Luce ed amor d' un cerchio lui comprende,
sì come questo li altri; e quel precinto
colui che 'l cinge solamente intende.   114

Non è suo moto per altro distinto;
ma li altri son misurati da questo,
sì come diece da mezzo e da quinto.   117

E come il tempo tegna in cotal testo
le sue radici e ne li altri le fronde,
omai a te può esser manifesto.   120

Oh cupidigia che i mortali affonde
sì sotto te, che nessuno ha podere
di trarre li occhi fuor de le tue onde!   123

Ben fiorisce ne li uomini il volere;
ma la pioggia continua converte
in bozzacchioni le susine vere.   126

Fede ed innocenzia son reperte
solo ne' parvoletti; poi ciascuna
pria fugge che le guance sian coperte.   129

Such virtue from that radiant look I won,
   as plucked me forth from Leda's lovely nest
   and to the swiftest heaven urged me on.
Its various parts, nearest and loftiest,
   so correspond in form, I cannot tell
   which one for entrance Beatrice deemed best.
But she, who my desire perceived full well,
   smiling the while, with so much gladness spake,
   that her delight seemed God's, made visible:
"The nature of the world, that fixed doth make
   the centre, and all circling it constrains
   to move, from here its starting-point doth take.
No other 'where' than God's own mind contains
   this heaven, for in that mind alone is lit
   the love that rolls it, and the power it rains.
Around it light and love in circle meet,
   as it does round the rest; and sole presides
   o'er that engirdment he who girdeth it.
Measured itself by none, this heaven decides
   the motion, swift or slow, of all the rest,
   as ten into its half and fifth divides.
And how in this same vessel have been placed
   the roots of time, its leaves in the other skies,
   will henceforth unto thee be manifest.
Oh covetousness that mortals in suchwise
   dost whelm beneath thy billows, that no power
   is left to any thence to lift his eyes!
The will in men bursts into glorious flower;
   but the true plums a never-ceasing rain
   turns into prunes, all withered up and sour.
To look for faith and innocence were vain
   except in children; later on, we find
   both fled, or e'er on cheek the down be plain.

Tale, balbuziendo ancor, digiuna,
 che poi divora, con la lingua sciolta,
 qualunque cibo per qualunque luna.   132
E tal, balbuziendo, ama e ascolta
 la madre sua, che, con loquela intera,
 disia poi di vederla sepolta.   135
Così si fa la pelle bianca nera
 nel primo aspetto de la bella figlia
 di quel ch' apporta mane e lascia sera.   138
Tu, perchè non ti facci maraviglia,
 pensa che 'n terra non è chi governi;
 onde sì svia l' umana famiglia.   141
Ma prima che gennaio tutto si sverni
 per la centesma ch' è là giù negletta,
 raggeran sì questi cerchi superni,   144
che la fortuna che tanto s' aspetta,
 le poppe volgerà u' son le prore,
 sì che la classe correrà diretta;   147
e vero frutto verrà dopo 'l fiore ".

CANTO XXVIII

Poscia che 'ncontro a la vita presente
 de' miseri mortali aperse 'l vero
 quella che 'mparadisa la mia mente,   3
come in lo specchio fiamma di doppiero
 vede colui che se n' alluma retro,
 prima che l' abbia in vista o in pensiero,   6
e sè rivolge, per veder se 'l vetro
 li dice il vero, e vede ch' el s' accorda
 con esso come nota con suo metro;   9

One that, while lisping yet, observes the enjoin'd
   fast-days, doth later, when his tongue's unbound,
   in every moon glut food of every kind.
And one, while lisping, is his mother's fond
   obedient child, who, when he speaks aright,
   longs then to see her dead and laid in ground.
Thus soon becomes the white skin dark as night
   in the first aspect of his daughter fair,
   who adds the morning to the evening light.
Do thou, lest thou shouldst marvel at it, bear
   in mind that earth no ruler hath to show
   the human family how it doth err.
But ere that through the hundredth, down below
   neglected, January shall have passed
   clean out of winter, these high spheres will so
shine, that the longed-for tempest, come at last,
   shall whirl the vessel, poop to prow, right round,
   so that the fleet run onward straight and fast;
and after blossom true fruit shall abound".

CANTO XXVIII

When she whose charms imparadise my mind
   had—ah, the contrast!—bared in all its shame
   the present life of miserable mankind,
as in the looking-glass a candle's flame
   is seen of one it lighteth from the rear,
   ere he beholds or dreameth of the same,
who turns to see if a real flame be there
   to match the image and finds this agree
   with that, as to its words is set the air;

così la mia memoria si ricorda
  ch' io feci, riguardando ne' belli occhi
  onde a pigliarmi fece Amor la corda.   12
E com' io mi rivolsi e furon tocchi
  li miei da ciò che pare in quel volume,
  quandunque nel suo giro ben s' adocchi,   15
un punto vidi che raggiava lume
  acuto sì, che 'l viso ch' elli affoca
  chiuder conviensi per lo forte acume: 18
e quale stella par quinci più poca,
  parrebbe luna, locata con esso
  come stella con stella si colloca.   21
Forse cotanto quanto pare appresso
  alo cigner la luce che 'l dipigne,
  quando 'l vapor che 'l porta più è spesso,   24
distante intorno al punto un cerchio d' igne
  si girava sì ratto, ch' avria vinto
  quel moto che più tosto il mondo cigne.   27
E questo era d' un altro circumcinto,
  e quel dal terzo, e 'l terzo poi dal quarto,
  dal quinto il quarto, e poi dal sesto il quinto. 30
Sopra seguiva il settimo sì sparto
  già di larghezza, che 'l messo di Iuno
  intero a contenerlo sarebbe arto.   33
Così l' ottavo e 'l nono; e ciascheduno
  più tardo si movea, secondo ch' era
  in numero distante più da l' uno;   36
e quello avea la fiamma più sincera
  cui men distava la favilla pura,
  credo, però che più di lei s' invera.   39
La donna mia, che mi vedea in cura
  forte sospeso, disse: "Da quel punto
  depende il cielo e tutta la natura.   42

even thus, I well remember, did I see
  a brightness mirrored in those glorious eyes
  whence Love had spun the noose to capture me.
And as I turned and mine were touched likewise
  by what within that volume leaps to sight,
  when its rotation well we scrutinise,
a point I saw which radiated light
  so sharp, no eye on which the ray is thrown
  can bear its keenness, past conception bright:
and of all stars in heaven the smallest known,
  as seen from earth, beside it set, as star
  is set by star, in size would seem a moon.
Maybe as distant thence, as seemeth far
  the halo from the light whose tints attire
  the mists that form it, when these thickest are,
there whirled about the point a ring of fire,
  more rapid than the motion which around
  the world revolveth with the swiftest gyre.
Another this enringed, the which I found
  girt by the third, that by the fourth, outside
  the fourth the fifth, which by the sixth was bound.
Followed the seventh now spread out so wide,
  that Juno's herald, if her course were run
  entire, would not contain it though she tried.
So too the eighth and ninth; and of them none
  but slower moved according as its post
  was numbered farther from the central one;
and of the clearest radiance that could boast
  which from the pure spark stood at least remove,
  I think, because it shares its essence most.
My lady, who perceived the doubts that strove
  within me, said: "On yonder point depend
  the heavens and nature, with all parts thereof.

Mira quel cerchio che più li è congiunto;
  e sappi che 'l suo muovere è sì tosto
  per l' affocato amore ond' elli è punto ".   45
E io a lei: "Se 'l mondo fosse posto
  con l' ordine ch' io veggio in quelle rote,
  sazio m' avrebbe ciò che m' è proposto: 48
ma nel mondo sensibile si puote
  veder le volte tanto più divine,
  quant' elle son dal centro più remote.   51
Onde, se 'l mio disio dee aver fine
  in questo miro e angelico templo
  che solo amore e luce ha per confine,   54
udir convienmi ancor come l' essemplo
  e l' essemplare non vanno d' un modo,
  chè io per me indarno a ciò contemplo ".   57
"Se li tuoi diti non sono a tal nodo
  sufficienti, non è maraviglia;
  tanto, per non tentare, è fatto sodo!"   60
Così la donna mia; poi disse: "Piglia
  quel ch' io ti dicerò, se vuo' saziarti;
  ed intorno da esso t' assottiglia.   63
Li cerchi corporai sono ampi e arti
  secondo il più e 'l men de la virtute
  che si distende per tutte lor parti.   66
Maggior bontà vuol far maggior salute;
  maggior salute maggior corpo cape,
  s' elli ha le parti igualmente compiute.   69
Dunque costui che tutto quanto rape
  l' altro universo seco, corrisponde
  al cerchio che più ama e che più sape.   72
Per che, se tu a la virtù circonde
  la tua misura, non a la parvenza
  de le sustanze che t' appaion tonde,   75

Observe the circle which doth round it bend
   most closely, and know it burns with love, the spur
   whereby its rapid motion is maintained ".
"Did the world-order ", I replied, " concur
   with that to which I see these wheels are brought,
   I should accept thy words without demur:
but in the world of sense one can but note
   God makes the revolutions more his own,
   as from the centre they are more remote.
To show me, then, all I would fain be shown
   within this wondrous and angelic shrine
   which hath for boundaries love and light alone,
thou must make further clear why in design
   copy and pattern tally not: for I
   gaze, but myself no reason can divine."
"That thy own fingers avail not to untie
   this knot, should cause thee no astonishment;
   so hard 'tis grown through lack of will to try!"
My lady thus; then, "Wouldst thou rest content,"
   she added, "lay these words of mine to heart;
   and on them whet thy subtle argument.
Ample or narrow are the orbs which dart
   material light, as more the power or less
   which permeates them all in every part.
The greater good will work more blessedness;
   more blessedness the greater bulk enclose,
   if like perfection all its parts possess.
Hence this one which sweeps with it as it goes
   the whole creation, corresponds, 'tis clear,
   unto the circle which most loves and knows.
Measure the virtue, then, which doth inhere
   within these rings, not their circumference—
   that which they are, not that which they appear,

tu vederai mirabil consequenza
di maggio a più e di minore a meno,
in ciascun cielo, a sua intelligenza ". 78
Come rimane splendido e sereno
l' emisperio de l' aere, quando soffia
Borea da quella guancia ond' è più leno, 81
per che si purga e risolve la roffia
che pria turbava, sì che 'l ciel ne ride
con le bellezze d' ogni sua parroffia; 84
così fec' io, poi che mi provide
la donna mia del suo risponder chiaro,
e come stella in cielo il ver si vide. 87
E poi che le parole sue restaro,
non altrimenti ferro disfavilla
che bolle, come i cerchi sfavillaro. 90
L' incendio suo seguiva ogni scintilla;
ed eran tante, che 'l numero loro
più che 'l doppiar de li scacchi s' immilla. 93
Io sentiva osannar di coro in coro
al punto fisso che li tiene a li ubi,
e terrà sempre, ne' quai sempre fuoro. 96
E quella che vedea i pensier dubi
ne la mia mente, disse: " I cerchi primi
t' hanno mostrati Serafi e Cherubi. 99
Così veloci seguono i suoi vimi,
per somigliarsi al punto quanto ponno;
e posson quanto a veder son sublimi. 102
Quelli altri amor che dintorno li vonno,
si chiaman Troni del divino aspetto,
per che 'l primo ternaro terminonno. 105
E dei saper che tutti hanno diletto,
quanto la sua veduta si profonda
nel vero in che si queta ogni intelletto. 108

and straightway will a marvellous congruence
   of more with more and less with less be seen,
   in every heaven, with its intelligence".
As, when from out his milder cheek the keen
   North-Easter blows a blast that scours the sky,
   our air is left transparent and serene,
and heaven, because it sees the rack whereby
   'twas overcast dissolved and put to rout,
   smiles on us, decked in all its pageantry;
even so did I, when Beatrice my doubt
   had by her lucid answer quite dispelled,
   and like a star in heaven the truth shone out.
After her words were ended, I beheld
   the circles scintillating, like as when
   sparkles the iron which a smith would weld.
Each spark accompanied its own burning train;
   in number such, that they out-thousanded
   the chess-board doubled o'er and o'er again.
From choir to choir I heard hosanna sped,
   as ever thus the fixéd point they hymn,
   which stays them aye where they shall aye be stayed.
And she who saw my understanding dim
   with doubt, said: "The two rings that met thy view
   first, are the Seraphs with the Cherubim.
Thus swiftly their own bonds do they pursue
   to grow as like the one point as they may;
   the which they may, the more their vision is true.
As for the loves that circle round them, they
   are called Thrones of the face of God, because
   the first trine found its term in their array.
And know thou that the joy which through them flows
   is as the depth to which they penetrate
   into the truth in which all minds repose.

Quinci si può veder come si fonda
  l' esser beato ne l' atto che vede,
  non in quel ch' ama, che poscia seconda;   111
e del vedere è misura mercede,
  che grazia partorisce e buona voglia:
  così di grado in grado si procede.   114
L' altro ternaro, che così germoglia
  in questa primavera sempiterna
  che notturno Ariete non dispoglia,   117
perpetualmente 'Osanna' sberna
  con tre melode, che suonano in tree
  ordini di letizia onde s' interna.   120
In essa gerarcia son l' altre dee;
  prima Dominazioni, e poi Virtudi;
  l' ordine terzo di Podestadi èe.   123
Poscia ne' due penultimi tripudi
  Principati e Arcangeli si girano;
  l' ultimo è tutto d' Angelici ludi.   126
Questi ordini di su tutti s' ammirano,
  e di giù vincon sì, che verso Dio
  tutti tirati sono, e tutti tirano.   129
E Dionisio con tanto disio
  a contemplar questi ordini si mise,
  che li nomò e distinse com' io.   132
Ma Gregorio da lui poi si divise;
  onde, sì tosto come li occhi aperse
  in questo ciel, di se medesmo rise.   135
E se tanto secreto ver proferse
  mortale in terra, non voglio ch' ammiri;
  chè chi 'l vide qua su gliel discoperse   138
con altro assai del ver di questi giri ".

Hence may it be seen, the beatific state
    has its foundation in the act of sight,
    and not of love, which must on seeing wait;
and, for this seeing, merit supplies the light,
    and merit is born of grace and of goodwill:
    'tis thus that one proceeds from height to height.
The second triad, which, in like manner still,
    doth burgeon in this sempiternal spring
    whose buds no nightly Ram can spoil or kill,
doth everlastingly 'Hosanna' sing
    in triple anthems, warbled by the trine
    orders of joy which binds their triple ring.
The three within this hierarchy divine
    are, first, Dominions; Virtues after these;
    then Powers, which here the third in order shine.
Ranked last but one, the Principalities
    with the Archangels whirl in measured dance;
    Angels at play the whole last circle is.
All, as they wheel in order, upward glance,
    and downward so prevail that, as all find
    themselves entranced by God, so all entrance.
And Denis with such passion set his mind
    to contemplate these orders, that he styled
    them all as I do, and their ranks defined.
But Gregory was in later times beguiled
    by other views; and, when he oped his eyes
    within this heaven, at his own error smiled.
Nor marvel that a truth which hidden lies
    with God, was by a man on earth forthtold;
    for one who saw it here did him apprise
of this and of much else these circles hold ".

CANTO XXIX

Quando ambedue li figli di Latona,
  coperti del Montone e de la Libra,
  fanno de l' orizzonte insieme zona,   3
quant' è dal punto che 'l cenit inlibra,
  infin che l' uno e l' altro da quel cinto,
  cambiando l' emisperio, si dilibra,   6
tanto, col volto di riso dipinto,
  si tacque Beatrice, riguardando
  fisso nel punto che m' avea vinto.   9
Poi cominciò: "Io dico, e non domando,
  quel che tu vuoli udir, perch' io l' ho visto
  là 've s' appunta ogni ubi e ogni quando.   12
Non per avere a sè di bene acquisto,
  ch' esser non può, ma perchè suo splendore
  potesse, risplendendo, dir 'Subsisto',   15
in sua etternità di tempo fore,
  fuor d' ogni altro comprender, come i piacque,
  s' aperse in nuovi amor l' etterno amore.   18
Nè prima quasi torpente si giacque;
  chè nè prima nè poscia procedette
  lo discorrer di Dio sovra quest' acque.   21
Forma e matera, congiunte e purette,
  usciro ad esser che non avia fallo,
  come d' arco tricordo tre saette.   24
E come in vetro, in ambra o in cristallo
  raggio risplende sì, che dal venire
  a l' esser tutto non è intervallo,   27
così 'l triforme effetto del suo sire
  ne l' esser suo raggiò insieme tutto
  sanza distinzione in esordire.   30

CANTO XXIX

WHEN of Latona's twins the one is found
   beneath the Ram, the other 'neath the Scales,
   and with the horizon both at once are zoned,
long as from when the equipoise prevails
   between them which the zenith makes, until,
   their hemispheres exchanged, the balance fails,
so long, her features painted with a smile,
   full on the point whose beams I could not bear
   gazed Beatrice; so long her voice was still.
Then she began: "Since I have seen it there,
   where centres every 'where' and every 'when',
   that thou wouldst learn, I ask not, but declare.
Not for himself a greater good to gain,
   which may not be, but that the beams thereof
   might, in resplendence, make his splendour plain,
shrined in his own eternity, above
   all time, all limits, as it pleased him, shone
   unfolded in new loves the eternal love.
Nor before lay he, as with nothing done;
   for ere God moved upon these waters, know
   that of 'before' and 'after' there was none.
Simple and mixed did form and matter go
   forth to a being which had no defect,
   like arrows three from a three-corded bow.
And as, if ye a beam of light project
   on crystal, glass or amber, all takes fire
   at once, nor stage therein may ye detect,
so the threefold creation from its sire
   into existence leapt, with no degrees
   in its beginning, but flashed forth entire.

Concreato fu ordine e costrutto
  a le sustanze; e quelle furon cima
  nel mondo in che puro atto fu produtto;   33
pura potenza tenne la parte ima;
  nel mezzo strinse potenza con atto
  tal vime, che già mai non si divima.   36
Ieronimo vi scrisse lungo tratto
  di secoli de li angeli creati
  anzi che l' altro mondo fosse fatto;   39
ma questo vero è scritto in molti lati
  da li scrittor de lo Spirito Santo;
  e tu te n' avvedrai, se bene agguati;   42
e anche la ragione il vede alquanto,
  che non concederebbe che i motori
  sanza sua perfezion fosser cotanto.   45
Or sai tu dove e quando questi amori
  furon creati e come; sì che spenti
  nel tuo disio già sono tre ardori.   48
Nè giugneriesi, numerando, al venti
  sì tosto, come de li angeli parte
  turbò il suggetto de' vostri elementi.   51
L' altra rimase, e cominciò quest' arte
  che tu discerni, con tanto diletto,
  che mai da circuir non si diparte.   54
Principio del cader fu il maladetto
  superbir di colui che tu vedesti
  da tutti i pesi del mondo costretto.   57
Quelli che vedi qui furon modesti
  a riconoscer sè da la bontate
  che li avea fatti a tanto intender presti;   60
per che le viste lor furo esaltate
  con grazia illuminante e con lor merto,
  sì c' hanno ferma e piena volontate.   63

Co-formed and stablished with the substances
   was order; some were made pure act, and heaven
   as apex of the world appointed these;
pure potency the lowest place was given;
   midway was potency with act clinched fast
   by such a rivet as may ne'er be riven.
In Jerome's writings you are told of vast
   aeons thro' which the angels lived, or e'er,
   for creatures else, one moment's life had passed;
yet do the Holy Ghost's own scribes declare
   in many a text that what I say is true;
   as thou'lt discover, if thou search with care;
and reason, in some measure, sees it too,
   which scarce would grant the movers could have stayed
   void of perfection all those ages through.
Now knowest thou where and when these loves were
   as well as how; and thus in thy desire   [made,
   already have three ardours been allayed.
Nor had the swiftest reckoner counted higher
   than twenty, ere of the angels no small part
   convulsed what lies 'neath water, air and fire.
The others, standing firm, were prompt to start
   the work thou sëest, which they love so well,
   that thus forever round and round they dart.
'Twas by the accurséd arrogance they fell
   of him thou sawest crushed by all the weight
   of all the universe in deepest hell.
Those here thou sëest, humbly owned their state
   dependent on the bounty which alone
   had framed them for intelligence so great;
thus by enlightening grace and by their own
   desert their vision was uplifted so,
   that will in them is full and steadfast grown.

E non voglio che dubbi, ma sie certo
    che ricever la grazia è meritorio,
    secondo che l' affetto l' è aperto.   66
Omai dintorno a questo consistorio
    puoi contemplare assai, se le parole
    mie son ricolte, sanz' altro aiutorio.   69
Ma perchè in terra per le vostre scole
    si legge che l' angelica natura
    è tal, che 'ntende e si ricorda e vole,   72
ancor dirò, perchè tu veggi pura
    la verità che là giù si confonde,
    equivocando in sì fatta lettura.   75
Queste sustanze, poi che fur gioconde
    de la faccia di Dio, non volser viso
    da essa, da cui nulla si nasconde: 78
però non hanno vedere interciso
    da novo obietto, e però non bisogna
    rememorar per concetto diviso.   81
Sì che là giù, non dormendo, si sogna,
    credendo e non credendo dicer vero;
    ma ne l' uno è più colpa e più vergogna.   84
Voi non andate giù per un sentiero
    filosofando; tanto vi trasporta
    l' amor de l' apparenza e 'l suo pensiero!   87
E ancor questo qua su si comporta
    con men disdegno che quando è posposta
    la divina scrittura, o quando è torta.   90
Non vi si pensa quanto sangue costa
    seminarla nel mondo, e quanto piace
    chi umilmente con essa s' accosta.   93
Per apparer ciascun s' ingegna e face
    sue invenzioni; e quelle son trascorse
    da' predicanti e 'l Vangelio si tace.   96

Nor would I have thee doubt, but surely know,
 that to receive grace is a virtuous deed,
 in measure as the heart inclines thereto.
Henceforth, if thou hast culled my words with heed,
 around this sacred college take thy fill
 of gazing; for no further help thou'lt need.
But since on earth your schoolmen argue still
 that the angelic nature is possessed
 of understanding, memory and will,
this will I add yet further, that thou mayst
 see in its purity a truth down there
 confused, when thus ambiguously expressed.
Since first they found the face of God so fair,
 these substances have never turned aside
 their gaze from it, which sëeth all things clear:
therefore no object not before espied
 cuts off their vision, nor need they to recall
 by memory aught to present sight denied.
Thus folk down there are waking dreamers all,
 some holding true, some not, the words they say;
 though these into the viler sin do fall.
Ye men in your philosophising stray
 down by-paths many; so much do love and thought
 of vain appearance carry you away!
This, tho' it angers heaven, provokes it not
 so much as when the holy scripture stands
 neglected or its doctrines are mistaught.
What blood the sowing thereof throughout all lands
 doth cost ye care not, nor how blest is he
 who humbly strives to do as it commands.
Each aims at outward show and fain would see
 his own inventions preached; which being done,
 the Gospel is passed over silently.

Un dice che la luna si ritorse
  ne la passion di Cristo e s' interpuose,
  per che il lume del sol giù non si porse;   99
e mente, chè la luce si nascose
  da sè; però a l' Ispani e a l' Indi,
  come a' Giudei, tale eclissi rispuose.   102
Non ha Fiorenza tanti Lapi e Bindi
  quante sì fatte favole per anno
  in pergamo si gridan quinci e quindi;   105
sì che le pecorelle, che non sanno,
  tornan del pasco pasciute di vento,
  e non le scusa non veder lo danno.   108
Non disse Cristo al suo primo convento:
  'Andate, e predicate al mondo ciance';
  ma diede lor verace fondamento.   111
E quel tanto sonò ne le sue guance,
  sì ch' a pugnar per accender la fede
  de l' Evangelio fero scudo e lance.   114
Ora si va con motti e con iscede
  a predicare, e pur che ben si rida,
  gonfia il cappuccio, e più non si richiede.   117
Ma tale uccel nel becchetto s' annida,
  che se 'l vulgo il vedesse, vederebbe
  la perdonanza di ch' el si confida;   120
per cui tanta stoltezza in terra crebbe,
  che, sanza prova d' alcun testimonio,
  ad ogni promission si correrebbe.   123
Di questo ingrassa il porco sant'Antonio,
  e altri assai che sono ancor più porci,
  pagando di moneta sanza conio.   126
Ma perchè siam digressi assai, ritorci
  li occhi oramai verso la dritta strada,
  sì che la via col tempo si raccorci.   129

One says that when Christ's passion was begun
    the moon was backward turned and stood between,
    so that on earth no ray of sunlight shone;
and thereby lies, for the light withdrew its sheen
    spontaneously; hence, as in Jewry, so
    in Spain and India too the eclipse was seen.
Florence of Bindi and Lapi cannot show
    such numbers as in pulpits every year
    fables like these are bandied to and fro;
so that the sheep, poor sillies, homeward fare
    from pasture fed on wind; nor merit they
    less blame, that of their loss they are unaware.
Christ to his first assembly did not say:
    'Go, preach to the world vain trifles'; but revealed
    the truth and bade them build on that alway.
Ay, and so loudly from their lips it pealed,
    that of the Gospel, when they went to war
    to light the faith, they made both lance and shield.
The preacher now provides himself with store
    of quips and gibes, and so a laugh be stirred,
    the hood puffs out, and he demands no more;
but in its angle nestles such a bird
    that, if the vulgar saw it, they would see
    the value of the pardon thus conferred.
Hence comes it that on earth such fools there be,
    that, without evidence to test it by,
    to every promise they would rush with glee.
Battens on this the pig, your Tantony,
    and others too, pigs of far baser sort,
    paying with money never stamped of die.
We have strayed far; the more doth it import
    us now to turn to the straight road again,
    that with the time the way be rendered short.

Questa natura sì oltre s' ingrada
   in numero, che mai non fu loquela
   nè concetto mortal che tanto vada: 132
e se tu guardi quel che si rivela
   per Daniel, vedrai che 'n sue migliaia
   determinato numero si cela.   135
La prima luce, che tutta la raia,
   per tanti modi in essa si recepe,
   quanti son li splendori a chi s' appaia.   138
Onde, però che a l' atto che concepe
   segue l' affetto, d' amar la dolcezza
   diversamente in essa ferve e tepe.   141
Vedi l' eccelso omai e la larghezza
   de l' etterno valor, poscia che tanti
   speculi fatti s' ha in che si spezza,   144
uno manendo in sè come davanti".

CANTO XXX

Forse semilia miglia di lontano
   ci ferve l' ora sesta, e questo mondo
   china già l' ombra quasi al letto piano,   3
quando il mezzo del cielo, a noi profondo,
   comincia a farsi tal, ch' alcuna stella
   perde il parere infino a questo fondo;   6
e come vien la chiarissima ancella
   del sol più oltre, così 'l ciel si chiude
   di vista in vista infino a la più bella.   9
Non altrimenti il triunfo che lude
   sempre dintorno al punto che mi vinse,
   parendo inchiuso da quel ch' elli 'nchiude,   12

This nature, mounting upward plane by plane,
   in number tops a height which mortal mind
   and language by no stretch could e'er attain:
and in the thousands thereuntó assigned
   by Daniel, if with care his words be read,
   thou wilt no clear, determinate number find.
The primal light, o'er the whole nature shed,
   impregns it in as many different ways
   as there are glorious beings with whom 'tis wed.
Hence, sith desire for that which draws the gaze
   follows the visual act, diversely bright
   do love's sweet ardours in it glow and blaze.
Consider now the broadness and the height
   of the eternal worth, which shines dispersed
   among so many mirrors, yet one light
abideth in itself as at the first".

CANTO XXX

HAPLY six thousand miles away is shining
   the hot sixth hour, and earth's dark shadow now
   is well nigh to the level plane declining,
when the mid-heaven, high over us, by slow
   degrees so suffers change, that here and there
   a star fades from our vision on earth below;
and as the sun's bright handmaid draweth near,
   so one by one the glittering azure loses
   its jewels, even those that loveliest were:
not otherwise the triumph which carouses
   for ever round the point of dazzling light,
   that seems enclosed by that itself encloses,

a poco a poco al mio veder si stinse;
 per che tornar con li occhi a Beatrice
 nulla vedere ed amor mi costrinse.   15
Se quanto infino a qui di lei si dice
 fosse conchiuso tutto in una loda,
 poco sarebbe a fornir questa vice.   18
La bellezza ch' io vidi si trasmoda
 non pur di là da noi, ma certo io credo
 che solo il suo fattor tutta la goda.   21
Da questo passo vinto mi concedo
 più che già mai da punto di suo tema
 soprato fosse comico o tragedo;   24
chè, come sole in viso che più trema,
 così lo rimembrar del dolce riso
 la mente mia da me medesmo scema.   27
Dal primo giorno ch' i' vidi il suo viso
 in questa vita, infino a questa vista,
 non m' è il seguire al mio cantar preciso;   30
ma or convien che mio seguir desista
 più dietro a sua bellezza, poetando,
 come a l' ultimo suo ciascuno artista.   33
Cotal qual io la lascio a maggior bando
 che quel de la mia tuba, che deduce
 l' ardua sua matera terminando,   36
con atto e voce di spedito duce
 ricominciò: "Noi siamo usciti fore
 del maggior corpo al ciel ch' è pura luce: 39
luce intellettual, piena d' amore;
 amor di vero ben, pien di letizia;
 letizia che trascende ogni dolzore.   42
Qui vederai l' una e l' altra milizia
 di paradiso, e l' una in quelli aspetti
 che tu vedrai a l' ultima giustizia".   45

little by little faded from my sight;
    till, seeing it no more, I turned to gaze
    on Beatrice, as well her lover might.
If all thus far related in her praise
    might now in one stupendous paean close,
    'twould serve me here but as a passing phrase.
The beauty I beheld so far outgoes
    conception, that its maker, I must deem,
    alone the full enjoyment of it knows.
Here, I confess, my theme defeats me—theme,
    such as no comic bard, no tragic, e'er
    was baffled by in his sublimest dream;
for, as on feeble eyes the sun's full glare,
    so to recall her smile's enchanting grace
    lays on my spirit more than it can bear.
From the first day that I beheld her face
    in this life, till this vision, my song with power
    unfailing hath pursued her loveliness;
but now, as poet, I must needs give o'er
    pursuit that every artist knows is vain,
    when, having done his best, he can no more.
She—such as I bequeath her to the strain
    of loftier trump than mine, now pressing on
    anigh the goal it long hath toiled to gain—
with gesture as of guide whose task is done,
    resumed: "We have left the world's last sphere, and
    now in the heaven composed of light alone: [move
light of the understanding, full of love;
    love of true goodness, full of ecstasy;
    ecstasy sweet all other sweets above.
Here shalt thou look on either soldiery
    of paradise, and the one host arrayed
    as at the final judgment it will be".

Come subito lampo che discetti
  li spiriti visivi, sì che priva
  da l' atto l' occhio di più forti obietti,   48
così mi circunfulse luce viva;
  e lasciommi fasciato di tal velo
  del suo fulgor, che nulla m' appariva.   51
"Sempre l' amor che queta questo cielo
  accoglie in sè con sì fatta salute,
  per far disposto a sua fiamma il candelo."   54
Non fur più tosto dentro a me venute
  queste parole brievi, ch' io compresi
  me sormontar di sopr' a mia virtute;   57
e di novella vista mi raccesi
  tale, che nulla luce è tanto mera,
  che li occhi miei non si fosser difesi.   60
E vidi lume in forma di rivera
  fluvido di fulgore, intra due rive
  dipinte di mirabil primavera.   63
Di tal fiumana uscian faville vive,
  e d' ogni parte si mettean ne' fiori,
  quasi rubin che oro circunscrive.   66
Poi, come inebriate da li odori,
  riprofondavan sè nel miro gurge;
  e s' una intrava, un' altra n' uscia fori.   69
"L' alto disio che mo t' infiamma e urge,
  d' aver notizia di ciò che tu vei,
  tanto mi piace più quanto più turge.   72
Ma di quest' acqua convien che tu bei
  prima che tanta sete in te si sazii."
  Così mi disse il sol de li occhi miei.   75
Anche soggiunse: "Il fiume e li topazii
  ch' entrano ed escono e il rider de l' erbe
  son di lor vero umbriferi prefazii.   78

Like to the sudden glare by lightning made,
   which doth the visual spirits so confound
   that from the eye the clearest objects fade,
a living glory compassed me around;
   and left me swathed in such a dazzling sheet
   of splendour that I nothing saw beyond.
"The love that calms this heaven is wont to greet
   after such fashion all it welcomes here,
   thus for its flame the torch to render meet."
Scarce had this brief assurance reached my ear,
   when I perceived myself with power endued
   surpassing that of any earthly seer;
and with such ardour was their strength renewed,
   that there exists no glory, shine it never
   so brightly, which mine eyes had not withstood.
And I saw light which flowed, as flows a river,
   blazing between two banks all gay with spring,
   but fairer spring than poet dreamed of ever.
Out of that torrent living sparks took wing,
   and settling on the flowers that by it grew
   glittered like rubies in a golden ring.
Then, as though drunken with the scents, anew
   they dived into the marvellous swirl; and lo,
   as one re-entered, forth another flew.
"The exalted wish, enflaming thee, to know
   the meaning of what here before thee lies,
   pleases me more, the more its ardours glow.
But, first, drink of this water, for thuswise
   alone canst thou thy raging thirst supply."
   So spake to me the day-star of mine eyes.
"The stream, the jewels that thence and thither fly",
   she added, "and the smiling herbage near
   are but dim proems of their reality.

Non che da sè sian queste cose acerbe;
  ma è difetto da la parte tua,
  che non hai viste ancor tanto superbe ".   81
Non è fantin che sì subito rua
  col volto verso il latte, se si svegli
  molto tardato da l' usanza sua,   84
come fec' io, per far migliori spegli
  ancor de li occhi, chinandomi a l' onda
  che si deriva perchè vi s' immegli.   87
E sì come di lei bevve la gronda
  de le palpebre mie, così mi parve
  di sua lunghezza divenuta tonda.   90
Poi come gente stata sotto larve
  che pare altro che prima se si sveste
  la sembianza non sua in che disparve,   93
così mi si cambiaro in maggior feste
  li fiori e le faville, sì ch' io vidi
  ambo le corti del ciel manifeste.   96
O isplendor di Dio, per cu' io vidi
  l' alto triunfo del regno verace,
  dammi virtù a dir com' io il vidi!   99
Lume è là su che visibile face
  lo creatore a quella creatura
  che solo in lui vedere ha la sua pace.   102
E' si distende in circular figura,
  in tanto che la sua circunferenza
  sarebbe al sol troppo larga cintura.   105
Fassi di raggio tutta sua parvenza
  reflesso al sommo del mobile primo,
  che prende quindi vivere e potenza.   108
E come clivo in acqua di suo imo
  si specchia, quasi per vedersi adorno,
  quando è nel verde e ne' fioretti opimo,   111

Not that these things are in themselves unclear;
  rather, with vision still too weak to soar
  at these great heights, 'tis thou that failest here."
No infant ever turned his face with more
  of a rush toward the milk, if wakened late
  from slumbering long past his wonted hour,
than I, to make mine eyes as mirrors yet
  more lucid, bent me to that river's bound,
  which pours its flood to aid us mend our state.
And as the eaves that edge mine eyelids found
  and drunk thereof, so seemed it that instead
  of being long it now was changed to round.
Then as a troop of maskers, an they shed
  the semblance not their own, are seen expressed
  in their true likeness, which before was hid,
thus changed, and in more dazzling beauty dressed,
  the flowers and sparks appeared, so that I saw
  both the high courts of heaven made manifest.
O splendour of God, by means of which I saw
  the truth triumphant reigning without cease,
  grant me now strength to utter how I saw!
There's light in heaven, and by means of this
  is the creator to all creatures shown
  that find in seeing him their only peace.
The light I speak of is diffused in one
  vast circle, of a rondure so immense,
  'twere even for the sun too loose a zone.
'Tis all one beam, that smites upon the sense
  reflected from the summit of the sphere
  first moved, which draws its power and motion thence.
And as a slope, rising from some calm mere,
  glasses itself therein, as though to espy
  its wealth of flowers and grass at the turn o' the year,

sì, soprastando al lume intorno intorno,
   vidi specchiarsi in più di mille soglie
   quanto di noi là su fatto ha ritorno.   114
E se l' infimo grado in sè raccoglie
   sì grande lume, quanta è la larghezza
   di questa rosa ne l' estreme foglie!   117
La vista mia ne l' ampio e ne l' altezza
   non si smarriva, ma tutto prendeva
   il quanto e 'l quale di quella allegrezza.   120
Presso e lontano, lì, nè pon nè leva;
   chè dove Dio sanza mezzo governa,
   la legge natural nulla rileva.   123
Nel giallo de la rosa sempiterna,
   che si dilata ed ingrada e redole
   odor di lode al sol che sempre verna,   126
qual è colui che tace e dicer vole,
   mi trasse Beatrice, e disse: "Mira
   quanto è 'l convento de le bianche stole!   129
Vedi nostra città quant' ella gira:
   vedi li nostri scanni sì ripieni,
   che poca gente più ci si disira.   132
E 'n quel gran seggio a che tu li occhi tieni
   per la corona che già v' è su posta,
   prima che tu a queste nozze ceni,   135
sederà l' alma, che fia giù agosta,
   de l' alto Arrigo, ch' a drizzare Italia
   verrà in prima ch' ella sia disposta.   138
La cieca cupidigia che v' ammalia
   simili fatti v' ha al fantolino
   che muor per fame e caccia via la balia.   141
E fia prefetto nel foro divino
   allora tal, che palese e coverto
   non anderà con lui per un cammino.   144

so mirrored in that light, and round it, I
  beheld in countless ranks above it rise
  all that of us have made return on high.
If pent within the lowest tier there lies
  so mighty a radiance, then how vast the space
  that the outer petals of this rose comprise!
And yet my vision suffered no distress
  at breadth or height, but could in full survey
  the range and quality of that happiness.
There, near and far nor add nor take away;
  for where God rules with nought to interpose,
  the natural law, being void, suspends its sway.
Into the yellow of the eternal rose,
  whose gradual leaves, expanding, waft sweet praise
  unto the sun that never winter knows,
as one who fain would speak, yet nothing says,
  Beatrice drew me, and "Lo there," quoth she,
  "what myriads of white robes confront thy gaze!
See the vast compass of our city! See
  our stalls so crowded, that we need but few
  fresh comers to complete our company!
On that proud throne, impressed upon thy view
  by the crown poised already o'er its state,
  ere at this marriage thou art feasting too,
shall rest the soul (emperor predestinate)
  of the great Harry, who, before her day
  be ripe, will come to set Italia straight.
Blind greed bewitches you, and 'neath its sway
  ye are like the peevish brat who, though half-dead
  with hunger, yet doth push the nurse away.
And o'er the sacred court will sit as head
  in those days one, that openly and by guile
  will not with him in the same pathway tread:

Ma poco poi sarà da Dio sofferto
   nel santo officio; ch' el sarà detruso
   là dove Simon mago è per suo merto,   147
e farà quel d' Alagna intrar più giuso ".

CANTO XXXI

IN forma dunque di candida rosa
   mi si mostrava la milizia santa
   che nel suo sangue Cristo fece sposa;   3
ma l' altra, che volando vede e canta
   la gloria di colui che la innamora
   e la bontà che la fece cotanta,   6
sì come schiera d' ape, che s' infiora
   una fiata e una si ritorna
   là dove suo laboro s' insapora,   9
nel gran fior discendeva che s' adorna
   di tante foglie, e quindi risaliva
   là dove 'l suo amor sempre soggiorna.   12
Le facce tutte avean di fiamma viva,
   e l' ali d' oro, e l' altro tanto bianco,
   che nulla neve a quel termine arriva.   15
Quando scendean nel fior, di banco in banco
   porgevan de la pace e de l' ardore
   ch' elli acquistavan ventilando il fianco.   18
Nè l' interporsi tra 'l disopra e 'l fiore
   di tanta plenitudine volante
   impediva la vista e lo splendore;   21
chè la luce divina è penetrante
   per l' universo secondo ch' è degno,
   sì che nulla le puote essere ostante.   24

whom in the holy office no long while
  will God endure, but hurl his guilty soul
  to Simon Magus, and so thrust the vile
man of Alagna deeper in his hole ".

CANTO XXXI

BEFORE me, then, in fashion as a rose
  of dazzling whiteness lay the soldiery
  of saints whom Christ by dying made his spouse;
but the other—those that ever as they fly
  behold and chant his glory, who fires their love,
  his goodness which exalted them so high,
like troop of bees that one while from above
  invade the flowers, and one while bend their flight
  there where their toil to sweetness they improve,
on the great flower, with leaves so richly dight,
  descending paused, then again upward flew
  there where their love dwells ever in their sight.
With faces all of living flame in hue,
  and wings of gold, their other portions shone
  so white, that never snow attains thereto.
From petal to petal, as they lit thereon,
  they imparted of the peace and the warm love,
  which, beating upward, they themselves had won.
And though, 'twixt flower and that which blazed above,
  the space was thick with wings in myriad flight,
  nought dimmed the splendour or the vision thereof;
because throughout the universe God's light
  so penetrates all parts in due degree,
  that nought avails to screen it from our sight.

Questo sicuro e gaudioso regno,
   frequente in gente antica ed in novella,
   viso e amore avea tutto ad un segno.   27
Oh trina luce che 'n unica stella
   scintillando a lor vista, sì gli appaga!
   Guarda qua giuso a la nostra procella!   30
Se i barbari, venendo da tal plaga
   che ciascun giorno d' Elice si cuopra,
   rotante col suo figlio ond' ella è vaga,   33
veggendo Roma e l' ardua sua opra,
   stupefaciensi, quando Laterano
   a le cose mortali andò di sopra;   36
io, che al divino da l' umano,
   a l' etterno dal tempo era venuto,
   e di Fiorenza in popol giusto e sano,   39
di che stupor dovea esser compiuto!
   Certo tra esso e 'l gaudio mi facea
   libito non udire e starmi muto.   42
E quasi pellegrin che si ricrea
   nel tempio del suo voto riguardando,
   e spera già ridir com' ello stea,   45
su per la viva luce passeggiando,
   menava io li occhi per li gradi,
   mo su, mo giù, e mo recirculando.   48
Vedeva visi a carità suadi,
   d' altrui lume fregiati e di suo riso,
   e atti ornati di tutte onestadi.   51
La forma general di paradiso
   già tutta mio sguardo avea compresa,
   in nulla parte ancor fermato fiso;   54
e volgeami con voglia riaccesa
   per domandar la mia donna di cose
   di che la mente mia era sospesa.   57

This happy realm, from every danger free,
   and thronged with folk of times both near and far,
   one object loved, one only turned to see.
Oh trinal light which in a single star
   sparkling upon them, so doth pacify!
   Look down on us, storm-beaten as we are!
If strangers, hailing from 'neath such a sky
   as every day by Helicë is spanned,
   revolving with the son she would fain be nigh,
on seeing Rome, so vast, so nobly planned,
   were wonderstruck, what time the stately fane
   of Lateran dwarfed all works of human hand;
in me, to heaven from the world of men,
   to the eternal from the temporal brought,
   from Florence to a people just and sane,
what wonder, think ye, must the scene have wrought!
   Truly, between sheer gladness and amaze,
   my pleasure was to hear, and utter, nought.
And like a pilgrim who with joy surveys
   the temple of his vow, while in him rise
   dreams of describing it in after days,
up through the living light I let my eyes
   range freely o'er the ranks from place to place,
   now upward, downward now, now circle-wise.
I saw there many a love-persuading face,
   in borrowed light and their own smiles arrayed,
   and gestures decked with every noble grace.
By now my glance had hastily surveyed
   the general form of paradise entire,
   and on no portion yet had firmly stayed;
I turned me, then, with new-inflamed desire
   to ask my lady many things that I,
   in keen suspense, was eager to enquire.

Uno intendea, e altro mi rispuose:
  credea veder Beatrice, e vidi un sene
  vestito con le genti gloriose.   60
Diffuso era per li occhi e per le gene
  di benigna letizia, in atto pio
  quale a tenero padre si convene.   63
E "Ov' è ella?" subito diss' io.
  Ond' elli: "A terminar lo tuo disiro
  mosse Beatrice me del loco mio;   66
e se riguardi su nel terzo giro
  dal sommo grado, tu la rivedrai
  nel trono che suoi merti le sortiro".   69
Sanza risponder, li occhi su levai,
  e vidi lei che si facea corona
  reflettendo da sè li etterni rai.   72
Da quella region che più su tona
  occhio mortale alcun tanto non dista,
  qualunque in mare più giù s' abbandona,   75
quanto lì da Beatrice la mia vista;
  ma nulla mi facea, chè sua effige
  non discendea a me per mezzo mista.   78
"O donna in cui la mia speranza vige,
  e che soffristi per la mia salute
  in inferno lasciar le tue vestige,   81
di tante cose quant' i' ho vedute,
  dal tuo podere e da la tua bontate
  riconosco la grazia e la virtute.   84
Tu m' hai di servo tratto a libertate
  per tutte quelle vie, per tutt' i modi
  che di ciò fare avei la potestate.   87
La tua magnificenza in me custodi,
  sì che l' anima mia, che fatt' hai sana,
  piacente a te dal corpo si disnodi."   90

But other than I purposed came reply:
　　I saw instead of Beatrice an old man,
　　like all the rest, apparelled gloriously.
Kindling his glance and o'er his cheeks there ran
　　a flush of joy benign, the while on me
　　he gazed as only a loving father can.
And instantly my cry was "Where is she?"
　　"I from my place by Beatrice was stirred
　　to come and crown thy longing," answered he;
"if thou look upward to the circle third
　　from the highest tier, once more she'll meet thy gaze
　　on yonder throne, for her high merit prepared."
He spake: I answered not by word or phrase,
　　but looked on high and there beheld her crowned,
　　reflecting from herself the eternal rays.
Not from that heav'n where highest the thunders sound
　　is mortal eye so distant, though within
　　what sea soever it lie deepest drowned,
as there was mine from Beatrice, I ween;
　　yet nought it mattered, for her image blest
　　came down to me unblurred by aught between.
"O lady in whom my hope is liveliest,
　　and who for my salvation couldst endure
　　in hell itself to leave thy footprints traced,
of all the sights that I have seen 'tis sure
　　that from thy power and from thy bounteousness
　　alone do they their virtue and grace procure.
Thou hast led me, thou, from slavery to the place
　　of freedom, making use, to serve thine aim,
　　of all the ways and means thou dost possess.
Preserve in me thy bounty still the same,
　　that so my spirit, healed by thy dear might,
　　may please thee when it quits this mortal frame."

Così orai; e quella, sì lontana
   come parea, sorrise e riguardommi;
   poi si tornò a l' etterna fontana.   93
E 'l santo sene "Acciò che tu assommi
   perfettamente" disse "il tuo cammino,
   a che priego e amor santo mandommi,   96
vola con li occhi per questo giardino;
   chè veder lui t' acconcerà lo sguardo
   più al montar per lo raggio divino.   99
E la regina del cielo, ond' io ardo
   tutto d' amor, ne farà ogni grazia,
   però ch' i' sono il suo fedel Bernardo".   102
Qual è colui che forse di Croazia
   viene a veder la Veronica nostra,
   che per l' antica fame non sen sazia,   105
ma dice nel pensier, fin che si mostra:
   "Signor mio Gesù Cristo, Dio verace,
   or fu sì fatta la sembianza vostra?";   108
tal era io mirando la vivace
   carità di colui che 'n questo mondo,
   contemplando, gustò di quella pace.   111
"Figliuol di grazia, quest' esser giocondo"
   cominciò elli "non ti sarà noto,
   tenendo li occhi pur qua giù al fondo;   114
ma guarda i cerchi infino al più remoto,
   tanto che veggi seder la regina
   cui questo regno è suddito e devoto."   117
Io levai li occhi; e come da mattina
   la parte oriental de l' orizzonte
   soverchia quella dove 'l sol declina,   120
così, quasi di valle andando a monte
   con li occhi, vidi parte ne lo stremo
   vincer di lume tutta l' altra fronte.   123

Thus I; and from that seeming far-off height
 she looked on me and smiled, then turning bent
 her gaze upon the eternal source of light.
And thus the holy elder: "To the intent
 that thou complete thy course (the end, whereto
 by prayer and holy affection I was sent),
fly swiftly with thine eyes this garden through;
 for thus thy vision before mounting higher
 on God's own radiance shall be focused true.
And she, with love for whom I am all on fire,
 the queen of heaven, will grant us every grace,
 since I, her faithful Bernard, so desire".
Like unto one who chance a Croat by race,
 drawn by the ancient legend, comes to see
 our *vera icon* of the sacred face,
and murmurs, while 'tis shown, "And can it be,
 my Lord, Christ Jesus, very God, that this
 was your true semblance?"—spell-bound, even as he,
was I and gazed with the like rapturous bliss
 on that great, loving soul who here below,
 by contemplation, tasted of that peace.
"Dear son of grace, if on the lowest row",
 he then began, "thou fixest still thy gaze,
 what heaven truly is thou wilt never know;
but rather towards the highest circles raise
 thine eyes until thou seest enthroned the queen
 whom all this kingdom worships and obeys."
I looked aloft; and as a brighter sheen
 at daybreak gilds the horizon where the sun
 rises than where his westering orb is seen,
so saw I, with my eyes still climbing on
 as if from vale to mountain, one far height
 outshining all that else I looked upon.

E come quivi ove s' aspetta il temo
   che mal guidò Fetonte, più s' infiamma,
   e quinci e quindi il lume si fa scemo,   126
così quella pacifica oriafiamma
   nel mezzo s' avvivava, e d' ogni parte
   per igual modo allentava la fiamma.   129
E a quel mezzo, con le penne sparte,
   vid' io più di mille angeli festanti,
   ciascun distinto di fulgore e d' arte.   132
Vidi a' lor giuochi quivi ed a' lor canti
   ridere una bellezza, che letizia
   era ne li occhi a tutti li altri santi.   135
E s' io avessi in dir tanta divizia
   quanta ad imaginar, non ardirei
   lo minimo tentar di sua delizia.   138
Bernardo, come vide li occhi miei
   nel caldo suo calor fissi e attenti,
   li suoi con tanto affetto volse a lei,   141
che i miei di rimirar fè più ardenti.

CANTO XXXII

Affetto al suo piacer, quel contemplante
   libero officio di dottore assunse,
   e cominciò queste parole sante: 3
"La piaga che Maria richiuse e unse,
   quella ch' è tanto bella da' suoi piedi
   è colei che l' aperse e che la punse.   6
Ne l' ordine che fanno i terzi sedi,
   siede Rachel di sotto da costei
   con Beatrice, sì come tu vedi.   9

And ev'n as there where heaves the pole in sight
  which Phäethon ill guided, all the sky
  flames, but on either side is far less bright,
so burned that peaceful oriflamme on high,
  intensest in the middle, and slackening
  its flame in all directions equally.
And, at that middle, angels on the wing
  saw I in thousands round it dance and play,
  each one in glory and function differing.
I saw there on their sports and roundelay
  such beauty smiling, that for joyousness
  no eye but sparkled in that blest array.
And ev'n did I such wealth of words possess
  as matched my imagining, I should not dare
  to attempt the least of her bewitching grace.
Then Bernard, seeing my eyes attentive were
  and fixed upon that unexampled blaze,
  his own with such affection bent on her
that he made mine more ardent in their gaze.

CANTO XXXII

Absorbed in his delight, the enraptured seer
  assumed the doctor's part with ready zeal
  and spake the holy words that follow here:
"The wound which Mary's ointment was to heal,
  yon lovely dame who sits at Mary's feet
  inflicted first and drave it deeper still.
Beneath her, where the stalls in circle meet
  to form the third row, sitteth Rachel, placed
  with thine own lady, look, in the next seat.

Sara e Rebecca, Iudìt e colei
   che fu bisava al cantor che per doglia
   del fallo disse ' *Miserere mei* ',   12
puoi tu veder così di soglia in soglia
   giù digradar, com' io ch' a proprio nome
   vo per la rosa giù di foglia in foglia.   15
E dal settimo grado in giù, sì come
   infino ad esso, succedono Ebree,
   dirimendo del fior tutte le chiome;   18
perchè, secondo lo sguardo che fee
   la fede in Cristo, queste sono il muro
   a che si parton le sacre scalee.   21
Da questa parte onde 'l fiore è maturo
   di tutte le sue foglie, sono assisi
   quei che credettero in Cristo venturo: 24
da l' altra parte onde sono intercisi
   di voti i semicirculi, si stanno
   quei ch' a Cristo venuto ebber li visi.   27
E come quinci il glorioso scanno
   de la donna del cielo e li altri scanni
   di sotto lui cotanta cerna fanno,   30
così di contra quel del gran Giovanni,
   che sempre santo 'l diserto e 'l martiro
   sofferse, e poi l' inferno da due anni: 33
e sotto lui così cerner sortiro
   Francesco, Benedetto e Augustino,
   e altri fin qua giù di giro in giro.   36
Or mira l' alto proveder divino;
   chè l' uno e l' altro aspetto de la fede
   igualmente empierà questo giardino.   39
E sappi che dal grado in giù che fiede
   a mezzo il tratto le due discrezioni,
   per nullo proprio merito si siede,   42

Sarah, Rebecca, Judith and the blessed
    great-grand-dame of the bard who with the cry
    'Have mercy upon me' his grievous sin confessed,
from rank to rank descending, even as I
    pass down the rose from leaf to leaf and name
    each one in turn, mayest thou in turn descry.
And downward from the seventh degree, the same
    as upward thence, there follows, parting all
    the locks o' the flower, dame after Hebrew dame;
for 'twixt the holy stairs from stall to stall,
    according as the faith of Christendom
    its aspect took, these form a severing wall.
On this side where the flower is in full bloom
    in all its petals, those are seated, who
    had faith in Christ while he was yet to come:
on that, where the half-circles are cut through
    by empty spaces, stationed are all they,
    who Christ, by faith, after his advent knew.
And as our lady's glorious chair this way
    distinction makes, and with the other chairs
    below her serves to part the whole array,
so, that way, the great John's this office shares,
    who, ever saintly, endured the wilderness
    and martyrdom, then hell for two long years:
and 'neath him chosen the same line to trace
    were Francis, Benedict and Augustine—these,
    then others, round by round, to the lowest place.
Now see God's foresight, how profound it is;
    for to this garden shall apportioned be
    both kinds of faith in exact moieties.
And know that downward thence, from that degree
    which cuts midway across the two partitions,
    none sitteth through his own desert made free,

ma per l' altrui, con certe condizioni;
  chè tutti questi son spiriti assolti
  prima ch' avesser vere elezioni.   45
Ben te ne puoi accorger per li volti
  e anche per le voci puerili,
  se tu li guardi bene e se li ascolti.   48
Or dubbi tu, e dubitando sili;
  ma io dissolverò 'l forte legame
  in che ti stringon li pensier sottili.   51
Dentro a l' ampiezza di questo reame
  casual punto non puote aver sito,
  se non come tristizia o sete o fame;   54
chè per etterna legge è stabilito
  quantunque vedi, sì che giustamente
  ci si risponde da l' anello al dito.   57
E però questa festinata gente
  a vera vita non è sine causa
  intra sè qui più e meno eccellente.   60
Lo rege per cui questo regno pausa
  in tanto amore ed in tanto diletto,
  che nulla volontà è di più ausa,   63
le menti tutte nel suo lieto aspetto
  creando, a suo piacer di grazia dota
  diversamente; e qui basti l' effetto.   66
E ciò espresso e chiaro vi si nota
  ne la Scrittura santa in quei gemelli
  che ne la madre ebber l' ira commota.   69
Però, secondo il color de' capelli
  di cotal grazia, l' altissimo lume
  degnamente convien che s' incappelli.   72
Dunque, sanza merzè di lor costume,
  locati son per gradi differenti,
  sol differendo nel primiero acume.   75

but through another's, under fixed conditions;
   for that all these are spirits enfranchised, ere
   they yet were capable of true volitions.
That they are children do their looks declare,
   an thou observe them well, as doth the sound
   their voices make, an thou but list with care.
Here doubtest thou; but, tho' thy doubts have found
   no utterance, I will loose the mighty chain
   in which thy subtle logic holds thee bound.
Within the ample range of this domain
   a thing of chance can no more easily
   find lodgment, than may hunger, thirst or pain;
for stablished by immutable decree
   is all thou sëest, in suchwise that here
   ring unto finger fits with nicety.
Hence these untimely comers to this sphere
   of true life are not *sine causa* placed,
   some in a higher, some a lower tier.
The king through whom this kingdom is at rest
   in love so great and in so great delight,
   that ne'er could will aspire to be more blest,
all minds creating in his own glad sight,
   with grace, at pleasure, variously endows:
   so be it, then, nor dream but God doth right.
And holy Writ expressly and clearly shows
   this truth in the twin boys we read of there,
   'twixt whom, while in their mother, strife arose.
Hence, even as such grace unto the hair
   its colour gives, so each, after his worth,
   the light most high must needs for chaplet wear.
Thus, wanting merit for their ways on earth,
   they are graded differently as differing
   but in the keenness of their vision at birth.

Bastavasi ne' secoli recenti
 con l' innocenza, per aver salute,
 solamente la fede de' parenti.   78
Poi che le prime etadi fuor compiute,
 convenne ai maschi a l' innocenti penne
 per circuncidere acquistar virtute.   81
Ma poi che 'l tempo de la grazia venne,
 sanza battesmo perfetto di Cristo,
 tale innocenza là giù si ritenne.   84
Riguarda omai ne la faccia che a Cristo
 più si somiglia, chè la sua chiarezza
 sola ti può disporre a veder Cristo ".   87
Io vidi sopra lei tanta allegrezza
 piover, portata ne le menti sante
 create a trasvolar per quella altezza,   90
che quantunque io avea visto davante
 di tanta ammirazion non mi sospese,
 nè mi mostrò di Dio tanto sembiante.   93
E quello amor che primo lì discese,
 cantando '*Ave Maria, gratia plena*',
 dinanzi a lei le sue ali distese.   96
Rispuose a la divina cantilena
 da tutte parti la beata corte,
 sì ch' ogni vista sen fè più serena.   99
"O santo padre che per me comporte
 l' esser qua giù, lasciando il dolce loco
 nel qual tu siedi per etterna sorte,   102
qual è quell' angel che con tanto gioco
 guarda ne li occhi la nostra regina,
 innamorato sì che par di foco? "   105
Così ricorsi ancora a la dottrina
 di colui ch' abbelliva di Maria
 come del sole stella mattutina.   108

Its parents' faith alone sufficed to bring
  salvation to the child, being innocent,
  in days while yet your world was at the spring.
After those early ages all were spent,
  behoved that males, their guiltless wings to plume,
  should seek the aid by circumcision lent.
But after that the time of grace was come,
  lacking the perfect baptism of Christ,
  such innocence had limbo for its doom.
Now to the face which most resembles Christ
  direct thine eyes, because its glorious light
  alone can make thee fit to look on Christ".
I saw, rained on her, joy so exquisite,
  borne in the holy spirits framed to soar
  forever to and fro across that height,
that whatsoever I had seen before
  held me not so much wondering, nor displayed
  appearance which to God such likeness bore.
That love which first had thither downward sped,
  singing 'Hail, Mary, thou with grace endued',
  hovered before her with his wings outspread.
His song divine the attendant saints renewed
  from all sides, so that every face was fraught
  thereby with more serene beatitude.
"O holy father who disdainest not
  for me to quit the pleasant place, far higher,
  wherein thou sittest by eternal lot,
who is that angel, in yon jubilant choir,
  who with such glee beholds our sovereign's eyes,
  enamoured so, that he seems all on fire?"
Thus once again I turned me to the wise
  instructor who in Mary's loveliness
  glowed like the morning-star in the sunrise.

Ed elli a me: "Baldezza e leggiadria
  quant' esser puote in angelo ed in alma,
  tutta è in lui; e sì volem che sia,   111
perch' elli è quelli che portò la palma
  giuso a Maria, quando 'l Figliuol di Dio
  carcar si volse de la nostra salma.   114
Ma vieni omai con li occhi sì com' io
  andrò parlando, e nota i gran patrici
  di questo imperio giustissimo e pio.   117
Quei due che seggon là su più felici
  per esser propinquissimi ad Augusta,
  son d' esta rosa quasi due radici.   120
Colui che da sinistra le s' aggiusta
  è il padre per lo cui ardito gusto
  l' umana specie tanto amaro gusta.   123
Dal destro vedi quel padre vetusto
  di Santa Chiesa a cui Cristo le chiavi
  raccomandò di questo fior venusto.   126
E quei che vide tutti i tempi gravi,
  pria che morisse, de la bella sposa
  che s' acquistò con la lancia e coi chiavi,   129
siede lungh' esso, e lungo l' altro posa
  quel duca sotto cui visse di manna
  la gente ingrata, mobile e retrosa.   132
Di contr' a Pietro vedi sedere Anna,
  tanto contenta di mirar sua figlia,
  che non move occhio per cantare osanna.   135
E contro al maggior padre di famiglia
  siede Lucia, che mosse la tua donna,
  quando chinavi, a ruinar, le ciglia.   138
Ma perchè 'l tempo fugge che t' assonna,
  qui farem punto, come buon sartore
  che com' egli ha del panno fa la gonna;   141

And he: "The boldest ardour, comeliest grace,
 that e'er in angel and in spirit lay,
 is found in him; nor would we have it less,
since he it is who did the palm convey
 to Mary, when the Son of God most high
 vouchsafed to assume the burden of our clay.
But follow now my words with heedful eye,
 as they the exalted senators disclose
 of this most just and loyal empery.
Yon twain, the chief in bliss, as suits with those
 that sit the nearest to the Imperial Dame,
 are, as it were, two roots unto this rose.
Him to the left doth his high seat proclaim
 to be the father through whose taste, o'erbold,
 mankind still tasteth so much bitter shame.
Upon her right that ancient sire behold
 of Holy Church to whom the two-fold key
 of this fair flower by Christ was given of old.
And he who ere his death was doomed to see
 all the afflictions of the lovely bride,
 won by the lance and nails upon the tree,
beside him rests, and on the other's side
 that leader under whom were fed on manna
 the fickle, thankless folk, puffed up with pride.
Confronting Peter, look, is seated Anna,
 so rapt in gazing on her daughter's face,
 she turns not from it e'en to sing hosanna.
And, fronting the first father of our race,
 sits Lucy, who moved the lady of thy troth
 to aid thee in thy time of dark distress.
But stop we here; and, as good tailor doth,
 in that thy time for slumbering swiftly flies,
 cut we the coat according to our cloth

e drizzeremo li occhi al primo amore,
　sì che, guardando verso lui, penetri
　quant' è possibil per lo suo fulgore.　　　144
Veramente nè forse tu t' arretri
　movendo l' ali tue, credendo oltrarti,
　orando grazia conven che s' impetri;　　　147
grazia da quella che puote aiutarti;
　e tu mi seguirai con l' affezione,
　sì che dal dicer mio lo cor non parti".　　150
E cominciò questa santa orazione.

CANTO XXXIII

"Vergine madre, figlia del tuo figlio,
　umile e alta più che creatura,
　termine fisso d' etterno consiglio,　　　3
tu se' colei che l' umana natura
　nobilitasti sì, che 'l suo fattore
　non disdegnò di farsi sua fattura.　　　6
Nel ventre tuo si raccese l' amore
　per lo cui caldo ne l' etterna pace
　così è germinato questo fiore.　　　9
Qui se' a noi meridiana face
　di caritate, e giuso, intra i mortali,
　se' di speranza fontana vivace.　　　12
Donna, se' tanto grande e tanto vali,
　che qual vuol grazia ed a te non ricorre,
　sua disianza vuol volar sanz' ali.　　　15
La tua benignità non pur soccorre
　a chi domanda, ma molte fiate
　liberamente al dimandar precorre.　　　18

and to the primal love direct our eyes,
   that, looking unto him, thou penetrate
   his beams as far as strength within thee lies.
But lest, while thinking to advance, thou yet,
   by beating thine own wings, shouldst backward go,
   we needs must pray for grace, and grace may get
from her who hath the power to aid thee so;
   thyself the while in my petition share
   by paying in heart the closest heed thereto".
And forthwith he began this holy prayer.

CANTO XXXIII

"Maiden and mother, daughter of thy son,
   lowly and high above all beings displayed,
   chosen of God, ere time had yet begun,
thine was the excellence which so arrayed
   man's nature that its maker thought no shame
   to make himself of that himself had made.
Within thy womb rekindled glowed the flame
   of love, that fed the germ from which this flower
   in endless peace to such perfection came.
To us in heaven like sun at day's mid-hour,
   thy charity is a well of hope on earth,
   whence mortal men draw draughts of quickening power.
Lady, so great thou art and such thy worth,
   that whoso longs for grace nor calls on thee,
   bids the wish fly, yet wingless speeds it forth.
Thy loving heart not only grants the plea
   of every suppliant, but ofttimes, ere yet
   'tis uttered, answers prayer spontaneously.

In te misericordia, in te pietate,
    in te magnificenza, in te s' aduna
    quantunque in creatura è di bontate.   21
Or questi, che da l' infima lacuna
    de l' universo infin qui ha vedute
    le vite spiritali ad una ad una,   24
supplica a te, per grazia, di virtute
    tanto, che possa con li occhi levarsi
    più alto verso l' ultima salute.   27
E io, che mai per mio veder non arsi
    più ch' i' fo per lo suo, tutti miei prieghi
    ti porgo, e priego che non sieno scarsi,   30
perchè tu ogni nube li disleghi
    di sua mortalità co' prieghi tuoi,
    sì che 'l sommo piacer li si dispieghi.   33
Ancor ti priego, regina, che puoi
    ciò che tu vuoli, che conservi sani,
    dopo tanto veder, li affetti suoi.   36
Vinca tua guardia i movimenti umani:
    vedi Beatrice con quanti beati
    per li miei preghi ti chiudon le mani!"   39
Li occhi da Dio diletti e venerati,
    fissi ne l' orator, ne dimostraro
    quanto i devoti preghi le son grati;   42
indi a l' etterno lume si drizzaro,
    nel qual non si dee creder che s' invii
    per creatura l' occhio tanto chiaro.   45
E io ch' al fine di tutt' i disii
    appropinquava, sì com' io dovea,
    l' ardor del desiderio in me finii.   48
Bernardo m' accennava e sorridea
    perch' io guardassi suso; ma io era
    già per me stesso tal qual ei volea;   51

Mercy, compassion, bounty without let,
   whate'er of good created being may boast,
   in thee, have all in thee, together met.
Behold this man, who from the nethermost
   abyss of all things up to this high place
   hath seen the realm of spirits, coast by coast,
and now beseeches thee that of thy grace
   strength be vouchsafed unto his eyes yet higher
   to raise him towards the final blessedness.
And I, who for myself was ne'er on fire
   more than for him, to see this vision, pray
   thee instantly—oh, spurn not my desire—
by means of thy own prayers to chase away
   all clouds of his mortality, that so
   he see the perfect joy in full display.
Further I pray thee, sovereign, who canst do
   whate'er thou wilt, after a sight so fair
   keep him from wishing aught less pure to know.
Control his human moods with watchful care:
   behold how many saints with Beatrice
   pray thee with claspéd hands to grant my prayer!"
The eyes which God reveres and loves, at this
   gazed on the pleader, and thus proved it right
   how dear to her all true devotion is;
then were directed to the eternal light,
   into whose essence we must deem no èye
   of creature pierces with such keen insight.
To the death of all desires now drawing nigh,
   I felt perforce the yearning, deep instilled
   within my heart, upon the point to die.
With nod and smiling visage Bernard willed
   that I should upward gaze; but his behest
   already of myself I had fulfilled;

chè la mia vista, venendo sincera,
e più e più intrava per lo raggio
de l' alta luce che da sè è vera.   54

Da quinci innanzi il mio veder fu maggio
che 'l parlar nostro, ch' a tal vista cede,
e cede la memoria a tanto oltraggio.   57

Qual è colui che somniando vede,
che dopo il sogno la passione impressa
rimane, e l' altro a la mente non riede,   60

cotal son io, chè quasi tutta cessa
mia visione, ed ancor mi distilla
nel core il dolce che nacque da essa.   63

Così la neve al sol si disigilla;
così al vento ne le foglie levi
si perdea la sentenza di Sibilla.   66

O somma luce che tanto ti levi
da' concetti mortali, a la mia mente
ripresta un poco di quel che parevi,   69

e fa la lingua mia tanto possente,
ch' una favilla sol de la tua gloria
possa lasciare a la futura gente;   72

chè, per tornare alquanto a mia memoria
e per sonare un poco in questi versi,
più si conceperà di tua vittoria.   75

Io credo, per l' acume ch' io soffersi
del vivo raggio, ch' i' sarei smarrito,
se li occhi miei da lui fossero aversi.   78

E' mi ricorda ch' io fui più ardito
per questo a sostener, tanto ch' i' giunsi
l' aspetto mio col valore infinito.   81

Oh abbondante grazia ond' io presunsi
ficcar lo viso per la luce etterna,
tanto che la veduta vi consunsi!   84

for, as it purer grew, my sight addressed
   itself more closely to the ray sublime
   wherein the truth of truth is found expressed.
Henceforth my vision far transcends what rhyme
   could trace in words, and memory in despair
   must yield to heights it strives in vain to climb.
As one who sees in dream, remains aware,
   when the dream's gone, of all it made him feel,
   while all he saw is lost beyond repair;
even such am I: my vision fails, until
   it all but ceases, yet my heart is awed
   by its sweet effluence which pervades me still.
Thus melts the imprinted snow by sunshine thawed;
   thus was the wisdom of the Sibyl, writ
   on frail leaves, to the breezes cast abroad.
O light supreme, so far above the wit
   of man exalted, let my thoughts again
   with some pale semblance of thy beams be lit,
and make my tongue so eloquent that when
   it chants thy glory, a future age may find
   at least one sparkle of thee inspire the strain;
for, by returning somewhat to my mind
   and sounding faintly in these verses, thou
   wilt make men to thy victory less blind.
Bewildered would mine eyes have been, I trow,
   by the keen living ray, whose utmost brunt
   they suffered, had they turned them from it now.
And I remember that on this account
   I endured more boldly, till my look grew one
   with infinite goodness at its central fount.
Oh abundant grace, whereby thus daring grown
   I fixed my vision through the eternal light
   so far, that sight I wholly spent thereon!

Nel suo profondo vidi che s' interna,
  legato con amore in un volume,
  ciò che per l' universo si squaderna;   87
sustanze e accidenti e lor costume,
  quasi conflati insieme, per tal modo
  che ciò ch' i' dico è un semplice lume.   90
La forma universal di questo nodo
  credo ch' i' vidi, perchè più di largo,
  dicendo questo, mi sento ch' i' godo.   93
Un punto solo m' è maggior letargo
  che venticinque secoli a la 'mpresa,
  che fè Nettuno ammirar l' ombra d' Argo.   96
Così la mente mia, tutta sospesa,
  mirava fissa, immobile e attenta,
  e sempre di mirar faciesi accesa.   99
A quella luce cotal si diventa,
  che volgersi da lei per altro aspetto
  è impossibil che mai si consenta;   102
però che il ben, ch' è del volere obietto,
  tutto s' accoglie in lei; e fuor di quella
  è defettivo ciò ch' è lì perfetto.   105
Omai sarà più corta mia favella,
  pur a quel ch' io ricordo, che d' un fante
  che bagni ancor la lingua a la mammella.   108
Non perchè più ch' un semplice sembiante
  fosse nel vivo lume ch' io mirava,
  che tal è sempre qual s' era davante;   111
ma per la vista che s' avvalorava
  in me guardando, una sola parvenza,
  mutandom' io, a me si travagliava.   114
Ne la profonda e chiara sussistenza
  de l' alto lume parvermi tre giri
  di tre colori e d' una contenenza;   117

Within its depths I marked how by the might
 of love the leaves, through all creation strowed,
 bound in a single volume, there unite;
substance and accidents with each its mode,
 fused as it were together, in such wise
 that as one undivided flame they showed.
Methinks I saw the essential form that ties
 this knot, because I feel, while saying this,
 a more abundant joy within me rise.
One instant dims my vision more, I wis,
 than Argo's voyage, which made old Neptune stare,
 is dimmed by five and twenty centuries.
So gazed my spirit, all suspended there,
 absorbed and steadfast, and the more it tried
 to see, the more its powers enkindled were.
In presence of that light so satisfied
 the mind is, that it never could consent
 to turn therefrom to glance at aught beside;
because the good, on which the will is bent,
 is all there; and, without it, incomplete
 are things which, in it, find their complement.
Henceforth my tongue, in struggling to repeat
 e'en what remembrance holds, will have less power
 than babe's, that yet is moistened at the teat.
Although there was one aspect, and no more,
 within the living light which met my view—
 for that is always what it was before—
yet as my vision, since it stronger grew
 the more I gazed, kept changing, so it found
 one sole appearance take on changes too.
In that exalted lustre's deep, clear ground
 methought that I beheld three circles glow,
 of threefold hue, in one dimension bound;

e l' un da l' altro come iri da iri
  parea reflesso, e 'l terzo parea foco
  che quinci e quindi igualmente si spiri.   120
Oh quanto è corto il dire e come fioco
  al mio concetto! e questo, a quel ch' i' vidi,
  è tanto, che non basta a dicer 'poco'.   123
O luce etterna che sola in te sidi,
  sola t' intendi, e da te intelletta
  e intendente te ami e arridi!   126
Quella circulazion che sì concetta
  pareva in te come lume reflesso,
  da li occhi miei alquanto circunspetta,   129
dentro da sè, del suo colore stesso,
  mi parve pinta de la nostra effige;
  per che 'l mio viso in lei tutto era messo.   132
Qual è 'l geometra che tutto s' affige
  per misurar lo cerchio, e non ritrova,
  pensando, quel principio ond' elli indige,   135
tal era io a quella vista nova:
  veder volea come si convenne
  l' imago al cerchio e come vi s' indova;   138
ma non eran da ciò le proprie penne:
  se non che la mia mente fu percossa
  da un fulgore in che sua voglia venne.   141
A l' alta fantasia qui mancò possa;
  ma già volgeva il mio disio e il velle,
  sì come rota ch' igualmente è mossa,   144
l' amor che move il sole e l' altre stelle.

and one by the other seemed as bow by bow
   reflected, and the third was like a flame
   which equally from either seemed to flow.
How scant is language, all too weak to frame
   my thoughts! And these are such, that, set beside
   my vision, 'faint' is word too weak for them.
O light that aye sole in thyself dost bide,
   sole knowest thyself and, being self-understood
   and knowing dost love thyself, self-satisfied!
That circle which appeared in thee endued
   with a reflected radiance, when I turned
   to scan awhile its shape and magnitude,
of that same hue with which it inly burned,
   seemed painted in the likeness of a man;
   to solve which wonder my whole spirit yearned.
As geometrician who tries all he can
   to square the circle and, without the clue
   he needs to guide him, ends where he began,
so I, before that marvel strange and new,
   strove to discover how the image lay
   within the circle, and how joined thereto—
flight too sublime for my own wings to essay,
   had not a flash of insight countervailed,
   and turned my blindness into sudden day.
The lofty phantasy here vigour failed;
   but, rolling like a wheel that never jars,
   my will and wish were now by love impelled,
the love that moves the sun and all the stars.

TABLE OF ARRANGEMENT
OF PARADISE

	Hier-archies	Orders		Classification of the Blessed
Primal Love (Holy Spirit)	III	9. Angels 8. Archangels 7. Principalities	Contemplate the 3rd Person with or without reference to the 1st and 2nd	Votive spirits (inconstancy) Active spirits (ambition) Loving spirits (earthly love)
Supreme Wisdom (Son)	II	6. Powers 5. Virtues 4. Dominations	Contemplate the 2nd Person with or without reference to the 1st and 3rd	Wise spirits (prudence) Militant spirits (fortitude) Judging spirits (justice)
Divine Power (Father)	I	3. Thrones 2. Cherubim 1. Seraphim	Contemplate the 1st Person with or without reference to the 2nd and 3rd	Contemplative spirits (temperance) 'All Souls' Angels

The Blessed contemplate GOD in three ways, as

These ways of contemplation are divided into *hierarchies* of three *orders* each

Heavens	Souls of the Blest encountered in the different spheres	Sciences		Time hrs.	Canti
Sphere of Fire				1	I–II
1 Moon	Piccarda, Constance	*Trivium*	Grammar	2	III–V
2 Mercury	Justinian, Romeo		Dialectic	2	V–VI
3 Venus	Carlo Martello, Cunizza, Folco, Rahab		Rhetoric	2	VIII–IX
4 Sun	Thomas (Aquinas), Albertus (Magnus), Gratian, Peter Lombard, Solomon, Dionysius (Areopagite), Orosius, Boethius, Isidore, Bede, Richard of St Victor, Siger	*Seven liberal arts*	Arithmetic	2	X–XIV
	Bonaventura, Illuminatus, Agostino, Hugh of St Victor, Peter Comestor, Peter Hispanus, Nathan, Chrysostom, Anselm, Donatus, Raban, Joachim of Calabria	*Quadrivium*			
5 Mars	Cacciaguida, Joshua, Judas Maccabeus, Charlemagne, Roland, William of Orange, Rainouart, Godfrey de Bouillon, Robert Guiscard		Music	2	XIV–XVIII
6 Jupiter	David, Trajan, Hezekiah, Constantine, William of Sicily, Rhipens		Geometry	2	XVIII–XX
7 Saturn	Peter Damian, Benedict, Macarius, Romualdus		Astrology	2	XXI–XXII
8 Fixed stars	Triumph of Christ—Mary, Peter, James, John, Adam	*Philosophy*	Physics	6	XXIII–XXVII
9 Primum Mobile	The nine angelic orders		Ethics	3	XXVII–XXIX
10 Empyrean	The celestial Rose		Theology	—	XXX–XXXIII
				24	

For EU product safety concerns, contact us at Calle de José Abascal, 56–1°, 28003 Madrid, Spain or eugpsr@cambridge.org.

www.ingramcontent.com/pod-product-compliance
Ingram Content Group UK Ltd.
Pitfield, Milton Keynes, MK11 3LW, UK
UKHW012335130625
459647UK00009B/301